DATE DUE

DATE DUE			
OCT 0 1 2002			
NOV 21 2002			
JAN 14 2003			
JAN 2 8 2003			
MAR 2 9 2003			
APR 2 8 2003			
MAY 1 2 2003			
OCT 2 7 2003			
2/18/05 ILL			
Sept 8, 2008 ILL			
OCT 1 0 2014			

RAISING
Blaze

ALSO BY DEBRA GINSBERG

Waiting: The True Confessions of a Waitress

RAISING *Blaze*

BRINGING UP AN EXTRAORDINARY SON
IN AN ORDINARY WORLD

DEBRA GINSBERG

HarperCollins*Publishers*

RAISING BLAZE. Copyright © 2002 by Debra Ginsberg. All rights reserved. Printed in the United States of America. No part of this book may be used or reproduced in any manner whatsoever without written permission except in the case of brief quotations embodied in critical articles and reviews. For information, address HarperCollins Publishers Inc., 10 East 53rd Street, New York, NY 10022.

The names of teachers, administrators, and other individuals in this book have been changed.

HarperCollins books may be purchased for educational, business, or sales promotional use. For information, please write: Special Markets Department, HarperCollins Publishers Inc., 10 East 53rd Street, New York, NY 10022.

FIRST EDITION

Designed by Jackie McKee

Printed on acid-free paper

LIBRARY OF CONGRESS CATALOGING-IN-PUBLICATION DATA
Ginsberg, Debra.
Raising Blaze : bringing up an extraordinary son in an ordinary world / by Debra Ginsberg—1st ed.
p. cm.
ISBN 0-06-000432-0 (hardcover)—ISBN 0-06-000433-9 (trade paperback)
1. Ginsberg, Blaze. 2. Parenting. 3. Mothers and sons.
4. Exceptional children. I. Title.

HQ769 .G65 2002
649'.132—dc21   2001051813

02 03 04 05 06 ❖/RRD 10 9 8 7 6 5 4 3 2 1

For Blaze
You bring me joy.

{ CONTENTS }

RAISING
Blaze

PROLOGUE

October 1997

$\mathcal{I}$'m standing in front of the frozen vegetables in my local supermarket, staring at the peas and corn and wondering exactly what it is that I need. My right foot is looped into the bottom rack of the shopping cart and I'm incredibly cold. This supermarket is kept at a temperature cool enough to preserve corpses. My sister Maya, my son Blaze, and I are on our weekly shopping excursion. Blaze calls this effort "the Big Shop" and it's become a routine we cannot stray from. Every Sunday at four we buy cereal and granola bars, bottled water and corn chips, apples and frozen pizza. We buy large quantities of the four foods that Blaze will consent to eat at any given time and sometimes—throwing caution to the winds—try to sneak in a cucumber, rice cakes, a banana. Anything to diversify Blaze's menu. We've actually managed to add celery and carrots in this way, although they're still not the foods of choice.

I spy one of the mothers from Blaze's school hovering over the snack cakes and I turn my head so that she won't recognize me, wheel her cart over, and start up a conversation. I find encounters with these other mothers extremely uncomfortable. They always know who I am before I can introduce myself.

"Oh, hey, you're Blaze's mother, aren't you?"

That's how it always starts and then I sense the inevitable unspoken subtext: *I know who Blaze is. He's that strange kid in special ed. You're his mother so you must be strange too. It must be difficult for you, having a kid like that. Of course, I wouldn't know, my kid is normal.*

I might be imagining this subtext but I doubt it. My years spent paying careful attention to body language and verbal nuances tell me I'm not too far off. Of course, none of these mothers would ever say these things out loud. They're all absurdly polite most of the time. It doesn't help that while I'm talking to them ("Oh, yes, I do think Mrs. Jones gives the kids too much/not enough homework. . . ."), I'm actually thinking that *they* are the strange ones and we are the ones who are actually normal. Whatever *normal* means. Then again, it's that very thinking that got me here now, hiding my face so that I won't have to speak to another mother.

The thought of having another one of those strained conversations is exhausting right now and I search for an escape. Blaze himself provides one as he runs over to me from the Wolfgang Puck display and says, "Mom, I want to pretend I'm being born again."

"What?"

"I want to pretend I'm being born again. You can be the Mom. Maya can be the baby. The baby me."

I look at him carefully. His round, brown eyes are fixed on mine and he's waiting for an answer. I can tell, with the understanding I've been able to hone over the ten years of this boy's life, that this is a serious question and an idea he's gone over in detail, not another repetitious request about why the garbage truck is so loud or why butterflies have to exist.

"But why would Maya be the baby?" I ask him back. "You can be the baby. Again."

"Okay, so can we do it? Can we pretend I'm being born again?"

"Why do you want to do this?" I ask him slowly. Aside from the obvious implications that "born again" suggests, I'm thinking about our recent visits to Dr. S., the child psychiatrist who told me and my father in the hush of his La Jolla office that, given the birth history I'd provided, it was his opinion that Blaze's difficulties, differences, whatever we wanted to call them, were caused by birth trauma. I've been vigilant in keeping this information from Blaze, who was in another room at the time it was delivered. Blaze records all the conversations he hears internally to be played back later at his own discretion. When the conversations involve him, his attention to them is that much greater. One of my goals this last year has been to avoid having Blaze think there is anything wrong with him at all, because, in fact, it is my belief that there is not. But Blaze is answering me now and his response has nothing to do with Dr. S. He is talking about another one of his three aunts, my twenty-year-old sister, Déja.

"Déja told me that when I was born I didn't have enough breath to cry. So I want to be born again and see what it was like not to have enough breath to cry. Is that true?" he asks, switching gears slightly, "did I not have enough breath to cry? Did I sound like this?" He makes a strangled, mewling sound in the base of his throat that sounds painful to my ears.

"Well, yes, it's true, sort of," I say wondering, with slight irritation, why my youngest sister always feels the need to present Blaze with these concepts. I'm always left to clean them up for him in the end.

(A recent discussion went something like this: "Déja says those two people in the movie were French kissing. What's French kissing, Mom? Why do people do it?")

"Well, we can try this," I say finally, "but maybe you want to do it differently this time. Maybe this time you can have enough breath to cry. Do you want to try it that way?"

Blaze is studying me again, measuring the depth of my interest in his proposal. He can see that the idea is taking root.

"Yes," he says, "sure."

Maya approaches us holding a box of Chinese restaurant tea. "I forgot this," she says. "Can't have stir-fry without it."

"Blaze wants to restage his birth," I tell her. Blaze looks over at her and nods.

"Okay," she says slowly, checking my expression to gauge the seriousness of what I'm saying before registering a reaction.

"We're going to do it differently this time," I tell her. Maya was present at Blaze's birth and so she suspects immediately what "differently" might mean. She nods again.

"Okay, sure," she says.

As we head off to the produce department, I start wondering if, in fact, we can do it differently this time. I wonder how much of his own birth Blaze remembers or senses in the recesses of his extraordinary mind. I have the feeling that he probably remembers most of it although I haven't shared these feelings with anyone outside my family. I smile to myself and shake my head. I remember that night in vivid detail. It might have happened only last week for the quality and clarity of my memory.

So much of Blaze's birth is tied to where we are now. Since our visit to Dr. S., I've been reliving those moments frequently. Now that Blaze has proposed this psychological experiment, I am thrust immediately into the wee hours of a summer night ten years past. And, after all, we were in it together, Blaze and I. Why wouldn't he remember it as well? I cast another look at my son and see him creating storms in his head as he watches a mist descend on the lettuce. As I watch him, I realize that his desire for rebirth is much more than an experiment. It's understanding he's after. Understanding and healing.

Chapter One

ENOUGH BREATH TO CRY

*A*ny story about a birth must have its origin in a story about conception. And if the story is about conception (at least, a conception that happens in the traditional way), then there has to be a story about the two people responsible. This is usually where the complications and intricacies come into play for the first time; two people creating a third. Our story is like this too—complicated, intricate, ongoing. If it had just stayed the two of us—John and me—this would have been a very short story, indeed. But, we created a third. And, despite our best efforts to dissolve the connection between us, that third person links us together forever.

I met John in the most mundane way possible; at a party in Portland, Oregon, where I was living in 1986, introduced by a mutual friend who thought we would hit it off because we were both aspiring writers. As we stood talking, drinks and cigarettes hanging casually from our hands, I didn't even think John was my type. He was good-looking, I thought, but not nearly dangerous enough for me. At that point in my life, I was still mostly attracted to men who were dark, edgy, and damaged in some way. In short, a challenge. John seemed a bit too smooth to fit this profile but I gave him my phone number anyway (like I said, he was good-looking and he could string an intelligent sentence together—both real bonuses) and when he called me a couple of days later, I agreed to a date.

It was during that first, very simple, just-coffee-and-dessert date that I decided I really liked John and the fact that he *wasn't* my type was probably quite a good thing. So there was a second, more elaborate date. We went to dinner and then to a play. John walked me home to my apartment and I asked him if he'd like to come up for coffee. He kissed me in the middle of my tiny kitchen and then everything just ignited.

The word *ignited* seems particularly appropriate to me. John and I didn't just start dating each other; we burst into flame. We fell into intimacy quickly, easily, and without thought. Our relationship was so passionate and so physical that I kept thinking we were getting along like a house on fire. But there was more to it than just remembering the aphorism: I could visualize the burning house, I could feel the two of us consuming each other.

Aside from the few hours every day when we worked at our separate restaurant jobs, John and I spent every moment together. When we weren't caught in the throes of passion, we were talking about it. We spent hours discussing how neither one of us had ever experienced the white heat we were generating between ourselves and what did that mean? What could it be? Was it love? Maybe something even deeper, we thought.

John started calling me "Juliet" and stood in the parking lot under my fourth-floor apartment, pitching small rocks at my window. "I can't leave you," he wailed up at me. "You are bliss." He read a draft of my novel and said I was a gifted writer. I read a draft of his novel and thought it was deep. He cooked lasagna for me in my little kitchen. I bought him a black wool sweater. Every time he appeared at my door, he brought a small gift; daisies, a bottle of red wine, a rare old book titled *Devil in the Flesh*. He had a "meet the family" dinner at my parents' house and seemed to enjoy the experience. He put me on the phone with his mother who said, "I've heard so much about you."

After three weeks of this intensity, John turned to me and said, "I think this might be *It*. You, I mean. You and I." It might be, I thought. Yes, it might indeed be. Admitting this felt frightening, as if I were relinquishing what little control I had over my fate. Falling in love is still falling and making that leap scared me. I remembered what a painful process picking myself up after one of those falls could be. Still, I let myself fall. I was twenty-four and not in the least bit concerned with protecting myself emotionally.

Nature is direct and its laws are specific. Anything that burns as ferociously as we did in those first couple of months will eventually consume itself and, ultimately, that is what happened. John and I began quarreling over issues that hadn't even factored in the previous weeks of passion. He became irritated with my insecurity. I thought he was lazy and moved on his goals too slowly. He said I was too impulsive. I accused him of being selfish. He said that I was the most demanding person he had ever met. I told him that he was unable to see a point of view other than his own. We began arguing late at night when we were tired and frustrated. Our barbs were sharpest then and most likely to do real damage. We fought in bed and we made up there too, but this roller coaster of emotions became nauseating after a while and we started showing signs of wear. That flaming house had burned to the ground and we were lying in the ashes.

I wasn't really surprised when John showed up one day dressed in tan slacks and a beige, cashmere sweater. This was breakup attire and I knew it. He started talking about how we had gone so fast—perhaps too fast—and now we weren't making each other happy and we should probably give each other some space. I have to say, John was terrible when it came to breaking up. He was predictable and showed none of the requisite tortured quality he needed to have to make it seem like the whole thing had been my idea. Every time he opened his mouth, I guessed at what he was going to say before the words fell out of it. All I really needed were the key words anyway: *space, time apart, not working out* and so on. It was a textbook speech and even had the obligatory kicker, "I hope we can still be friends," attached at the end.

"No!" I screamed at him, "we most definitely *cannot* be friends!"

I was hurt, not so much by the fact that John was ending our relationship, but by the sheer unoriginality of his words. I thought I warranted something more careful, some greater showing of emotion. I was also angry, too angry to even cry about my lost love. I let the Portland skies do that for me. I spent days walking the downtown streets, rain streaking my face, taking the place of the tears I couldn't shed. When I got home from these walks, I stared dumbfounded at my unblinking answering machine. I couldn't believe that he hadn't called, wasn't sorry, wasn't missing me so badly that he couldn't wait another second to see me. But, of course, I hadn't called him, either.

A week after our breakup, I discovered I was pregnant. For a few days, I just sat on the information, trying to figure out what shape my future was going to take with the addition of a child. For me, there was no decision whether or not to have the baby, but there *were* decisions to be made about how to tell John. For a while, I entertained the notion of not telling him at all. But then I remembered a conversation we'd had early in our relationship, after we'd compared various scars but before we'd declared our love for each other. I had told John that if, despite our best efforts at prevention, I happened to become pregnant, I wouldn't consider an abortion. I had my reasons, I told him, and I wouldn't change my mind. It was a risk, I told him.

"Well, we'll have to be very careful," he told me.

Clearly, we hadn't been careful enough. Matters of care aside, however, he had a right to know. Before I could contact him, though, John finally called me to see how I was doing and to tell me that he missed me. We made a date for dinner.

"But I don't want to spend the evening arguing," he told me.

"Don't worry," I said. "I don't think that will happen."

John did not react well to the news that he was going to become a father. He demanded that I have an abortion immediately, claiming it was completely unfair that I make a decision that would affect his life permanently, against his wishes. My point, that it was quite clearly my body we were talking about, fell on ears deafened by anger. Sure it was my body, he said, and I was using it as a weapon to demolish his future. I reminded him of the discussion we'd had about what I would do if I became pregnant and, after denying that such a conversation had ever taken place, he claimed that if I'd felt so strongly about abortion, I should have been much more careful from the start. He'd done his part, he said. It was obvious to him that I'd gotten pregnant on purpose and, he said, I must have been trying to rope and tether him from the very beginning.

I tried to answer John rationally and spoke as if I had even the vaguest notion of what I was getting into. I told him that I had no desire to "tether" him, didn't want to marry him, and didn't even particularly care if we were even romantically involved. But I stressed that he should think carefully about what his role was going to be in the life of his child.

John was furious. How could I even consider having a child when my own financial prospects were bleak and his were worse? Why would I want to raise a child that was unwanted by at least one of its parents? How could I, in good conscience, intentionally ruin three lives? He held fast to his position and said that if I insisted on keeping the baby, I was going to have to go it alone.

John and I had several conversations over the next couple of weeks, each more bitter and filled with recriminations that the last. No, he wouldn't help, didn't want to be with me, was outraged at me and my senseless, irresponsible actions. I stopped trying to be rational after the first conversation. He was a big boy, I maintained, twenty-eight years old, and he knew better. He was acting like a spoiled baby. Hadn't he realized that he couldn't give me directives on what to do with my own body? I became as angry as he and ended most of the conversations with the inelegant instruction that he should go fuck himself.

John moved to California shortly afterward and some time after that, I received a letter from him, telling me where he was and that he hoped I'd come to my senses and changed my mind. We exchanged a few hostile missives after that and then, finally, there was nothing but a yawning silence between us.

By the time John left, I had convinced myself that I was much better off without him. Buttressed by the unconditional support of my family, I decided that "going it alone" was entirely preferable to the misery I would likely feel if I pursued any kind of relationship with John. I had plenty of time, I reckoned, to get used to the idea of being a single mother. On balance, I was quite happy. I *wanted* my baby and I couldn't wait to meet him.

There was only one moment during my pregnancy when I faltered and felt a hint of something I had to call grief. I was in the middle of my first prenatal checkup. The doctor had given me a due date and a prescription for vitamins. He told me that I was in great health and that I should have an easy and trouble-free pregnancy. He put a stethoscope to my still-flat belly and instructed me to listen. I heard a quick, pulsing heartbeat that wasn't mine coming from within my body. It was a reality then, that very soon I would be responsible for a completely new person. There was an intense joy in this but, at the same time, I experienced deep pain at being separated from John. It was really the two of us who had made this third, I thought, and I wished he had been there with me, listening. That heartbeat belonged to his baby as well as mine. If only he could hear this, I thought, he wouldn't be able to find a place for his anger. How could anyone be angry in the face of such magic?

I was convinced I was going to be a champion in delivery, just as I was smugly sure I had orchestrated the perfect pregnancy. Blaze, however, had different ideas from the start. He was very late, for one thing. My original due was set at the beginning of July, so from the middle of June I was anxiously looking forward to his arrival.

I'd shut myself up at home for the last few weeks of my pregnancy. I was so large I could balance a teacup and saucer on my protruding belly. It was the hottest summer on record in Portland that year and I had no air-conditioning. For the better part of three weeks I lay on my sweaty bed directly facing a fan, watching the interminable Iran-Contra hearings, which promised to be as endless as my pregnancy. Every evening I stared at the little trunk I'd filled with tiny baby clothes and blankets. I folded and refolded them, arranged them according to color, tossed them around my bed and put them back again. And waited.

Two weeks after my due date, I was frantic. I could barely breathe and sleeping was out of the question. The baby's endless hiccups ("An excellent primitive breathing reflex," my doctor assured me) kept me awake, staring at the changing colors of the sky every night. I couldn't eat more than a single piece of fruit at a sitting owing to my squashed stomach and I was in the bathroom every fifteen minutes. Besides all of these mundane physical discomforts, I was beginning to think I was carrying an alien life-form within me. I could see the outline of feet against the tight skin of my belly as the baby moved around in his limited space, but as the days and nights stretched on and on, *baby* became *intruder* in my mind. My grandmother had an accurate (if somewhat cold) Yiddish term for this. She called the unborn baby a *mitfresser*, which translates, roughly, into eat-along.

"Who are you?" I asked the rolling skin of my midsection, although I wasn't entirely ignorant of the answer. There were at least a couple of things I did know about this baby. An ultrasound taken a week after my due date showed that the baby was a boy, something I'd assumed from the beginning. I fully agreed with a friend of mine who said, "It would just be so out of character for you to have a girl."

I also knew that this baby's name was Blaze. The name had come to me in the middle of a bad first-trimester cold. I couldn't take any pain relievers or decongestants so I lay in a miserable heap on my bed watching TV shows that I would never normally watch. A character on one of these shows was named Johnny Blaze. I knew immediately and without any kind of reason that Blaze would be my baby's name. It was almost as if he'd named himself.

Being a suspicious type, though, I wasn't confident enough in the choice of name to forgo researching its origins. I didn't want to brand my kid with a name that had negative connotations. Aside from mine, names were quite a big deal in my family. Every one of my siblings had spent time explaining the origins of their names. I didn't want my child to experience even the most subtle problems because of his name (yes, I had really thought of everything—what a well-prepared mother-to-be!).

The first few baby name books I consulted listed *Blaze* as a derivative of the Latin *Blasius,* meaning "one who stammers," which was totally unacceptable. Fancy laying terrible communication skills on a kid from the get-go. Because I was so attached to this name, though, I kept searching. Finally, I found what I'd been looking for, a mention of Saint Blaze, a fourth-century Armenian bishop who had hidden in a cave during the persecution of the Christians and tended to wounded animals. He was one of the patron saints of physicians, invoked against ailments of the throat. This was good enough for me.

Despite my preparedness with a name, baby clothes, crib, and an almost desperate desire to deliver, I began to have a sneaking suspicion that I was never going to go into labor naturally. It was in this state that I found myself in the hospital's waiting room on the morning of July 22.

"I'm not leaving until he's out," I warned Maya. "I don't care if they have room or not. I'll give birth right here if I have to."

There was one other, nonpregnant, woman in the waiting room listening to this frenzied conversation I was having with my sister. She waited for a lull before she said, "Is this your first baby?" I admitted that it was and she asked me when I was due. When I told her that I was already two weeks past my due date, she nodded sympathetically.

"They going to induce you?" she asked. I answered that this was my fervent hope.

"Make them do it," she said stridently. "I was three weeks late with my first and they did nothing about it. The baby ran out of oxygen in there. He died. My baby died. They could have saved him if they'd given me an induction."

I stared at her, horrified. What a thing to say to a pregnant woman! And what was the proper response to such a statement? "I'm sorry?" "Thanks for letting me know?" I felt a panic coming on as I searched my brain for something appropriate to say.

"Stand your ground," she added, before I could say anything. "You wouldn't want that to happen to you."

My obstetrician mercifully rescued me at that point. She appeared like a guardian angel at my shoulder and said, "Good news. We've got room for you downstairs. Looks like you're going to have your baby today."

I was totally unconcerned about the pain of labor, despite what I'd heard from other mothers about the agony of childbirth. I had vowed to avoid any drugs during the process. As far as I was concerned, pain meant that birth was imminent and, therefore, not a bad thing. Besides, my own mother had given birth to all of her children without any pain medication. She'd assured me that her labors had been short and uncomplicated and I saw no reason why my own should be any different. I thought women who complained of endless labors and excruciating pain were wimps who were too emotionally detached from childbirth to appreciate the process. I was actually *looking forward* to birthing my baby. I felt fearless.

My family arrived at the hospital in stages. Maya was with me from the beginning, alternately watching TV, eating snacks from the cafeteria, and keeping a running commentary about the shrieks of pain from other women in labor, all of which we could hear through the walls. Our favorite among these was the woman who kept yelling, "Ow, ow, ow-ee, ow-ee! Shit! Shit!" over and over again, her words in the exact same pattern each time.

"*Ow-ee?*" Maya questioned, eyebrows raised.

"Just don't let me do that, okay?" I begged her. "Just shoot me if I start screaming."

"Ow-eeeeeeeeeeeeeeeeeeee!" came the wail from the next room.

"Yup, okay," Maya said, staring ruefully into her plastic foam cup. "You know, this is supposed to be hot chocolate, but you'd never know it. Everything comes out of the same nozzle down there: hot chocolate, tea, coffee, soup. I can't tell what this is. Want some?"

By the time the drugs I'd been given to induce labor had really kicked in and I was having contractions every minute, my parents and my siblings were all there, wandering in and out of the room, eating potato chips and chocolate and arguing with each other.

It was then that I realized fully that having a baby is a completely solo effort. There was no way to drag anybody else in and have them take over. I could barely see and certainly could not move with all the equipment strapped to my body. There were several IV lines and a fetal monitor that amplified the baby's heartbeat to a level that was impossible to ignore. That rhythmic *thump* was so loud and elemental I continued to hear it hours after Blaze was delivered.

After three hours of solid one-minute contractions, my legs started to shake uncontrollably and I worried about losing control completely and screaming in agony. I felt as if I were being slowly torn in half, from the inside out, and started to wonder how any woman could survive this kind of pain. I wondered if *I* was going to survive it. Visions of camels passing through the eyes of needles danced through my head. This is too hard, I thought several times, I can't do it, make it stop. Every time this thought crossed my mind, it was immediately followed by the terrible realization that I *had* to do it, that there was absolutely nowhere to go and nobody who could make it stop.

My mother, worry etched into her face, stood at the end of the bed and grabbed hold of my feet, the only part of my body she could really reach, squeezing hard. I looked at her and felt an immediate and deep sense of betrayal. I couldn't believe that, as my mother, she hadn't seen fit to tell me about a pain that was—as close as I could equate it—like having my legs tied to two trucks that were driving off in opposite directions.

"Why," I panted between contractions, "didn't you tell me it was going to be like this?"

"Would you have believed me?" she answered.

After several hours of hard labor, I demanded that Maya kick everybody out of the room. "I need drugs," I told her. "Now."

"But you told me you didn't want—"

"Now!" I had thirty seconds before the next contraction was going to overtake me completely and I couldn't afford to waste time telling her how I'd totally given up on the concept of a drug-free childbirth. I was only four centimeters dilated after ten hours of labor and quite certain that I would never make it without the kind of chemical help that only a day earlier I had sworn I would never take.

The anesthesiologist who gave me an epidural was easily the most popular person in the hospital. Laboring women who saw him greeted him with the fervency of disciples. It was no different for me. Ten minutes after he painlessly inserted a needle into my lower back, I was completely pain-free and briefly entertained the notion of naming my baby after *him*. I could feel my entire body relax in the absence of that intense pain and I was prepared to go through many more hours of labor, but within twenty minutes, I had progressed to full dilation.

That was the moment that things began to go wrong for Blaze. The fetal monitor began showing dips in his heart rate with every contraction and, as the minutes passed, the dips became more sustained. Because I had Blaze at a teaching hospital, I met the doctor who would deliver him only an hour before it happened. This doctor began looking at the monitor's printout with concern and started talking over my body to the nurse on the other side of the bed.

"Have her tracings been like this all night?" he asked and the nurse murmured something about the last half-hour.

Alert now that I was free of pain, I asked him what was going on.

"He's probably caught the umbilical cord around his neck," the doctor told me. "Looks like he came down pretty fast after the epidural." He went on to assure me that I wouldn't have to worry, that the baby was on his way out now and that he didn't think it was severe. He also told me that I should start pushing immediately.

I pushed on command, totally removed from any physical cues. The doctor, intern, and labor nurse in the room had all become very serious, engaged in the clipped, instructions-only dialogue peculiar to crisis. In a very small unoccupied portion of my brain, I realized that had I not been caught in the middle of the most difficult act I'd ever performed, I would have been completely terrified. I could see nothing over the equipment I was buried under and relied on the reflection in my sister's eyes to see what was going on in my own body. She was rapt, occasionally prompting, "Come *on*, I can see the head."

I heard the labor nurse say, "Lots of hair on this baby."

I felt my ribs stretching and my body tearing.

I said, "I can't do this," and was ignored.

The doctor said, "There it is, there's the cord." I asked if I should push and they all yelled "No!" in unison. The umbilical cord was tightly wrapped twice around the baby's neck. The doctor had to literally cut it off his throat before pulling him out of me and laying him on my stomach. He had entered the world strangled by his own lifeline.

Blaze was positioned so that his face was turned up to mine. His eyes were very dark but wide open and I looked directly into them. They were full of brand-new life and they were gazing right into mine as if to say, "Here I am, it's me." I could see his very soul in that moment, shining and silently beckoning to me. My hands went out to him automatically and I cupped them around his small body. "Oh, it's *you*," I said out loud. "I know you." And then I started weeping.

Women talk about falling in love with their newborns. There was all of that for me too and more, because, in that instant, I recognized him. He let me in at that very first moment and I understood completely the connection between the two of us. In doing so, I missed the flurry of activity going on around us. I didn't notice that Blaze wasn't making any sound at all. I missed the nurse calling out an Apgar score of 3 (a scale of 1–10 measuring heart rate, respiration, and muscle tone on a newborn—3 being not that far from dead). I never heard anyone say "blue and floppy," although Maya did, and moved back from the delivery table. All I saw was the life, startled but intelligent and powerful, in his slate-colored eyes. That look was a gift to me, an unbreakable bond between us. My faith in Blaze was born in that very moment.

I was still weeping tears of joy when the nurse lifted him carefully from me and said gently, "We'll bring him right back. We're just going to give him some oxygen. He needs a little jump-start."

It was many weeks before I learned what happened to Blaze next. My parents, afraid of sending me into frightened hysterics, waited until then to tell me the following scene: My mother, who was waiting outside the door with my father, realized that the baby had been born when she heard me crying. Those tears were familiar to her. They were both waiting anxiously to be let into the room, but moments later the nurse came out holding the baby and ran across the hall to the neonatal-care unit. My mother, predictably, went into a panic. My father was rather more decisive about things. He strode across the hall after the nurse and walked into the unit capless, maskless, and unscrubbed. He leaned over Blaze, who was surrounded by doctors and nurses administering oxygen, drawing blood, and requesting a section of the umbilical cord for blood gases.

My father, who had sworn that, after five children, he was definitely not becoming attached to another (he'd have fun with his grandchild, sure, but no "heavy" attachments), moved through all the doctors and put his finger into Blaze's tiny hand so that the baby would have somebody from his family touching him. He started speaking to Blaze then with words that have not changed in meaning to this day. "Come on, Blaze," he said, "get it together. Look at all these other babies; they're small and red and premature. That's not you. You don't belong in here. Your mother's waiting for you. You're big and fat and healthy. Come on and breathe now. Come on, Blazicle, breathe."

A nurse finally had to physically detach my father from Blaze and push him out of the room, saying, "It's okay, Mr. Ginsberg, he's not going to die."

When the same nurse came back into my room to get information from me for Blaze's birth certificate, she gave me an update on his condition.

"He'll be fine," she said. "We're just trying to get a good, solid cry out of him. Your dad's in there talking to him."

"He is?"

"Yes," she said, smiling. "It's really cute."

A team of doctors and nurses blew oxygen on Blaze for several minutes. They poked and prodded him, beginning a series of tests for possible infection, but he never did capture enough breath to cry that morning. When they brought him back to me, wrapped up like a burrito in his blanket, he was making little growling noises, his eyes closed firmly against the glare of his new world. He refused to nurse. He refused to do anything but lie in the little Tupperware-like container they set him in, breathing fast and shallow.

I lifted him out of the Isolette and put him beside me in the bed so

I could lie next to him and study his face. His eyes were still shut tight and his miniature brow was slightly furrowed. His tiny mouth was set in an expression I could only have described as disgusted had I not been so entranced by the cuteness of it. He was one pissed-off newborn. When he continued his hunger strike and irregular breathing over the next several hours, his body temperature dropped and a concerned nurse took him away from me again. "We'll need to do some more tests," she said.

A few hours later, I hobbled into the hospital's elevator and went upstairs to see my son. When I got to the neonatal-care unit, I found a knot of physicians and nurses clustered around Blaze's crib. I stood there dumbly, until a nurse noticed me and said, "Ginsberg's mom is here." The doctors shifted slightly to look at me while I tried to process the fact that the word *mom* now applied to me. I moved a little closer to the crib and saw that Blaze was lying on his side, held into a fetal position by a couple of nurses.

"We're going to give him a spinal tap," a nurse said to me by way of explanation. "We need to rule out an infection." Without any warning (to myself as much as to the hospital staff), I burst into loud, hysterical sobs. I was totally unable to control myself and couldn't even stop long enough to scream at the doctors to stop, which was what I wanted to do. A nurse took me by the arm and made me sit down at the far end of the room so that Blaze and the hideously invasive procedure about to be performed on him were no longer in my view. "It will be okay; he's not going to die," she said sternly. Her words only made me sob louder.

"He's . . . not . . . going . . . to . . . die," she said again, louder this time, as if speaking to someone with a hearing problem. It hadn't occurred to me that dying was even an issue to be reckoned with until that point, so I didn't find anything particularly comforting in her words. I tried to talk to the nurse and when that proved futile, I tried to get up out of the plastic yellow chair I was sitting in. My hospital gown came undone and I scrambled to pull it around me. I cast my eyes around frantically, trying to find a familiar marker, something to remind me of what my life had been like less than forty-eight hours ago, but there was nothing. Even my body, swollen and unfamiliar, had betrayed me.

I couldn't see Blaze through the doctors any longer and I could not stop crying, despite my best efforts. My chest was heaving and my face was completely wet with tears. I hadn't shed tears like this in front of another person for at least ten years. Sure, I'd oozed the obligatory crocodile droplets over lost loves and existential angst (almost required crying in my college days), but real tears, the kind that come from so deep a place they hurt when they fall, hadn't made an appearance since I was fourteen, when I'd decided that tears were a sign of emotional weakness I didn't want to show. Now the tears poured out regardless of any decisions I had or would ever make. It would be like this forever more with Blaze. Once he was born, a wound opened inside me that would never close. I would never break down again so completely, but from then on, the tears would always be close to the surface, ready to spill.

"Do you have anybody here with you?" the nurse asked me. "Baby's dad?"

"*N-n-no,*" I managed to hiccup, "there's n-n-no d-dad."

"Well, honey, is there anyone I can call for you?"

"M-m-my father," I managed to get out. Surely, I thought, my father would be able to sort things out, find out what was really going on. At the very least, I thought, I would have to stop the hysterical sobbing long enough to speak to him. I heard the nurse dialing the number and asking for Mr. Ginsberg. I tried to imagine who'd answered the phone and hoped it wasn't my mother. This wasn't the kind of phone call she dealt with particularly well. Despite the sudden thickness in my head, I could hear the nurse talking to my father, telling him that I was upset, could he assure me that everything would be all right, that the baby was in no danger of dying.

When I got on the phone with my father, he sounded tired. He asked me if I had slept at all and I realized it had been almost two days since I had. He told me that Blaze would be fine and that I should go to sleep.

"But what's wrong with him?" I asked my father. "Why is he in here?"

"Don't worry," my father said. "Go to sleep. There's nothing wrong with him, he's fine."

Seeing that I was sufficiently calmed, the nurse led me, like a child, back to my room. I was given a small red pill and descended immediately into a black, dreamless sleep.

I was discharged from the hospital the following morning. Alone.

"Some more tests" turned into five additional days in the neonatal-care unit. Blaze was tested for infection, for lung problems, for blood problems. After the spinal tap he had an IV inserted in his scalp. His breathing continued to be rapid and shallow and he grunted instead of crying. He wouldn't take formula from a bottle. He didn't wet his diaper. The doctors found nothing to indicate what the problem might be.

When I left the hospital, my first stop was at the dark, underground office of a local astrologer. This was my particular way of seeking answers to the unanswerable questions that had suddenly been thrown my way. It would be the first—but by no means the last—time I'd seek enlightenment regarding Blaze outside the traditionally accepted means and professionals. Although I'd been casting horoscopes for years, I needed the astrologer to calculate Blaze's birth chart, since I was in no condition to start figuring mathematical equations. But I would be doing the interpretation myself. I walked into the office uncertainly and with my eyes full of tears. The astrologer was there with an associate, both of them nudging seventy years of age.

"Wait a minute," the astrologer said to me, "you mean you just had this baby *yesterday*?"

"Yes," I said feebly. "He's having some problems. I want to have a look at his chart." I explained that he had been strangled by the umbilical cord and that he was having difficulty breathing now. The astrologer presented me with Blaze's chart and told me that Blaze was lacking the element of air in his chart.

"That must be the problem," she said. I tried to imagine walking into the neonatal-care unit and explaining to the doctors that my baby was born without air in his chart and that, clearly, was why he was having trouble getting enough of it to breathe. The thought was almost funny enough to make me laugh. I thanked the astrologer for the chart and paid her but when I headed toward the door she stopped me.

"You know, you're very lucky," she said. "I lost my first child in this way, with the umbilical cord around his neck. A few years ago they couldn't have done anything for you and your baby. You are very lucky."

I walked as fast as I could toward the door and my mother, who was waiting for me in the car.

I spent the next five days going back and forth to the hospital, trying to persuade Blaze to take my breast and whispering in his ear that I wanted to bring him home. I started spending longer hours in the neonatal-care unit because I just couldn't stand to be separated from him. Every time I left the hospital, I felt as if I were leaving my own beating heart alone in a plastic crib on the fifth floor. When I got home, I was incapable of any conversation that didn't involve the minutiae of Blaze's care or what time I would be returning to see him. Sleeping was impossible. I would wake up, startled by bright lights, feeling as if I had wires attached to me pinning down my arms. Of course, there were no lights and no wires in my bed, but this is what Blaze was experiencing in the hospital and I took his experiences into my own body. He had only just *left* my body, after all. Besides feeling that I was still physically attached to him and that I was now missing a large portion of myself, I also felt truly guilty about leaving my newborn son in the care of doctors and nurses. He needed his mother, I kept thinking. There are no substitutes. I knew all about infant bonding and was really worried that I wouldn't achieve it with my own child.

In the constant glare of the neonatal-care unit, I saw the same feelings reflected on the faces of the parents who shared a similar situation. We followed the same drill on the way in, all of us stopping first to scrub our hands and arms with microbe-killing soap and then donning a hospital gown over our clothes. Everybody learned the nurses' names very quickly. The nurses, on the other hand, referred to us as "Blaze's mom," "Justin's mom," "Kelly's mom," and so on. We'd get a rocking chair and our babies to hold. When the nurse handed Blaze to me, she covered his head with a receiving blanket so that I wouldn't have to look at the IV stuck into his scalp. I was one of the luckier ones. Most of the babies in the unit were covered with IVs and monitoring devices. Some parents had to drag half a roomful of equipment around with them when they sat down to hold their babies.

Although most of the babies in the unit were actually getting better, since the unit was a step down from intensive care, many of the babies were still sick and underweight. It was a sad place and most of the parents who came to visit spent some time weeping. I did not cry after that first night.

The tears started only when I had to leave Blaze. In between visits to the hospital, I sat with my mother in her kitchen, weeping into my teacup. "I want him back," was all I could say.

By way of comforting me, my mother hauled out the story of my own birth. I'd heard the details before, how I'd been sick, had trouble breathing and nobody knew what was wrong. I was blue first and then yellow from jaundice. I didn't leave the hospital for two weeks, but then I was fine.

"You don't know what this is like," I moaned. "You can't imagine what it's like to have to leave without him."

"I also had to leave you in the hospital and go visit you every day before I could take you home," my mother answered. "It was even worse because I didn't have my mother there to help me. And see, everything turned out all right in the end, didn't it?"

"Sure," I said, feeling incredibly sorry for myself, "everything turned out just great." I folded my hands over my deflated belly, a posture I'd come to assume naturally over the last several months whenever I felt the baby kicking.

"Take your hands off your stomach," my mother told me, "you're not pregnant anymore. You have to get used to the fact that you're not carrying him now. He's his own person now."

She was right, of course. He was on his own, but knowing that I couldn't protect him in the shelter of my own body made me feel even worse.

Nothing ever did turn up on all the tests administered to Blaze. *Birth trauma* was the best and most general term anybody seemed to come up with to describe Blaze's lack of enthusiasm at being alive.

"I think he's angry at being born," I told a nurse late one night as I held him in the artificial hospital glow.

"Well, that may be," she said with the weary tone of someone who had heard more than her share of whispered and frantic pacts made with God, "but if he doesn't start eating soon he's going to become a 'failure to thrive' baby. We're going to have to put in a feeding tube."

I thought about the phrase *failure to thrive* and decided it was unacceptable. "Please, Blaze," I whispered desperately, "please eat. I don't want them to put a tube down your throat. Please." I held the bottle to his mouth and nudged it against his lips.

At that moment, Blaze snapped out of his resistance and began to take formula greedily from the hospital bottle. I couldn't yet sell him on my breast, but the fact that he was finally taking nourishment was enough for me right then. I could have said it was because he heard me somehow and responded to me directly, but I sensed he was just following his own time schedule. He finally made up his mind to give it a go at five days of age and so he did.

When Blaze was discharged from the hospital shortly thereafter, I was given a few caveats. Watch his breathing. Check his eating. I had to pass a crash course in infant CPR before they would let him go. Let us know, they cautioned, if anything seems abnormal. Of course, *abnormal* was a relative term. I had no clue what was normal to begin with so it was impossible to determine what wasn't.

When I finally got Blaze home, he seemed no more comfortable than he had been in the hospital. He screamed the wail of the damned through the night, refusing the breast, bottle, and pacifier. He writhed around and refused to be comforted. Because he'd spent a week in the bright lights and constant bustle of the hospital, he had no day-to-night schedule and slept for only twenty minutes at a stretch. Every time he cried, I was convinced there was something radically wrong with him and made several frantic calls to the neonatal-care unit in the middle of the night. There had been times before in my life where I thought I'd been scared, but in those dark hours when nothing I did seemed to quiet my newborn, I experienced real fear for the first time. Often during those endless nights, I simply cried along with him. "What?" I blubbered out loud in the wee hours of yet another day. "What is it that you want?"

In a rare moment of rationality, it occurred to me that Blaze and I were out of synch because of our weeklong separation. It would take some perseverance, I realized, to recapture that moment right after his birth where he had introduced himself to me with his eyes opened to mine. I made a promise to him then that I would never leave him alone again, no matter what the circumstances.

It took four weeks for me to get reacquainted with my son and for me to stop believing that every time he cried he was going to cease breathing. I learned to trust myself and he learned to trust me. Although it terrified me when he wouldn't eat, I stopped giving him a bottle, forcing him to learn how to nurse. I kept him in my bed with me even though every baby book I'd read said to leave him in his crib. I wanted him to feel me next to him all the time. I wanted to make sure that his baby brain told him he was safe. I talked to him. I wrapped him tightly in blankets and let him sleep against my chest so that he could hear my heartbeat. Slowly, he started developing a routine and started crying less. After a month, I had learned a new language. I could tell exactly what each little grunt and cry meant. I knew when he was hungry and when he was just restless. My fear subsided and in its place was a love so strong, it sometimes hurt me to look at him. (In characteristically neurotic fashion, I worried about that, too. It seemed a sin against nature to love anything with that kind of intensity.)

Blaze became nothing less than a perfect baby in my eyes. He ate well, he slept well, and he seldom cried. He smiled often. Because of his low Apgar scores, a nurse was dispatched to my apartment after six weeks to check on his neurological development. When she arrived, she explained that oxygen-deprived babies sometimes had "difficulties." She didn't tell me what she was looking for at that point and, basking in the glow of my beautiful baby, I didn't think to ask her. After all, he was quite obviously flawless, wasn't he? Surely anybody could see that. The nurse seemed to think so, smiling broadly as she picked him up and held him out to look at him. Everything seemed just fine, she assured me and, oh, isn't he cute?

When Blaze was six months old, John came to Portland to visit us. I couldn't tell if he was coming to test his feelings about fatherhood or if the reason was sheer curiosity. My feelings about him were in total confusion. Hours after Blaze's birth, a nurse had given me a sheet of information to fill out for his birth certificate. I was still very angry at John and asked the nurse if I had to fill out the spaces that asked for the father's name and the father's place of birth.

"You're on your own, aren't you?" the nurse asked me and I told her that I was.

"Well, honey, you can put down anything you want there. The state of Oregon doesn't require any information on the father for the birth certificate. You can list the president of the United States on there if you want. It makes no difference."

I drew a thick line through the offensive spaces. Blaze's birth certificate arrived some weeks later with his name, my name, and a row of asterisks where his father was supposed to be. I was unprepared for the grief I felt at the sight of these little stars. The shame of not providing Blaze with a father hit me for the first time. I wanted desperately to share this gift with the other person responsible for creating him. When Blaze was born he looked a great deal like John. They shared the same olive skin and there was a bit of play around their mouths that was identical. I had an almost physical tug of sadness when I saw the father reflected in the son.

I had no idea what I wanted from John or what I would say to him. I was angry that he'd left me, but so proud of our beautiful baby. I had spent months hating him, but I loved what we had made together. When I saw him standing at my door, holding a bottle of red wine and a small stuffed toy, I just started to cry.

John looked at Blaze but didn't want to hold him, citing that he felt too awkward. We drank a toast and talked about the pattern of our days. I told him about Blaze's rocky birth and he said he was sorry that it had been so difficult for me. He said that he'd been hurt that I didn't call him to tell him when Blaze was born and that he'd had to hear it from the Justice Department, which was looking for him to start paying child support. Because I was living more or less on the poverty line, I'd had to take advantage of state-sponsored medical aid. The Justice Department knew where and who John was because I'd told them as part of my application for aid. I told John that he hadn't exactly shown a great deal of interest in Blaze's existence, never mind the date of his birth. Still, I added, "I'm sorry you had to hear about it that way."

We talked some more and John drank more wine. The room grew a little warmer. I gushed on about Blaze, what an amazing baby he was, how completely besotted I was with him.

"I have no doubt that you're an excellent mother," he said. "I've always thought you would be."

I was drawn to him again, not now as the man I had originally met, but as the father of our child, a child I loved beyond words. In the heat of this glow, I moved toward John and kissed him. After a moment, he pushed me away.

"What's the matter with you?" he said angrily. "How can you think I'd ever do *this* again? You disgust me."

I watched his wine-stained lips move around these words and had to blink back sharp, painful tears. If he'd punched me with his fist it wouldn't have hurt as much. His rejection was fundamental and complete. I felt savaged.

We had a vicious argument then, filled with recriminations, threats, and accusations. He told me I was an evil manipulator who had used him as a stud and he would never support my wicked plan to rope him in. I called him the sorriest son of a bitch who ever walked the face of the earth and that my biggest regret was that *he* was the father of my child. For good measure, I threw in that he hadn't exactly excelled in his duties as stud, if that was what he felt he was.

John left in a rage. For the first time in my life, I threw things at the wall in frustration—the first item being the empty wine bottle he'd left behind. It took several hours for me to calm down enough to stop shaking.

A few months after this episode, I learned through the Justice Department that John had requested a paternity test. For me, this was the final insult. John knew that he was Blaze's biological father beyond the shadow of a doubt. Demanding a paternity test was just an ill-conceived attempt to avoid paying child support.

To make matters infinitely worse, I was forced to take Blaze to a lab where an inept phlebotomist stabbed him mercilessly for two hours before getting enough blood for the test. Blaze contracted a terrible fever afterward and started vomiting. He was very ill for one terrible week. Even his normally stoic pediatrician seemed alarmed when I brought him in with a spiking temperature of 104.

I really resented John after that but, as much as I wanted to, I couldn't bring myself to hate him. It was impossible to hate a man who was present, in whatever form, within my son. I knew I couldn't bear another scene like the one we'd had when he'd come to visit, but some part of me still believed that, eventually, John would play some part in Blaze's life.

Mostly, though, I avoided thinking too much about that part of the future. Blaze and I had already weathered the storm of his birth and I was sure that we could get through anything else that was thrown our way. If it were just the two of us, that would be all right as well. Blaze's presence gave me strength. His total dependence on me never made me feel helpless or alone; it invigorated me. Mothering Blaze, for me, was turning out to be a joint effort and it was Blaze who was helping me. Every time he smiled at me, I saw the echo of his first look at birth and felt the same joy. Here I am, that look said, and each time I saw it, I responded in kind. Yes, I told him, I know you.

Chapter 2

SCHOOLED

$\mathcal{M}$any of my childhood memories involve my father telling me, my sisters, and my brother that we were unusual. Not just run-of-the-mill bright, artistic, or beautiful, mind you, although he believed we were all of those. We were, he said, different from any other family. He never articulated exactly what this quality was; it came merely from being part of the seven-member team that was our nuclear group. When we went "out there" (meaning any place that wasn't home), he said, we had to play by the rules set up by the world, even if those rules weren't necessarily the same ones that governed our household. For a long time, my sense of what my father was saying was that we were a little island of alien beings masquerading as regular humans and, to my mind, he wasn't that far off the mark.

"Figure out what your teachers want," was his advice for performing at school, "and give it to them." In his opinion, school was where we learned how the rest of the world behaved; as for academics, it was just a given that we would all excel. His advice on most schoolwork began with the statement: "Any idiot can do this." Any idiot could do long division, for example, or tell time, or write a paper, or, later, drive a car. The things we learned at home were things that "any idiot" would never have access to, like the weekend nights we spent playing board games as a group. My parents often changed the parameters of the games to include some different concepts. We played "Clue" as a psychic exercise, for example. We would take turns selecting cards from the deck and psychically transmitting the images (be they Dining Room, Wrench, or Professor Plum) to another player. Masterpiece, a game where famous artworks are auctioned off, also got a few modifications. Nobody was allowed to play until they could identify, by artist and title, every one of the eighteen paintings in the game box.

Of course, this wasn't the only thing that made us different. None of my classmates had mothers who busted out a deck of Tarot cards or threw the *I-Ching* on a regular basis. For that matter, none of my peers had mothers who wore miniskirts and snakeskin platform shoes but who were also fluent in Yiddish and enjoyed a nice jar of pickled herring from time to time. None of the other dads knew how to cast horoscopes or listened to the Doors. And none of the other families moved around as often as we did.

We moved regularly, sometimes as often as yearly, and not just across town. My parents moved across continents. We went from England, where I was born, to Brooklyn, New York, and back again a couple of times. We moved to South Africa for a year and then to Los Angeles. We ended up in the Catskill Mountains for a few years, but even then, we moved from town to town several times. By the time I graduated from high school, I had attended thirteen different schools in three different countries. My parents weren't moving because of their jobs, because of schools, or to be closer to their own parents. When my classmates asked me if I was an army brat, I was baffled. I didn't have any idea what the term meant. No, my young, freethinking, nomadic parents were looking for the perfect place to raise their own tribe. Every time we relocated, my mother would sew together several Indian-print bedspreads and stuff them with colored foam. Bits of green-and-pink foam flecks dotted our carpets for at least a decade. "The big pillows," as we called them, functioned as couches.

My father bought a giant redwood picnic table and benches while we were living in Los Angeles and that traveled with us for years as our dining-room set. There was never a feeling of permanence in the places we lived and we owned nothing that couldn't be packed up quickly and shipped off to the next location.

Friends were equally transient. There was never time to form long-term friendships with schoolmates and not much of an inclination to bring anybody home. When friends came for dinner or for rare sleep-overs, they would inevitably be grilled, their eating habits criticized, their value systems judged. None of this was done in an overt, mean way. No, it was subtle enough to be missed by the guests but we would squirm under the light of that scrutiny on their behalf.

Above all else, my parents stressed our connectedness to each other and reinforced our need to support each other in every possible way. This too set us apart from the other families I knew growing up. The results of my parents' efforts can be seen in the terms we now use to classify anyone who is not a member of our immediate family:

1. Not one of us.

2. Could, maybe, with some work, be *like* one of us.

It seems as separatist now as it did then, but this philosophy has resulted in an extraordinary closeness and affection among all the members of my family. I have lived with my sister Maya for over a dozen years. We share almost everything. Although the rest of my siblings live in other houses, we all eat dinner together at least once a week. We speak to each other daily in a sort of shorthand relay. There is always somebody to talk to if need be and there is always a burgeoning story of interest to share. Of course, there are a few odd little anomalies and we do have our idiosyncrasies. One of us doesn't drive. One has a secret passion for the romance novels she keeps stashed under the bed. One only feels comfortable working the graveyard shift when nobody else is awake. One of us hides chocolate all over the house (actually, a couple of us do this). But we are comfortable in our peculiarities because, in my house, to be average was to be disappointing. To be different was good. We are products of our differences and this is what we have always known. If any of us felt as if we never quite fit in (as I did for most of my life), it was all right, because there was always home to retreat to. Home, where the rest of our kind resided.

I was in no way alarmed, then, when my own child exhibited some very specific differences early in his life. For example, Blaze never crawled. He preferred to slide backwards on his head to get where he was going. At twelve months he just got up and walked.

He had an acute sensitivity to loud noises and an extraordinary appreciation for all kinds of music by the time he was four years old. Although Maya is the only bona fide musician, music has always played a large role in my family. I listened to all kinds of music with Blaze, wanting to expose him to everything. By the time he approached his fifth birthday, he could single out the styles and voices of specific artists and showed a definite preference for jazz. I could never get Blaze to initiate dressing himself and it was very difficult for him to put his own shoes on, but when it came to picking out and playing music, he was adept with tapes and CDs and was more or less in control of the playlist in our house.

Unlike me, he never showed any kind of interest in drawing pictures. I bought him colored pens and markers just as my mother had for me, but he was much more interested in making up his own names for the different shades and gradations of color and then playing with the pens as if they were building blocks.

He toilet trained himself in the space of a week when he was two years old but preferred to sit backwards on the toilet until he was seven. Of course, this position necessitated taking off a fair amount of clothing, but I wasn't about to complain. I'd heard horror stories of parents who couldn't get their kids potty trained even after a year of trying so I considered myself lucky.

I read to Blaze daily and, by five, he knew the alphabet and the numbers to ten. I bought a map puzzle of the United States and before long he'd learned the names of all fifty states but he refused to put the puzzle together. He started speaking late, around the age of three, but early on he was able to replicate various sounds such as trains, bells, air brakes, and sirens.

None of these oddities seemed disturbing to me when Blaze was younger. He was beautiful, luminous, and receptive. He was special, yes, undoubtedly. I expected this. He was, after all, one of us.

When I enrolled Blaze in kindergarten in the fall of 1992, I expected that he would be a star in his class. He seemed ready, willing, and even happy to start. Although I had never minded the constant moving of my childhood, I planned to stay in one place and let Blaze put down his own roots in what I considered a safe, pleasant neighborhood. Four years before, my family left Portland and moved to California. Maya and I followed a few months later.

Now, she and I had just moved into a rapidly developing upper-middle-class neighborhood near the Pacific Ocean. We didn't exactly fit the community profile. We were a couple of waitresses among white-collar families with SUVs and mortgages and, according to the school directory, I was the only single mother with a child in kindergarten that year.

It was the elementary school itself that had attracted me to the area. The year before, Blaze and I had watched it being built as we rounded the neighborhood on our daily walks. I loved the look of it and the fact that it was so new and fresh. I met Blaze's teacher at the orientation for parents. She was very cool, very pretty, and very young. The school day for kindergartners was short, she told us, only three hours. I had no idea what I would do to fill the time. Aside from my time working, Blaze had been with me all five years of his life. I was thrilled for him and couldn't wait to see what adventures he'd have "out there."

As I took Blaze to his first day of kindergarten, we were both in high spirits. It was the first bridge to his life as an independent individual and we were happy to cross it. Just like everybody else.

Blaze and I arrive in front of his classroom fifteen minutes before school is due to start. The parking lot is jammed with Ford Explorers and Chevy Suburbans. Outside his classroom, the scene resembles a press briefing before an Academy Awards ceremony. Parents swarm the playground with video cameras and flashbulbs, photographing their children from every possible angle.

"Smile, Ashlyn, look at Daddy!"

"Honey, go stand by your teacher so Mommy can get a picture."

Blaze lets go of my hand as soon as we arrive and starts darting around, taking in the bustle of color and movement. Although I feel like the panorama in front of me is a little ridiculous, I have a twinge of regret that I haven't thought to bring a camera of my own. It looks bad, I think, showing up without some kind of recording device, like I don't care as much as the other parents, even though I'm convinced I probably care more. And I've shown up without a husband, either. Every other kindergartner here is represented by two parents. This is definitely not the first time I've felt different, but it *is* the first time I've ever felt guilty about it.

Some children are crying, unwilling to leave their parents but most—scrubbed, coiffed, and wearing their best designer duds—just appear vaguely stunned. There is not a single man, woman, or child of color in this entire panoply. This observation flits through my consciousness and settles somewhere in the back of my brain. Blaze's teacher emerges from her room like a movie star making her first entrance on the red carpet and directs the children to form a line.

"Go on, honey," I tell Blaze, "get in line." My voice is choked and there's a lump in my throat. I struggle to control myself because I don't want Blaze to think that I'm sad to see him go off to school. It turns out I've got nothing to worry about; Blaze gives me a perfunctory "Bye, Mom," and marches off into the classroom without a moment's hesitation. I watch him disappear and stand outside for a few minutes, sentimental tears rolling down my cheeks, listening to the click and whir of thirty cameras.

When I get back home, I haul out my own video camera. I may not have had one at the beginning of the day, but I'll be there to record the moment when he gets off the bus. Yessir, just like everybody else. My mother comes over to help me welcome Blaze home after his first day. I have tea with her and Maya and we talk about how exciting it is that Blaze is in school and he's already five, can you believe it, seems like it was just yesterday he was a newborn wrapped up in his bunny suit all snug in a front pack. When the time comes, all three of us walk to the corner, tape rolling, to wait for the bus. When it pulls up, we squeal with delight and start clapping.

The bus grunts to a halt in front of us and a couple of kids disembark. After a moment, Blaze bounces off too but his teacher appears at the top of the steps right behind him and she looks mighty concerned.

"Turn the camera off," my mother orders.

"What's wrong?" I ask the teacher.

"Hi, there," she offers by way of answering me. "Blaze is fine, but there's a little problem. We're wondering if you could come down to the school this afternoon for a meeting."

"What kind of problem?" I ask, a cold sweep of panic racing through my body. "Hi, Mom," Blaze says, "I like the bus." He turns around and starts to reboard, but my mother grabs his hand and walks off with him and Maya, leaving me with the teacher.

"What is it?" I ask her again.

"It would really be easier to explain at the meeting. Will it be possible for you to come at about four o'clock this afternoon?"

"No, I can't, I've got to go to work at four. Can you just give me an idea what this is about?" I ask her a third time. I can read nothing in the expressionless oval of her face and nothing from the well-modulated tone of her voice.

"Blaze seems to be having some problems adjusting to the class-room environment," she concedes finally. "He's kind of all over the place. We have a special day class right on site and we think that maybe that would be a better placement for him."

"What does that mean?"

"Look," she says, a little desperation of her own creeping into that tightly controlled tone, "it will really be easier to explain at the meeting and I've got to get back to the school right now. Will you be able to come earlier? Maybe around three o'clock?"

"Yes, yes, of course I'll come," I tell her. "Three o'clock. Fine."

Stunned, I walk back to the house. I have a very bad feeling about this and it's growing larger and blacker by the minute. I feed Blaze lunch and attempt to grill him on his first day of kindergarten, but I get less information from him than I did from his teacher. There is a slide, he tells me, and a sandbox. After that, he remains mute. I ask him if anything went wrong and he says no. He reiterates that he likes the bus. I am left to fill in the rest of the blanks myself.

I ask my mother, "What could possibly have happened in three hours?"

The meeting is held in a little room stuffed with several adults. I've had to attend in my black-and-white waitress work clothes because I'll have to go straight to work from here. Maya is at home with Blaze. Most nights, she is the one who stays with him while I work. One by one, I am introduced to the principal, the speech therapist, the special-education teacher, and the school psychologist, who also doubles as the special-education administrator. The kindergarten teacher, who I have now secretly dubbed "the Ice Princess," is here as well. These staff members compose the individual education program (IEP) team and

I will be meeting with them from now on, they tell me, to discuss Blaze's progress. Looking at them from my end of the long conference table, they remind me, vaguely, of a parole board. They have folders bulging with papers and carefully constructed looks of concern pasted onto their faces. Instead of receding, the wave of panic I felt a few hours ago is now a full-scale tsunami that threatens to drown me in adrenaline.

After the introductions, the school psychologist, Dr. Roberts, takes the lead. Blaze, she tells me, is not able to handle a regular kindergarten class and it is "the team's" recommendation that he be transferred to a special-education class immediately, pending further evaluation.

"We have an excellent special-education program here," the principal interjects with the cadence of a politician, "and Sally"—he gestures to the special-education teacher—"is one of the best. Her kiddos really do wonderfully in that environment."

"We think it's important that Blaze get some special attention at this point," Dr. Roberts adds.

"What did he do?" I am finally able to ask after clearing the boulder in my throat. "This was only the first day of school." They are well prepared for this question. Notes are pulled out and observations are shared. Dr. Roberts speaks in the slow, deliberate, well-enunciated sentences that are common to those in the psychiatric profession. I keep waiting for her to ask me, "And how does that make you feel?"

"He doesn't seem to be able to follow teacher-directed activity," she says. "When the teacher asked the children to sit in the circle, Blaze wandered around and didn't want to sit down."

"But he's never been in school before," I say. "He has no idea what he's supposed to do."

"He's never been in preschool?" Dr. Roberts asks, eyebrows raised.

"No, I've kept him home with me. I thought that was better for him." My voice sounds squeaky and tight, betraying my state of mind. Keep control, I tell myself, keep it together.

"And you're a single mom, is that right?"

"Yes, I'm a single mom."

"And does Blaze see Dad at all?"

"No, Blaze does not see Dad. There is no Dad."

Dr. Roberts makes several notes on the paper in front of her. Others shuffle papers of their own. Ice Princess maintains a glacial silence. This meeting is starting to feel less like a parole hearing and more like a trial. I still have no clue what Blaze has done to warrant such attention. Did he hit someone? Start a fire? Threaten the president of the United States? What?

"So we're here because Blaze didn't sit in the circle?" I ask.

"Well, no, there's a little more to it than that," Dr. Roberts says. "In my observation of him today, he didn't initiate play with any other children."

"He's never been around any other children," I tell her.

Ice Princess finally chimes in. "Blaze does not seem able to cut with scissors," she says. "Is that something you've noticed at home?"

"No, it isn't," I say. "He's never used a scissors at home. He's never *had* to."

But Ice Princess is not finished. "When I asked the children to form a line, Blaze could not take his place. He ran out the door without waiting for the rest of the group."

"You know, he really doesn't have any experience in a classroom environment," I tell them. "He's really not used to lining up and cutting and all those things. There are really a lot of things that he *can* do."

"Really?" Dr. Roberts says, smiling. "Why don't you tell us some of those?"

I'm wondering if it's her tone that's making me feel like jumping across the table and throttling her or if I'm just having a psychotic break. Surely, she's said and done nothing that warrants the fury I'm starting to feel.

"He knows the names of all fifty states," I say feebly.

"That's wonderful," Dr. Roberts says. "Does he have any other special talents?"

Her tone indicates that she doesn't necessarily think "special talents" are such a good thing, but I answer her anyway, unable to stop myself. I am proud of the things Blaze knows, proud of the fact that he is special. I tell Dr. Roberts that Blaze loves jazz and that he can tell the difference between Billie Holiday and Ella Fitzgerald. I mention that I've been showing him a big illustrated book of Impressionist painters and he can now identify Degas and Monet. Dr. Roberts continues to take notes. I glance around the room at the impassive faces surrounding me and I want to cry. I must sound like a complete fool. I'm protesting too much. They must think I'm lying or at least exaggerating. Maybe they think I'm deranged. Anger creeps in again. These people probably don't even know who Ella Fitzgerald and Billie Holiday *are*, I think, especially Ice Princess who is now telling the group that she doesn't think Blaze is mature enough to follow the rules of a kindergarten classroom. I respond, pointedly, that Blaze knows all his letters and numbers.

"Blaze seems uncomfortable making eye contact," Dr. Roberts pipes in. "Have you noticed that at home? Does he dislike being touched?"

"No," I tell her emphatically, "I've never noticed that, not ever. Blaze is a sweet, happy kid. He's really very bright. He's clean and neat . . ."

"Really?" Dr. Roberts asks. "Is he very neat? Does he like to have things ordered? Like his toys? Does he line his shoes or building blocks up in a row?"

"No," I tell her through clenched teeth. I can see where she's going with this. "He's neat, he's not obsessive."

I tell the group at large that Blaze is a completely contented child, that he'd shown no signs of distress about going to school or leaving me this morning. I am practically begging them to believe me, and I hate the sound of it. I finish by saying I can't understand how some confusion over what to do on his first ever day at school justifies being referred to special education.

Dr. Roberts, it seems, has been anticipating this and has saved the best for last.

"Blaze refused to come inside after recess was over," she says. "The teacher was unable to persuade him and so I went out there. When I tried to coerce him, he became very agitated. He yelled at me to go away and pushed me. He pulled at my nylons when I tried to remove him from the slide."

I look at her aghast. Pulled her nylons? Who is this child she is describing? A parallel universe version of Blaze? I can't even fully bring myself to believe her, although after she delivers this proclamation (more like a sucker punch, I'm thinking), I feel like I want to pull her nylons and hit her myself. There isn't much I can say now to dig Blaze out of the hole that he's in. There's no offensive strategy I can come up with. From now on, it's all going to be about defense.

"Blaze is a very happy child," I tell Dr. Roberts. "I've never seen him hit or push anyone. I really don't know what could have happened to make him react that way."

It seems that everybody has suddenly started talking at once. The speech therapist is saying Blaze might not have adequate communicative skills. Sally, the special-education teacher, offers the fact that her class is much smaller than the regular kindergarten class and, therefore, Blaze would be able to receive much more one-on-one attention. Dr. Roberts says that, of course, they'd want to do a thorough evaluation to determine "the best possible placement" for Blaze.

As a final trump card and as if to prove what an utter failure Blaze has been in her classroom, Ice Princess brings out some work samples. The assignment was to draw yourself and your family, she says. The first few she shows are typical kindergarten drawings, some stick figures, some bodies filled in. Blue skies, yellow suns. Then she brings out Blaze's drawing, a formless swirl of color.

"He doesn't like to draw," I say, almost in a whisper. "I don't make him draw at home."

"Coloring is an important prewriting skill," Dr. Roberts says. "Children need to be able to color appropriately at the kindergarten level to prepare them for first grade. First grade is very challenging academically."

She assures me, again, that special education is the best placement for Blaze. I can't help but feel that all of these people are implying, or at the very least trying to make me admit, that there is something wrong with Blaze. Nobody has mentioned what, exactly, but now I certainly am not lacking examples of what a catastrophe his first day has been. Tears start welling in my eyes and I struggle to keep them back. I begin to lose focus on the specifics of what is being said. I feel an unbridgeable chasm opening between how these people see my child and how I do and I am not sure that it is going to close anytime soon. I see nothing wrong with him and they see nothing right.

Dr. Roberts tells me that we will have to decide on a "handicapping condition." The law requires that, to qualify for special education, a child has to meet certain criteria. Some of my choices here include specific learning disability, deaf/blind, multiple handicaps, autistic, mentally retarded, severely emotionally disturbed, and speech/language impaired. How can I possibly pick from one of these categories? I have gone from having a beautiful, bright child to a handicapped kindergartner in the space of a few minutes. I don't know how this has happened or why I let it happen at all. It's the evidence they pulled out, I think. The evidence was damning. Dr. Roberts suggests we go with speech and language impaired since Blaze seems to have trouble processing language and expressing himself. Fine, I tell her, speech and language. At least she hasn't suggested that he's mentally retarded. I suppose I should consider myself lucky. I debate protesting some more, telling them that this is a mistake, that there's nothing wrong with Blaze, that he's a special, wonderful kid and part of a special, different family, but I stop myself. The faces in this room show no signs of yielding. They've made up their minds. Ultimately, it is the implacable gaze of the Ice Princess that does it for me. I don't know much about the special-ed class, but I sense that it will be better than what Blaze will get with her. Although I feel foolish for feeling it, in this moment, I hate her completely.

I sign papers to transfer Blaze into the special-education class where he will start tomorrow morning. Sally encourages me to come and see the classroom when I bring Blaze in so we can both feel "comfortable." Fuck comfortable, I want to tell her. We left comfortable behind as soon as this meeting began. I agree to a full evaluation by the speech therapist, and Dr. Roberts and I make an appointment with the school nurse who will take a full medical history (part of me is convinced that in the course of these evaluations, Blaze's native intelligence will shine through and they'll all be able to see what a mistake this has been). Everybody seems happy with the results of the meeting. I am not smiling. I walk away from the building so fast, I am almost running. The tears have started now but I wipe them away. I will have to wait until I finish working to go home and get into bed. I can't share the pain I am feeling now, it is too close to the bone. I want to be able to cry in private.

It took days for me to come to a full acceptance that Blaze was in a special-education class. Even after the description of his behavior on his first day of school, I still couldn't figure out what he had done that was so bad. I kept looking at him, searching for clues to what they were talking about and what I could have missed in the five years since his birth. I had never so much as suspected that what I had considered "special" could be regarded as "wrong." I was forced to sift through all his behaviors (and my own) to see if I could even vaguely reconcile my version of Blaze with the school's. The first order of business was to figure out what I had done incorrectly as his mother.

I knew that I'd done everything I *thought* was right for my child. I'd kept him with me throughout his first five years because I thought it would give him a sense of security to know that I was always there. He should get the full benefit of the one parent he did have. Despite the fact that he had lots of attention from a big and loving family, I felt bad that he didn't have a father and I wanted to make up for it by being both mother *and* father to him. I actually scoffed at mothers who put their kids in child care even when they didn't have to work. Why have a kid at all, I'd always wondered, if you weren't going to spend any time with him?

I'd disciplined Blaze but let him develop at his own pace. I wanted him to be whoever he wanted to be. I had never noticed behavior from him that seemed unacceptable to me. I had always assumed that when Blaze started school he would be able to follow the rules, adapt, find his way in the world just as I had. But it was clear from that very first day that Blaze was not going to fit this profile at all. He was operating from his own rule book and it had nothing to do with what the school thought was "normal" or "appropriate."

Although I agreed to place Blaze in special ed, I didn't think he would have to stay there. I thought if I just gave him enough time to figure out what was expected of him in school, he would pull it together and go back to the regular kindergarten world where he belonged. I suppose Dr. Roberts and company would have considered this deep denial. I thought he was brilliant and didn't belong in special ed at all. But aside from this, I had a host of prejudices about special ed based on my own experiences.

Special-ed kids didn't mix with the general population when I was in school. The remedial kids attended the "stupid class" but the real tough cases went to school in separate institutions far away from public view. These institutions were so removed that I wouldn't have known they even existed as a child but for the fact that my father worked briefly in one of them when we lived in upstate New York. It had been an intense and draining experience for him. He became too emotionally attached to the kids, my mother informed me much later, and descended into a deep depression that manifested itself in physical illness.

Those who weren't bad off enough to warrant placement outside public school in an institution such as my father worked in but who still needed "extra help" got the brunt of the teasing schoolchildren are famous for. These kids—the ones who needed remedial English or math—who had to attend summer school or vocational school, were "retards" or worse. The worst mark of failure was to have to ride the small school bus—a dead giveaway that you were a hopeless social write-off at best, functionally retarded at worst. Because the stigma was so severe, especially as we advanced through the grades, the kids who needed this extra help or who continued to fail in regular classes, merely dropped out of school early or joined a tough crowd, taking up smoking or drinking or delinquency. I had no intention of signing my child up for thirteen years of this kind of torment. My goal was to get him the hell out of special ed before he could realize that he was even in it.

Ironically, the ultimate goal of the special-ed class and the special-ed teacher, I was told, was quite similar. Their directive, Dr. Roberts told me, was to get the kids "mainstreamed." That is, normal enough to fit into a regular classroom. Whatever time they could spend outside the special-ed classroom was to be encouraged. Therefore, Blaze would be spending some quality art and recess time with the Ice Princess and her class.

I liked Sally, the special-ed teacher. She seemed to me to have all the qualities that Ice Princess was missing. She smiled and laughed, for one thing. The tone of her voice changed, encompassing some highs and lows instead of remaining at a steady, hospice-worker level, and she actually seemed to *like* the children. She would be one of very few teachers in Blaze's school career who wouldn't look at him as if he were an alien life-form she'd never seen before. Sally was creative and she took a creative approach to solving problems in her class. When I came to pick Blaze up after his first day in her class, for example, she informed me that she felt the two of them were going to get along just fine. She had asked Blaze to do some work, she said, and Blaze had responded that he would work if she took her long blond hair out of its ponytail. Sally complied and Blaze performed whatever task it was that she was requesting. Sally wore her hair down for the rest of the year.

Because she was the special-ed teacher, I learned later, Sally was allowed to think outside the box. Teachers in regular ed are allowed very little creative latitude. Therefore, Ice Princess became "very concerned" when Blaze said something like "The floor hurts my feet"; no matter how much I explained that he was trying to tell her that his ankles hurt from sitting cross-legged on the hard floor, she was convinced that he was having delusions of the floor attacking him. Sally, on the other hand, was likelier to ask me what I thought Blaze meant if he used language in a metaphoric way. She'd tell me that he'd mentioned having "red lasers" in his stomach and I was able to tell her that he used that term whenever he was nervous about something. She'd think about this for a moment and then tell me that, yes, that nervousness did sort of feel like red lasers, didn't it?

Above all, Sally was determinedly cheerful but not in the false, fabricated way I was starting to recognize from other school staffers. Sally's cheerfulness was both positive and genuine. This was more than I could say for her class. Since there was only one special-ed class in the school, Sally had a mix of at least four grade levels in her classroom and what seemed to be an astonishing array of "issues." There was one little girl in a wheelchair and one boy who had severe vision problems. There was an older, bigger boy who continuously shouted out a pattern of loud sounds in an unchanging loop. A couple of kids sat at the edge of the room, desperately working on computers as if their lives depended on it. The rest of the class merely looked tired and dispirited as if they had already had enough of the whole school experience. Despite Sally's creativity and her innate warmth and compassion for her students, I don't remember them ever looking happy when I dropped Blaze off there every morning. They looked, to me, like prison inmates waiting for a reprieve. I liked Sally but I hated leaving Blaze there every day. It was depressing and I was depressed about the whole situation.

As the days wore on, I wondered how long it would take Blaze to come around to my father's philosophy of "give your teachers what they want" or if that would ever even happen. Blaze's placement in special ed right out of the gate underscored the feeling I'd always had that I'd never really fit in and that, although I'd been able to cover it well, whenever I went "out there," I was merely visiting. Obviously, I now thought, the same applied to my son and he was apparently less able to camouflage his differences than I had been. Although I'd always tried to see Blaze as his own person, always listened to him when he spoke to me, and constantly defined my role as his mother, I still had his identity very much tied up with my own when he started school. I filtered his experiences through my own impressions, which was all I had to go on. Blaze was stingy with the details of his life at school. If I demanded information, I got nothing. If I waited a few hours after he got home, when he finished processing his day, I'd get some odds and ends, such as what book the teacher was reading or who cried on the playground, but never more than that. I had to rely solely on what the teachers told me and what I personally could observe and interpret. I was in the position of being both his defender and translator on a daily basis.

Sally, Dr. Roberts, and the speech therapist began the series of psycho-educational tests that I'd signed off on. Blaze was uncooperative in the extreme. For Dr. Roberts's tests, he refused even to remain seated, let alone finish drawing triangles or squares.

"Blaze had great difficulty staying seated and attending to the directions of the standardized tests given," she later wrote in her report. "During the testing session, the reinforcer offered was time to play in the playhouse outside the examiner's door; this reinforcer was not powerful enough to motivate Blaze to cooperate. He threw the testing booklet on the floor and began to kick the filing cabinets, the door, and the examiner."

I was very disappointed in these results. Blaze was proving me to be a liar. Even though I begged him to cooperate and even sat in the room while Dr. Roberts administered one of her tests, Blaze was as intractable as he had been in the days following his birth when he'd refused to nurse or cry or get on with the general business of living. He had decided not to take the tests and so he didn't. No amount of cajoling or pleading would get him to change his mind.

Sally was only slightly more successful in obtaining any kind of valid information from the tests she administered. No matter how carefully a test was disguised, Blaze always seemed to know exactly when his abilities were being measured against a standard and immediately shut down. At least, it seemed that Sally was beginning to understand that Blaze did have some academic skills. "He knows his letters and most of his sounds," she told me, "it's just really difficult to know what else he knows because he won't tell us."

I considered the speech therapist an absolute lunatic. She jumped up and down, alternately told Blaze that his behavior was inappropriate and that she thought he was a wonderful boy, and sang show tunes out loud. For once, Blaze seemed totally stunned into silence, if not submission. His fascination with the speech therapist was short-lived. After the first few sessions with her, he refused to work with her and simply hightailed it out of the room whenever he was scheduled with her. Luckily, she was reassigned to another school shortly after this and another, much calmer, woman took her place.

None of the teachers who tested Blaze got what I felt were accurate results in determining his intelligence, potential, or what was "wrong" with him. In a way, it was like a repeat of the medical tests given to him right after his birth. Again, no conclusive results, nothing specific, no diagnosis. Only Blaze, it seemed, knew what was really going on and he wasn't saying.

I attended a series of meetings during those first few months of school to review the findings of the tests and assess placement for Blaze. Not surprisingly, all the school staffers felt that Blaze should remain in special ed. "What's really important," Sally told me, "is that he start forming some peer relationships and learning appropriate social skills." I couldn't imagine how Blaze was going to learn "appropriate" social skills from the kids he was now in class with. He seemed most intrigued by the boy who made noises and shouted out non sequiturs and had taken to imitating him. In fact, Blaze found the most *inappropriate* behaviors very appealing and sought to mimic them whenever possible. If he wasn't acting like a total nut when he entered school, I reckoned, he certainly would be by the end of kindergarten.

I began taking my father with me to the meetings at school. I had a paranoid hunch that my status as waitress–single mom wasn't helping me when I tried to get answers from the staff about what exactly they thought was wrong with Blaze and why, exactly, they thought he needed to be in special education. My father was a big hit at the meetings. Dr. Roberts thought he was just wonderful and for the first time, I actually heard some of the other (all female) staff giggle. I found it vaguely repulsive that it seemed I could only get taken seriously with a man present, but I accepted it as fact and, from then on, I wouldn't attend a meeting without him.

Although I ran the gamut of emotions that year, from depressed and angry to ashamed and then vaguely hopeful, I never felt that Blaze would spend his school career in special-ed. I saw very few of the other parents in Blaze's class on a daily basis, but I felt no kinship with those I did speak to occasionally. When the mother of the little girl in the wheelchair asked me if I would like to join a support group for parents of children with disabilities, I was actually insulted. My child did *not* have a disability—he was just not cut out for a regular classroom. He was not a round peg. He wasn't even a square peg. The board for his shape peg hadn't been built yet. And I had a nagging feeling that this was all a big joke to Blaze, that he understood the drill and could have followed it if he'd wanted to. But since the moment of his birth, Blaze has been both stubborn and unyielding. If his behavior was under his control, he wasn't letting on—not to Sally, not to Dr. Roberts, and not to me.

I could tell that most of the staff thought that I just couldn't accept my son's problems and most of them treated me as if I were likely to become hysterical at any moment. It would be years later, when I found myself working in special education, that I would finally be able to see what they saw or even have a point of view other than the one I held to then.

Talking to the Ice Princess was especially horrible. Every time we had a meeting, she brought out more examples of Blaze's "work," which looked like textbook illustrations from the loony bin. There were Smoky the Bear puppets with eyes glued where the mouth should be, drawings of houses that looked like they'd been through Hurricane Andrew, and the letters of his name drawn in fragile, shaky lines. She seemed bent on making me understand that my son was really damaged in some way. All the while, that pitiless demeanor of hers never changed, no matter if I was cheerful, teary, angry, or distant. During one meeting, I asked her if she had any children of her own because I just couldn't see a human baby coming out of that sub-zero body. She admitted that she hadn't yet had children but she was

planning to and—in any case, she added defensively—it made no difference to her ability to teach kindergarten or love her students. I thought
perhaps if her students were all robotic Popsicles that might actually be
true. What I told her, though, in a rare moment of honesty, was that I
hoped that if she did someday have children, she would never have to face
the kind of parent-teacher conferences I was having with her.

I'll never know exactly why Blaze's first day of school resulted in such
a complete disaster. I can't tell whether or not he would even have
been noticed if the school were in an urban area or catering to a different demographic. Sometimes I think that if the Ice Princess had
been slightly warmer and willing to give him a chance at a second day
in her class, perhaps things would have been different. Then I wonder,
if Blaze's behavior had sent up so many red flags, why had nobody ever
mentioned them to me before? And I wonder why, although Dr.
Roberts et al. asked me questions that were clearly geared to elicit certain responses (Does he line up his toys? Does he make eye contact
with you? Does he cry when he hurts himself?), nobody ever told me
what *disorders* they thought Blaze might have. The fact that I had
never suspected school problems would be in store for Blaze made me
ill equipped to handle what I felt was a full-scale attack the first day
and I do believe that the tenor of those early meetings have affected
my attitude toward the school system ever since.

Many years after those first dark days of kindergarten, when Blaze
was nearing the end of sixth grade, I requested a copy of his school
file that was, by then, several inches thick. The special-education secretary was very busy that week and I was working at the school at
that point, so I volunteered to copy it myself. The secretary happily
complied since there aren't many school jobs as onerous as copying
(the copier's always broken, the upper-grade teachers always have
something more important and more urgent ot copy, and the staples
are always getting caught). Parents of children in special education

always get copies of all the IEP forms they sign at all the meetings they attend, but there are other pieces of paper in the file that most parents don't see. There are notes between teachers, for example, work samples, written observations of the child's behavior and other odds and ends. I would never have had the chance to read any of these if the secretary had copied the file herself. As I yanked staples out of paper packets and tried to catch floating Post-its, I paid careful attention to the beginning of the file. Dr. Roberts had since moved on to less stressful pastures, but I could picture her all over again when I saw her incredibly controlled, neat handwriting, not a dash or comma out of place. What intrigued me the most were the notes of her initial observation of Blaze on his first day of school. She had observed him from 9:00 A.M. to 9:20 A.M. and decided his entire school future in less than half an hour. She wrote:

Does not understand the process of lining up and following other children or keeping same place in line (runs ahead of others when placed in line).

Would not sit on his name spot.

Had difficulty accepting limits; he wanted to eat another cracker and asked repeatedly for a cracker although he was told that it was not time to have a cracker; repeatedly tried to pull a chair over to get the crackers down from the shelf in spite of clear statements "No, you may not have a cracker."

I laughed about the crackers in spite of myself. To me, pulling out a chair and trying to reach the crackers sounded like good problem-solving—something Blaze hadn't exactly excelled at since. I could just picture the Ice Princess having a meltdown over the sheer irregularity of it all. But I was curious about the rest. Dr. Roberts, the Ice Princess—even Sally—had always maintained that Blaze was unaware of his actions and unable to control his behavior. By that point, Blaze had demonstrated a vaultlike memory many times over so I wanted to know how much of kindergarten he remembered and what details were prominent in his recollections. I asked him to tell me about that year.

"Well, Mom," he began, "you know kindergarten wasn't exactly the best time of my life. I don't really want to talk about it." I knew this better than anybody, but I urged him to continue.

"I hated lining up," he said. "We had to line up every day, all the time, for everything. Always lining up. I wouldn't do it. I hated it. The teacher read us a story every morning and we all had to sit on our names in the circle. I didn't like sitting on my name, either. There was a better place to sit on the carpet near the playhouse. I got put in time-out. Dr. Roberts came in and then I had to go sit in her office." He stopped and took a breath. "I don't want to talk about kindergarten, Mom." I didn't make him continue, although I was sure that if I pressed him, he could have come up with a few more tidbits, especially in his memories of the Ice Princess which, I knew, were almost as fond as mine ("I really hated her, Mom, she was the evil character of my school"). The point was that he remembered it all and was conscious of his behavior at the time. I'd always suspected as much but this knowledge hadn't helped either one of us when Blaze started school. The classroom is the one place where Blaze has always kept his talents well hidden.

Of course, I knew none of this at the time and had no experiences with which to compare Blaze's entry into public school. After he'd been in school for a few months, I didn't even know what was normal behavior for a five-year-old boy anymore and had to rely on Dr. Roberts and Sally to tell me. I don't think I'll ever really be sure whether Blaze's behavior that first day warranted his immediate transfer into special ed or if that transfer precipitated other behaviors that really were worthy of a special-ed classroom. It's a chicken-and-egg conundrum that will likely never be solved for me.

As Blaze came to the end of his first year and we headed into the start of the second, I started looking outside the school for some answers as to why he didn't fit into the expected classroom mold. This would mark the real beginning of our journey and an entry into the world of doctors, specialists, medications, and diagnostic labels. By the end of that first year too my father had changed his instructions for performing at school. Instead of "Give your teachers what they want" he told Blaze, "Pretend you're like everybody else while you're in school."

In my heart, I knew that my father's advice was tailor-made for Blaze because the one thing I *was* sure of was that Blaze really wasn't like everybody else. I could even see it when I dropped him off at school and came to pick him up. Around the other kids, he even looked different, less solid somehow, as if his physical body wasn't quite all there. To me, Blaze looked like a character from one of the old *Star Trek* episodes who was in the process of being transported to a new planet. He looked as if he hadn't quite beamed in all the way, as if there were still parts of him floating through space. I'd leave him at school and he'd smile at me, watching me as I left, waiting patiently, I assumed, for transmissions from the mother ship.

Chapter 3

THE GOOD DOCTORS

*M*y relationship with those in the medical profession has long been an uneasy one. This stems partly from my parents, who have never liked or trusted doctors and have always had serious misgivings about the way most doctors practice medicine. My mother and father both had negative associations with the medical profession based on their own experiences and have never forgiven or forgotten. My mother had a grisly tale of a nearly botched tonsillectomy when she was a child. After the death of his own father in one, my father viewed hospitals as places where people went to die, not recover. An obstetrician pressured my parents into inducing labor when my mother was pregnant with her last child because he was afraid an approaching snowstorm would make travel to the hospital more difficult. My parents acquiesced and my sister was born a few hours later, not quite ready to come out, with a slightly underdeveloped liver that required two extra days in the hospital. Without ever explaining why, a series of gynecologists tried to convince my mother to have a hysterectomy after the birth of her last child. She was told that she would regret not having the surgery. Terrified, my mother got as far as the preoperative suite before climbing off the table and checking herself out of the hospital, never to return.

When I was growing up, my parents transferred many of their misgivings to my siblings and me. Aside from clinic visits for immunizations, none of us ever visited a pediatrician. I didn't go to a doctor for a physical, sick call, or checkup until I was an adult. My sisters and brother followed the same course. None of us took antibiotics until we were in our twenties. Most of us didn't even know what antibiotics *were* until then. My father's attitude was always clear. "Doctors are like mechanics," he used to say. "If you take your car to a mechanic, he'll find something wrong with it and if you go to a doctor, he'll find something wrong with *you*. That's his job."

Both my parents also believed that most ailments could be controlled by attitude and neither one of them was particularly tolerant of colds, flu, sprains or the like. "Get over it," my father used to say. "Stop coughing." I realize this sounds a little draconian in the telling. It wasn't. My parents would never have denied any of their children medical attention if we needed it and we knew that. (When my brother had appendicitis, he went immediately to the hospital and when my sister fell out of a tree, nobody stopped on the way to the ER to question whether her leg was really broken.) However, we weren't about to get extra attention and coddling if we got sick. My parents saved positive reinforcement for getting better or beating a cold before it turned into a fever.

Long before it became trendy, my mother started exploring alternative methods of healing. Our kitchen cabinets were always stocked with homeopathic remedies, essential oils, and vitamins. She is the only woman I know who gave herself mustard plasters for catarrh (and honestly, who even knew what catarrh was?). Doctors, clinics, and hospitals were always a last resort.

By their own admission, my parents were extremely lucky. Out of five children, there was only one broken leg and one appendectomy. In retrospect, this kind of health record seems nothing short of a miracle to me. Of course, growing up, it didn't seem like a miracle; it seemed normal not to be sick and not to trust doctors. Blaze changed all of that—not just for me, but for my entire family.

From the outset, Blaze had odd medical issues that required trips to, and conversations with, pediatricians and specialists. These began with the drama of his birth and the series of inconclusive tests. I was constantly on the verge of weepy hysteria the first few days of Blaze's life and didn't question much of what the nurses and pediatricians were doing. I just wanted to get my baby home. When he was finally released, looking no worse for the wear, I assumed that Blaze would need no more medical supervision than I had as a child. I was further off the mark than I could have imagined.

When Blaze was four weeks old, I got a call from his pediatrician who said she wanted to discuss some test results with me. Please, I begged her, it's not anything bad, is it? Please, tell me it's not something bad. No, nothing terrible, she assured me. Did I remember Blaze taking the PKU test? Of course I didn't. He'd had so many tests, it was impossible to recall this one. Patiently, the pediatrician explained that the PKU test was given to all newborns at birth and then again at two weeks and it screened for some congenital abnormalities. Too frightened to speak, I looked over at Blaze, rolled up in a blanket and tucked into his straw carry basket. He was chubby and healthy and gorgeous. There couldn't possibly be anything abnormal about this baby. One of the things the PKU screened for, the pediatrician continued, was hypothyroidism, or low levels of thyroid hormone in the blood. Congenital hypothyroidism could result in mental retardation, she explained, but it was treatable, so the test was an extremely important one. She barreled ahead, not giving me a chance to react to this information. Blaze's test had *not* shown significantly low thyroid hormone, she said, but his levels were not as high as they should be. In fact, she added, the levels were exactly on the borderline between normal and low. After delivering this piece of news, she stressed that I didn't need to worry, that he was still just in the normal range and that before she did anything she'd like to test him again in case his birth trauma or some other testing glitch had affected the outcome.

I hung up and stared blankly at the wall. The test was wrong, I repeated to myself. The test was wrong. Consciously, I believed this, but on a deeper level I suspected that this simple test might only be the beginning, that Blaze and I were not going to get off so lightly.

Blaze began what would be an endless series of diagnostic tests. Extracting blood from him proved to be an almost insurmountable challenge for even the most skilled pediatricians in the hospital. Blaze's veins were buried beneath his baby fat and refused to yield to the assault of a needle. His doctor tried veins on the hand, wrists, arms. After thirty minutes of this, Blaze was a screaming pincushion and I had bitten tiny holes in my lip. The doctor looked pale.

"I'm sorry," she said. "I think I'm going to have to try his neck. You might want to wait outside."

"No," I told her. "I'm not leaving him."

I watched as the doctor and several nurses held Blaze down on an examining table and tipped his head back so that his neck was exposed. To me, he looked like nothing less than a sacrificial lamb being readied for slaughter. Blaze was crying so hard he was almost choking. The pediatrician prodded his neck with her finger for a moment and quickly slid a needle into what I assumed was his jugular vein. Terror produces no tears and so I remained dry-eyed and trembling. At the same time, watching this horrific tableau, I realized that if I hadn't allowed this procedure, it wouldn't be happening at all. There were things Blaze didn't have to suffer, I decided, and it was my job to figure out what those things were. I was his mother. He couldn't say no but I could. I would never have felt so empowered for myself, but the total trust and dependence on me that Blaze had was inviolable.

"I hate to have to do it that way," the doctor told me after she was finished and Blaze was returned to my arms.

"Have you taken blood from the neck often?" I asked.

"Once," she said, cheerfully.

"I don't want to do that again," I said. "We'll have to find another way."

"I agree," she said and made a notation on Blaze's chart. It said, *Difficult Draw.*

After three separate blood tests, Blaze's thyroid levels remained exactly where they had been the first time, on the border between low and normal. Blaze's pediatrician and the pediatric endocrinologists at the hospital were stumped, unsure what was causing the low levels and why they didn't move in either direction. We'll keep testing him over the next few months and see what happens, they said. When Blaze was seven months old, the doctors advised me to start giving him synthetic thyroid hormone, "just to be on the safe side." My parents advised against it.

"Don't give him hormones, you don't know what they can do," my father said.

"I don't know what *not* giving them will do, either," I told him.

"You can't trust these doctors," my mother said.

"I have to trust them," I told her. "At least a little."

Finally, we struck something of a compromise. I agreed to take Blaze to a naturopath my mother had found. Although he seemed reasonable enough, I didn't have much faith in the naturopath and it wasn't because he wasn't an M.D. I told him the results of Blaze's blood tests and he suggested I take thyroid hormone from a natural source and Blaze would get it through my breast milk. I had all kinds of problems with this. The first was that there was no way to measure the amount of hormone Blaze would receive this way and the second was that the "natural" hormone came from actual desiccated thyroid. Forget it, I told my mother. You eat somebody's dried-up thyroid gland; it's not for me. I put Blaze on the synthetic hormone and his next blood test showed normal levels. I was advised to follow up regularly with a pediatric endocrinologist as Blaze would likely need to keep taking the hormone for a long time. But what was it that could cause this kind of thing, I asked. Heredity? Genetics? Blown over fallout from Chernobyl? Would there be long-term effects? What would they be?

Don't worry, I was assured. Everything looks good. Could be any number of factors contributing, but it doesn't matter. Don't worry. Don't worry.

In March of 1990, when he was almost three years old, Blaze developed a series of colds accompanied by a constant dry cough, wheezing, and struggling for breath. The symptoms got a little worse each time he got sick. I took him to a pediatrician, but she wasn't particularly helpful. She wrote me a prescription for Ventolin syrup, which sometimes helped but often didn't. Blaze always seemed to get the sickest in the darkest, most unforgiving hours of the night when there was nobody to call and no buffer between me and my fear. I'd spent many moments cataloguing my sins and making wordless promises to God at two and three o'clock in the morning while Blaze lay next to me, feverish, wheezing, coughing. Just let him get better. It was every mother's midnight prayer. Just let him get better and I'll do anything.

I hated to leave him at all when he was sick but I had to work. I was a waitress and a day off meant no pay. A few days off translated to a loss of seniority. Other waiters would start getting the night shifts and I would get demoted to lunches. There were no "sick days" in this restaurant and sick kids didn't count, either. I was the only waitress working there with a child and one of very few women working the dinner shifts. It wouldn't take much time off to change this exalted status permanently.

One particularly cold, windy night, I arrived home from a long dinner shift to find Blaze lying on the couch with Maya, gasping for air.

He was sucking his chest in and out with short, tortured breaths and couldn't even hold enough air in his lungs to speak. He was whimpering and seemed totally exhausted.

"I'm really worried," I told Maya, but this was a lie—I was terrified. I called my father, waking him.

"Blaze needs to go to the hospital," I told him.

"Are you sure it's that bad?" he asked me. No, I told him, it was much worse than that. My father, hater of hospitals, intolerant of illness, took one look at Blaze when he arrived and said, "Which emergency room is closest?"

On the way to the hospital, I held Blaze close to me in the backseat of the car. I could feel his small heart beating wildly and the warmth of his little body through his sweater. I tried to send strength through my arms to him and tried not to let my fear seep through to him. I held my breath and let it out, trying to breathe for him. If only it were me, I kept thinking, I could handle this if it were me. I would have some control.

The emergency room was a bright rush of sounds. Blaze was immediately given two injections of epinephrine. His arms and legs went rigid and he cried out. A cluster of technicians crowded around him, stringing wires and tubes. I tried to get close to him to take his hand and tell him it would be all right; I was there, but he couldn't hear me above the din of voices and equipment.

"He's in pretty bad shape," the on-call pediatrician told me. "We're going to have to transport him to the children's hospital. He's definitely not going home tonight."

I searched my father's face for reassurance and he said, "He'll be okay. They know what they're doing."

I was not allowed to ride with Blaze in the ambulance that took him to the children's hospital. It was two o'clock in the morning and a light rain had started to fall. I watched the paramedics load my child into the ambulance and close the doors and I felt like my insides were falling out right there in the parking lot. It was a sickeningly familiar feeling, just like the one I had when Blaze was born and I had to leave the hospital without him. Since then, he had never been alone with anyone who wasn't family.

I couldn't hear my father's words of comfort as we followed the ambulance on the freeway. I kept thinking, he's only two. He's only two years old.

In the early hours of the morning, the light in the children's hospital had an eerie, pale green glow. The sound between the walls was that of tender, muted grief. There were fuzzy bears and colorful posters everywhere, but they couldn't make up for the total absence of cheer. I followed Blaze to the intermediate care unit where he would stay until the doctors could determine whether he needed a bed in the regular ward or in intensive care. Both Maya and my father were showing signs of exhaustion so I told them to go home. It was only me then, peering over a crowd of doctors, trying to catch a glimpse of my son. A specialist entered the room briskly and asked, "Is this the asthmatic baby?"

This was the first time I had heard the word *asthma* and I was stunned. Is that what it was? Asthma? Why didn't I know that? What did I forget to ask? What else didn't I know?

I didn't have time to voice any of these questions because I was quickly hustled off to the main office to discuss insurance and how I would be paying for Blaze's treatment.

"I really need to get back to my child," I told the automaton in the office. "Can we discuss this in the morning?"

"I understand that this is difficult," she told me, "but we do need to discuss the financial aspects of your son's care. Where do you work again?"

"I'm a waitress," I told her. "I work in a restaurant." I was still in my work clothes; black pants, black tie, and white shirt. The night's tips were folded into my front shirt pocket because I hadn't even had the presence of mind to move them into my purse. I smelled like roasted duck. I didn't want to be discussing "financial aspects" with this calmly efficient woman while my son was struggling for each breath he took, but I had to hand it to her—for a moment she actually got me distracted and I started thinking about money and visualizing the huge sums that were already accumulating. I wondered where the hospital found people to work in the middle of the night asking distraught parents about cash flow. I knew it wouldn't be high on my list of career choices.

I told her, finally, that I needed to speak to John, Blaze's biological father, about insurance. I hadn't seen him since the last ugly scene we'd had in my apartment over two years ago, when Blaze was still a newborn. He didn't pay child support and we argued every time we spoke. He was still angry with me for having Blaze against his wishes. His anger made me furious and then communication broke down completely. John had moved to northern California before Blaze was even born and I had only a vague notion of where he lived.

When I had moved from Oregon to California eighteen months before, the district attorney's office had sent John a letter demanding he pay me $275 a month and provide health insurance for Blaze. John had been enraged and called me, screaming that he couldn't possibly afford such a sum and, besides, I had no right to demand it of him. No right at all! Did he ask for this kid? This was *my* decision. *I* was the one who wanted a baby and now I had one and goddamn it if he was going to pay for that decision. If I persisted in making him pay it, he yelled, he would take full advantage of his parental rights and start taking Blaze on holidays and summers and weekends and who knows when else. All of this was highly unlikely, because he lived six hundred miles north and lacked even the slightest inclination to interact with his son, but his fury was enough to terrify me into agreeing that I would write a letter to the district attorney's office and drop the case. Just please send me something, I asked him, and please provide health insurance. Without health insurance, I would be headed toward social services and I didn't think I could stand to go through that. John agreed to this and I wrote the letter. He never sent any money and I hadn't heard anything about insurance for a while. It was possible that he had it but I wasn't sure. I wouldn't know until I called him. This was what I told the woman in the financial office, hardly believing that I could spill these ugly details all over her nice, neat desk. There was no cause for worry, though. After my tirade, she merely looked up and said, "Is your son's father employed? Do you have his employer's address?"

By the time I returned to Blaze's room, he had been infused with a cocktail of anti-inflammatory drugs, including theophilline and prednisone. He was lying in a large crib, wrapped in wires and monitoring devices, crying that he wanted to go to sleep. The drugs were keeping him awake, a nurse told me, but he would be able to rest more comfortably soon. I reached my hands through the bars of the crib and stroked his head, trying to soothe him.

"It's okay," I told him, "I'm not going anywhere. I'm going to stay right here with you."

"Lie with me," he whimpered.

"He wants me to lie with him," I told the nurse. "Can I get in there with him and hold him? I think it's the only way he'll be able to sleep."

The nurse looked at me quizzically. "Well, I don't know," she said. "You're not really supposed to be in this room at all. We don't have beds for you in here." I stared at her, daring her to try to make me leave. I'll scream, my eyes told her, and I'll throw things. I won't leave. Perhaps she could sense this because she said, "But, I guess . . . well . . . poor thing. All right, go ahead and get in there with him. But don't tell anybody I let you."

Climbing into the hospital crib was quite a feat, but I managed to get next to Blaze and curl around him, tucking him into the hollow of my body—wires, equipment, and all. This was how Blaze had taken naps almost every day of his life, tucked into me, my arms around him, ready to catch him as he fell into sleep. After whimpering and wriggling for a while, Blaze was finally able to drift off. I held him tight, the aftereffects of too much adrenaline keeping my arms rigid. My thoughts were loose, muddled, and edged with anxiety and fear but holding him next to me like this, I felt, finally, like I might have some control over our fate.

Dawn came sneaking through the room and I could hear two nurses whispering to each other.

"Mom's in there with him," one of them said. "Can you believe it?"

"How did she fit?" the other asked.

"I don't know, but it worked. He's sleeping now, poor thing. He was only saturating eighty-five percent on full oxygen when he came in."

"Mm-mm. Poor little thing."

I was suddenly so grateful for these two nurses and the moment of sheer comfort their words gave me. Their concern made a soft pillow to lean into after a terrible night and I found safe harbor in their voices.

Blaze remained in the hospital for almost a week. I spent the time sleeping in fits and starts next to his bed, calling work to tell them that I wouldn't be in again tonight, and questioning doctors, nurses, and respiratory therapists. I learned everything I could about asthma and cursed myself repeatedly for not realizing that my own child had this illness in the first place.

There was a free phone in the upstairs lounge. From there, parents could call anywhere in the world at no cost. There was a certain irony in this, I thought. Where is there to call and who is there to speak to when your child is sick in the hospital? If the line extended to heaven, it would be one thing, but to call someone in Zambia just to chat . . .

I used the free phone to call John and find out about the insurance. It was a horrible conversation because I couldn't keep from crying and he seemed totally unmoved on the other end. Not that I really wanted him to be moved; I just wanted some kind of relief. I wanted to think that maybe, at some point, somewhere, I could shift just a fraction of my load to someone else. John was obviously not that person, but then again, that didn't come as much of a surprise.

"Oh, I had asthma as a kid," he said. "Yeah, really bad. I was in the hospital a lot. Is he allergic to olive trees? That was my problem."

"You had asthma?" I asked him. "That would have been nice to know beforehand."

There was silence on the other end. He was pissed off again. I asked him if he could think of any other medical issues that he might have passed along to Blaze, but he stonewalled me. There was so much information I was missing, I thought. How long would it take to learn everything? At least, I found out, John had finally added Blaze to his insurance. It was an afterthought, he told me, but a pretty lucky one in retrospect. He asked me for all of Blaze's information to give the insurance company because he didn't know the correct spelling of Blaze's name or his date of birth. I wanted to hurl epithets through the phone but I didn't. I merely recited the data and hung up.

John wasn't the only one holding back on information. I couldn't seem to get any straight answers from the doctors, either. Every one of them had a different angle on what the causes of Blaze's asthma were and how best to manage it. One doctor was convinced that allergies were to blame and told me I should take him to a specialist to figure out what those were. Another, swayed by the results of Blaze's chest X rays, told me that he had pneumonia and that was what was responsible. I asked if asthma was hereditary and the doctor told me it wasn't. Then why do medical questionnaires always ask if there is asthma in the family—which I now know there is? I asked. It's probably not hereditary, the doctor repeated. Blaze's original pediatrician, the one who sent me home with Ventolin syrup, was on rounds at the hospital and stopped in to see him. She asked me if Blaze had been tested for cystic fibrosis, her question sending me into an immediate, choking panic. None of the doctors seemed willing to tell me anything other than bare essentials. It was as if they felt I simply didn't need to know. I was supposed to feel some sense of security with these professionals surrounding me, but I didn't. I felt alone and ignorant and I started losing my ability to trust them at all.

Maya and my father came to visit and bring me food and changes of clothes. My mother was out of the country, attending her father's funeral in South Africa. My father knew I hadn't slept, knew that I went to the hospital rest room regularly to cry.

"I know how hard this is for you," he said. "I wish you could share this with a partner or a mate, but what can you do? You are strong enough for this. If you weren't, Blaze never would have chosen you as his mother. Think about it. There is a reason that you are his mother."

After five days in the hospital, Blaze was thin and pale. He wouldn't eat anything served off the scary institutional trays and I was forced to spoon-feed him soup brought from home. He didn't even trust ice cream because the nurses crushed bitter steroid pills and sprinkled them on top. He became stoic and silent. When I walked with him down the halls, trailing his little tank of oxygen, I could see his ribs showing through the gaps in his hospital gown. He looked at me with big, sad eyes, and I saw no joy there, no will to keep going. He was checking out, I realized with horror. I had to get him home before he faded away altogether.

It took excessive wheedling on my part to convince the doctors that Blaze wouldn't improve any further in the hospital, but I was finally able to get him released. I was sent home with a stack of instructions, the portion of the bill not covered by insurance (I calculated that it would take at least two years to pay it off), and enough drugs to stun a team of oxen. Blaze was very quiet when we got home but he was breathing. I didn't know how long it would take for him to recover fully and become the fat happy toddler he was less than two weeks before. I took him in my arms and held him, free, finally, of the wires, tubes, and oxygen.

"I'm sorry," I whispered. "I'll never let that happen to you again."

Blaze's hospitalization shook me deeply. It wasn't his asthma that disturbed me as much as my own shocking ignorance. After all, I reckoned, asthma wasn't some weird endocrine thing involving mysterious hormones and blood tests, it was extremely common. I hadn't been paying attention and had let my own medical prejudices blind me to symptoms that should have alarmed me. The worst realization was that I hadn't asked enough questions of Blaze's doctor before he wound up in the hospital. Perhaps I could have prevented it if I had known more. I became vigilant about monitoring Blaze's health. He seemed very weak after he came home from the hospital and it took him months to fully recover his vitality.

My father asked, "He's not going to become one of those sickly kids, is he?" which I interpreted to mean, "You're not going to coddle him and make him want to be sick, are you?"

My mother told me that I could help him by using natural methods and diet. "You shouldn't give him all those harsh drugs," she said. I told her I wasn't about to wait for him to quit breathing while I waved burning sage over him, but I tried some alternatives as well as the pills I'd been sent home with. So I cooked cactus (which was supposed to help open bronchial tubes) disguised in spaghetti sauce and I gave him prednisone. I gave him warm baths with oils of eucalyptus and hyssop and breathing treatments with albuterol. I gave him theophilline and massaged his back so he could relax and breathe easier.

Blaze's asthma attacks got fewer and further between but they still came and they still terrified me. I noticed that each attack was preceded by a seemingly mild cold. I tried to keep him hermetically sealed off and away from viruses but that was hardly possible. A few months after his hospitalization, he started wheezing and I took him to a pediatrician to get a prescription for the asthma drugs.

"We don't use theophilline anymore," she told me. "We've found that it can build too quickly to toxic levels in children."

"What happens when it gets toxic?"

"Seizures," she said. "Brain damage."

I started researching every drug I gave Blaze after that and I became quite an unpopular parent with all of his doctors. I had too many reservations and too many fears. I asked too many questions and wasn't satisfied with the answers.

"I wish you parents would stop reading all this stuff about medicine," one doctor told me after I questioned the safety of the hepatitis B vaccine. "It's dangerous for your children."

It was my insistence on questioning everything, however, that told me something was wrong when, at the age of seven, Blaze was still the size of a five-year-old. He had simply stopped growing. Back to the endocrinologist we went for another battery of tests. After almost a year of these, Blaze was proclaimed growth-hormone deficient. Could be any number of reasons, the endocrinologist told me, but most likely it's his pituitary. We can't be sure. "Idiopathic etiology," he said. My dictionary defined this term as *a condition of unknown origin* which, as far as I was concerned, described Blaze's condition perfectly.

This time, however, I got lucky. Blaze's regular endocrinologist, who had a horrible bedside manner with Blaze and spoke to me in small, monosyllabic words as if I were a not-very-bright child, was on sabbatical, bicycling through Italy, when all of Blaze's test results were completed. The doctor filling in for him understood my need to know as much as possible about growth-hormone treatment and what it would mean for my son. He directed me to a medical library where I could have access to every scrap of available literature on the subject.

"Read as much as you can," he said, "and I'll try my best to answer your questions afterward." He knew I would discover that, without growth hormone replacement, Blaze would never grow and would become a "pituitary dwarf." He knew I would never allow this to happen and he was right. After my own investigation I learned how to give the injections Blaze would need on a daily basis and I started administering them. Blaze grew five inches in the first year.

What I considered this doctor's greatest gift to us, however, was not his diagnosis, respect for my wishes or even his gentle treatment of Blaze. Rather, it was his response when I pressed him about what could have caused Blaze's conditions and what effects he thought they might have on Blaze in the future.

"Look," he said, "there are some things we just don't know. In fact, there are a lot of things we don't know. We don't like to admit it because it makes us look bad, but we are constantly learning. If you've read all the literature on this then you probably know almost as much as I do. All we've got to work with is what we have now."

There was liberation for me in his words. I felt I could not only trust myself but I trusted him more as well. I had long relied on my intuition when it came to Blaze, but it was then I realized fully that my intuition alone would never be enough to navigate the maze of doctors, diagnoses, and treatments; I needed knowledge as well. Knowledge, I realized, was a very powerful tool and I planned to use it.

Chapter 4

WHAT COLOR IS TUESDAY?

I'm in Blaze's room, picking up stuffed animals and books, attempting to sort them all by size and shape so that they will fit onto the white melamine shelves on the wall. Blaze sits on the floor, leafing through a Dr. Seuss book, not helping me. This is what we call cleaning up his room. I sort, he watches. His room is fairly small, but then, so is mine. Maya's bedroom is slightly larger but so packed—with instruments, sheet music, and canvas bags full of things she can't bear to throw out—it appears much smaller. We have to live compactly in this pink-and-beige stucco condominium. I don't hang pictures. Tall white walls give the feeling that there is more space here, more room to breathe.

I like it here, despite the space constraints. There are two swimming pools and a couple of hot tubs available to all the residents of this little condo city and we use them all the time. There are narrow little driveways lined with streetlights running between the units. The lights go on at dusk and give a twinkling Grimm brothers feeling to the whole place.

The streetlights are on now and I'm looking out the window, holding something fluffy and red in my hand. I'm not thinking about anything at all, just existing in the peacefulness of the moment. So when

Blaze looks up from his book and says, "Tuesday is light blue," I respond without analyzing his statement first. I picture Tuesday and see it as I have always seen it, a deep indigo.

"It's dark blue," I tell him. "Wednesday's the light blue one."

"Oh, okay," he says. He gets up and appears ready to move on to another topic, but I stop him.

"Wait a minute," I tell him. "What color is Monday?"

"It's brown," he says.

"Yes, it is," I say. "Monday is definitely brown." I'm smiling now and so is he. I feel like we've stumbled onto something big here. This is the first time I have realized that, for as far back as I can remember, I have always assigned colors to the days of the week, months of the year, even numbers and letters of the alphabet. The fact that Blaze does this as well gives me a fresh understanding into the way he sees the world around him. For the moment, I can see what he sees. Blaze is happy about this, too. It's as if I have suddenly started speaking to him in his native tongue.

"What about Sunday?" he asks me.

"White," I tell him.

"Mine is silver," he says. "What about Thursday?"

"Bluish green," I say.

"I think it's more green."

"Maybe it is more green," I say, giving Thursday a good, hard look. "But Friday is definitely pink."

"No, it's red."

"Saturday's red."

"Mine's yellow."

"Hmm," I say. "What about July?"

"July . . ." he says, contemplatively. He's just started first grade and hasn't had a whole lot of exposure to the months of the year yet. He's still trying to get the sequence down and so his colors for them are not firmly established. He wants to know all of mine, though, so I share them with him. January is a dark, dark blue; February is an icy green; March is orange; April is peach colored; May is cream; June is royal blue; July is purple; August is gold; September is reddish brown; October is reddish orange; November is gray; December is white.

We move on to the letters of the alphabet. He does have colors for all of those. As he tells me what they are, I imagine words forming out of the letters and realize that when I read, the words have colors too, based on the colors of the letters within them. It has never interfered with my reading. After all, I've only just noticed it now. Yet, the words do have color and the color affects their meaning for me. I don't like to eat cake, but I like the word *cake*. I like the word because I like the color pink and, for me, *cake* is a pink word. Part of my love for words, in general, is based on the way they look to me, the colors that they create in my mind.

This information comes to me in a rush of realization. All the while Blaze looks up at me with his big brown eyes as if to say, You're just getting to this now? It must all seem so obvious to him. Of course Tuesday is blue and cake is a pink word. This is a system that helps both of us order the world, only I've never understood it until now and Blaze seems to have known it all along. What's more, the system seems like a pretty good one to me. After all, who hasn't found peace and symmetry in color coding? But before I can get too excited about my new insight, I remember something and stop short.

"Blaze, you don't tell your teacher about the colors, do you?" I ask him. I design my words so that he will understand that telling the teacher might not be such a good idea (*You don't* instead of *Do you*).

He looks up at me and says, "No, Mom. She doesn't know."

"That's okay," I tell him. "She doesn't have to know. You can talk to me about it."

"Okay, Mom."

Make sure you never tell anyone on the outside about these things that make you different. This is what I'm teaching him, I think bitterly.

This is what he needs to know. I spend only the briefest of moments debating whether or not to tell the teacher myself. Maybe she'd find it useful? Interesting? I share Blaze's unique method of coloring words and letters and I'm all right, aren't I? Shouldn't that mean something? But no, Blaze has been in school for two years now and I've learned not to share any information with the school staff that might make him seem odder than he is. Sally, the special-ed teacher, is open to listening and the closest to reaching an understanding of my son, but Dr. Roberts and the other teachers start looking concerned, pull out bits of paper and start taking notes. I hate those damn notes.

This newfound information will have to stay between me and Blaze for now. Maybe later, when he's finally gotten himself secure in school, it will be safe to share these things. In the meantime, there is more territory to cover. I sense that the colored letters are just a tiny piece of Blaze's unique worldview. There is so much I have yet to learn.

Blaze had his first neuropsychological evaluation when he was five. I didn't think he needed an evaluation at all, but I took him to avoid appearing uncooperative toward the school staff. It was all right for me to seethe in private, I sensed, but if I let my anger or frustration show, it wouldn't bode well for Blaze. This was the attitude I adopted for most of Blaze's first two years of school. I was still laboring under the delusion that he would magically snap out of his resistance to the classroom rules and start exhibiting his innate brilliance. At the same time, I didn't make any efforts to change him. Despite the horror of his first day, I still felt that my role was to encourage and applaud his individuality. Although I wouldn't admit it, even to myself, I secretly admired the way he defied authority, something I could never have done myself at any age. He was an innovator and would be a leader one day, I thought, the system be damned.

Midway through kindergarten, the IEP team met again to discuss Blaze's progress. Although Ice Princess was present, she had little to contribute. She represented the regular-education class and Blaze was still on her class list, but she had very little interaction with him (to her pleasure, I assumed). This meeting was more or less Sally's show and she had made several copies of her notes for distribution.

Blaze's classroom behavior is becoming more appropriate at a pre-academic level, she wrote in her report. *He is able to sit for longer periods of time without creating a disturbance and participates in desirable group activities like singing, counting, and reciting his address.*

(I'd never thought of reciting one's address as a desirable group activity, but so be it.)

Blaze's social skills have improved dramatically. He is a friendly child who says "hello" and "good-bye" to teachers and peers. He is able to follow teacher direction, but often chooses not to.

(Well, I didn't need her to tell me *that*, but I was glad that she was aware that there was some thought behind his action.)

Blaze no longer demands a cracker for sitting with the class. Staying in school is a strong reinforcer for him. He is highly suspicious of any adult on the phone for fear he will be sent home.

(Poor thing, I thought. The kid *likes* school. How long before he doesn't?)

Dr. Roberts hastened to tell me that these signs of progress indicated that the special-ed class was the best placement for Blaze and that he should remain there to continue reaping the benefits. She added that, although Blaze was improving, he was still exhibiting inappropriate behaviors. What kind of behaviors, I wanted to know.

"He leaves class when he hears a garbage truck or another large vehicle in the parking lot," she said.

"He's very intrigued by loud noises," Sally added.

"Is that really so unusual?" I asked.

"It is a problem if it becomes a safety issue," Sally said.

"Blaze also exhibits very idiosyncratic language," Dr. Roberts said. "We're concerned about this."

"Yes," the speech therapist said excitedly. "I'd really like to talk about this."

"Idiosyncratic?" I asked.

"When he's frustrated, he will say things like, 'the puppies are on fire,' or 'the teacher's on fire,' or 'I'm standing in garbage.' These are inappropriate responses to his frustration," Dr. Roberts said in that unshakably calm tone of hers.

"But I know what he means," I said.

"Do you?" Dr. Roberts asked.

"Well," I began, knowing that I could be digging myself a nice little hole, "he's been watching *101 Dalmatians* and so that's where the puppies come in. And fire is scary, so if he's upset, he associates the puppies being scared or on fire. And when he says he's standing in garbage, it means that he feels like he's surrounded by something unpleasant, something rotten."

There was a silence in the room as Sally, Dr. Roberts, the speech therapist, and Ice Princess stared at me with identical expressions of naked dismay.

"That makes sense, doesn't it?" I asked feebly.

Dr. Roberts broke the mask her face had become by smiling and said, "It makes sense to you, but you can probably see how it wouldn't make sense to an outsider."

"Yes, I suppose I can," I said, although I didn't, really. Blaze made sense to me, I knew that. Why would it be so difficult for an "outsider"? Because, I thought grimly, we *were* the outsiders. I decided to remain as silent as possible for the rest of the meeting.

Dr. Roberts continued speaking, saying that neither she nor Sally had been able to cull any definitive data from the pyscho-educational tests that they'd given Blaze. He remained totally noncompliant when it came to testing, she said, and they didn't want to give him short shrift by basing their findings on partial results.

"I've had a little better luck," Sally piped in. "He *will* work for food."

She held out the stash of M&M's she kept handy and smiled but I was unable to smile back. Her words created a terrible vision in my head. I saw Blaze, many years older, sitting on a freeway off-ramp, holding a cardboard sign in dirty hands that said, *Will Work For Food.*

"I'd prefer it if he doesn't get too much of that," I told Sally. "I don't like him to eat too much sugar."

"Oh, it's not too much," she said quickly and the smile faded from her face. I thought I detected something wounded in her voice and I immediately felt guilty. I knew she was trying to help and that she wasn't responsible for my hallucinations of catastrophe.

Dr. Roberts interjected again and asked me if I had thought about getting an outside assessment for Blaze from a psycho-educational specialist or psychiatrist. She said she knew two offhand whom she recommended highly. You never knew what kinds of things a professional evaluation could turn up, she stressed. I might find that there were behavior-management strategies I could use that the school hadn't thought of or possibly even some medications that might help.

"What kind of medications?" I asked her sharply. "He doesn't have to take anything for his asthma on a daily basis. He's fine unless he has an attack."

"I was thinking of some of the other medications that have been very useful for some children who find the attention and focusing demands of the classroom difficult."

"You mean like Ritalin?" I asked, trying to spit out the word with as much disgust as possible. "I would *never* consider giving that to Blaze."

"You know, there's an awful lot of literature on medications like this," Dr. Roberts said. "You might want to—"

"No," I said. "I really don't want to even explore it as a possibility."

Dr. Roberts assessed me quickly. In her eyes, I could see the responses of hundreds of parents—their hope, desperation, pain, and guilt. She filtered mine through all the others in her memory and must have seen a warning because she dropped the medication issue for the time being.

"Well, the important thing is to see that Blaze becomes successful at school," she said. "Anybody who can help with that would really be beneficial."

I didn't trust Dr. Roberts enough to send Blaze to anyone she recommended but I stopped myself from telling her this. Instead, I told her that the cost to see one of her specialists was completely out of my range, which was also the truth. But there was another possibility, I told her. Blaze's HMO had a center for school problems. (It was on the same floor as his endocrinologist and I'd noticed the closed door and ominous title every time I took him for a checkup). Perhaps, I asked Dr. Roberts, I could take Blaze there?

Oh yes, Dr. Roberts said, she was familiar with the center for school problems and knew the director. They had a good reputation. I was momentarily stunned. Did all these people know each other? Was there some kind of underground network? Dr. Roberts thought it would be a splendid idea to take Blaze to see Dr. Whoever-was-in-charge and the school would be happy to provide any forms, interviews, or information. Dr. Roberts seemed happy. I was absurdly pleased. Blaze didn't want to impress her in any way, but, I realized suddenly, it seemed that I did.

Before Blaze's appointment at the center for school problems, I received a packet of medical-history forms to fill out. In the interest of total accuracy, I answered each question meticulously. I described the length of my labor and how, at delivery, the umbilical cord was wrapped in two loops around Blaze's neck. I listed his low Apgar scores. I knew when he got his first tooth (seven months), when he first crawled (never), when he started walking (twelve months), when he spoke his first word ("shoes," two years old). I described his hospitalization for asthma and his thyroid function tests. Then there were the questions about family history. I found some of these a little more difficult to answer. Had anyone been hospitalized, treated for, or suffered from depression, epilepsy, nervous-system disorders, alcoholism, drug dependency? Suicide? I could only answer for my own family, having almost no information about John's. And what did they mean by *depression*? Didn't everyone get depressed sometimes? Wasn't depression, well, kind of normal? Better not check that one off, I thought, sure that my interpretation of feeling blue was nothing like theirs. When I was finished, the family-history section of the form was pristine, not one item checked. By the looks of it, we were clearly the happiest, healthiest, most well adjusted family on earth.

This was also the picture I tried to paint verbally for Dr. F. at the center for school problems when we arrived for our appointment. I told Dr. F., a clinical neuropsychologist, that, in my opinion, Blaze's school difficulties were based on the fact that he'd had little interaction with other children and, had I known that there were so many rules and restrictions for kindergarten, I would surely have tried to prepare him better. Silly me, I told Dr. F., I thought kindergarten was a year to ease into school. Who knew that kindergartners had to meet high academic standards to prepare them for first grade? I shut up then, aware that I was starting to sound slightly bitter. Dr. F. asked me some more questions: how did I view Blaze? What, if anything, did I think were causing his school problems? What was my opinion of what was going on in the classroom? Was his behavior different at home than it was in school? I answered all of these in depth, never holding back on the fact that I thought there was a large gap between my view of Blaze and the school's. After jotting down notes and listening to me carefully, Dr. F. took Blaze into his office.

"Shouldn't I come with?" I asked, slightly alarmed.

"Probably better if you don't," Dr. F. said. "It'll be easier to get valid results without you present. Don't worry, we won't be long."

After I spent forty minutes staring at the closed door, Dr. F. summoned me into his office. Blaze was sitting at a computer, randomly clicking the mouse and watching a series of geometric images on the screen.

"How'd he do?" I asked Dr. F.

"Oh, fine," Dr. F. said, smiling. "Didn't seem to miss you at all."

Dr. F. was bearded and bearish, friendly and soft-spoken, but I felt vaguely uncomfortable around him. My parents' misgivings about the medical profession paled in comparison to their skepticism of those in the psychiatric profession and I was raised to believe that psychotherapy was a lot of malarkey. For the most part, I shared their opinion, although I'd never explored the field in any depth. Of course, I'd never really *had* to before Blaze came along and it had always been easy to dismiss therapy from a slightly smug, superior position. Now I was forced to journey through this unfamiliar territory with Blaze, just as I had with his medical conditions and, once again, I felt out of my depth. What were the right things to say to these people and what could I say that would convince them that there was nothing wrong with Blaze? Was there a code, a language, a secret handshake?

"Blaze was a little reticent at first," Dr. F. told me. "He didn't really care for my tests."

"They've had a terrible time trying to test him at school," I said. "They can't seem to get any results. That's part of the reason we came today."

"Well, it was certainly not impossible," Dr. F. said, "but I did have to convince him. I made some jokes; we played a little. Once he got a little more comfortable, it was no problem. He liked the joking around quite a bit."

"He's got a great sense of humor," I said, brightening.

Dr. F. told me that he wasn't particularly concerned, that Blaze seemed very bright and certainly capable of performing kindergarten tasks. It was most likely his social immaturity that was hindering him, Dr. F. added, and that could be easily remedied.

"And he seems to be pretty strong-willed," Dr. F. added. "Is that something you've noticed at home?"

"You have no idea," I said, laughing. "*Strong-willed* is an understatement."

Dr. F. told me that he would speak to Sally and then write up his evaluation. Was that all, I wanted to know? No other tests or interviews?

"Do you feel shortchanged?" Dr. F. asked, smiling. "I could probably come up with some other tests if you do."

Dr. F.'s report was only three pages long, but I felt entirely vindicated once I read it and wasted no time making copies for Dr. Roberts and Sally.

Blaze is a young boy of above-average intelligence who is presently without any sign of neuropsychological dysfunction and is intellectually quite capable of grade-level work but who emotionally may have a difficult time, he wrote.

See that, I wanted to scream, *above*-average intelligence! What did I tell you? Ha! The report went on:

Language based pre-academic skills are above both age and grade expectations and certainly within the parameters predicted by his general cognitive development. Blaze was able to recite, write and recognize his letters and numbers, write his own name, and has well mastered serial conversations, and can perform simple addition and subtraction.

These were all things that everybody at school swore Blaze could *not* do and I was sure they thought I was lying when I insisted that he could. Finally, I had proof. Dr. F. had concluded his report with what I felt were some very astute observations about Blaze, and I was highly impressed that he'd come to such a good understanding of my son in the limited amount of time they'd spent together.

Blaze is both timid and stubborn with a relatively strong perfectionistic streak, he wrote. *If Blaze is in a large classroom in which the teacher is unable to draw him out and build his confidence, or in unfamiliar settings, Blaze would likely withdraw and appear far less capable than he is. . . . Blaze can be a stubborn little boy who turns to silence when he doesn't wish to comply with an environmental request or is unsure of himself. In a busy classroom, with a wide variety of developmental and emotional needs, this silence can unintentionally result in his being overlooked and/or assumed to not really understand the class material. . . . A smooth transition to the regular class for next year is paramount.*

Of course, this wasn't all Dr. F. had written. He'd also mentioned that Blaze's motor skills were "low average" and that "his visual-motor integrative skills were relatively weak." He'd said that "Blaze's medical history is worth noting and may bear upon the reasons for this referral," but, in the report, he'd gotten most of the medical details wrong, and had entirely left out what, exactly, he thought was worth noting and why. Nowhere in the report did he mention the details of Blaze's birth even though I had gone over them on paper and during the interview. But I had no quarrel with any of this, nor were the motor issues a big concern for me. Blaze simply hadn't practiced with scissors, pencils, shoelaces, and buttons. I'd done all of those things for him. All he needed, I was sure, was training. What I chose to focus on—and what I pointed out to Sally and Dr. Roberts—was that Dr. F. had clearly seen evidence of Blaze's intelligence and capabilities. Surely this opinion had merit, I thought.

The school staff wasn't nearly as enthusiastic as I was about Dr. F.'s evaluation. While Blaze may have performed well for him in a one-on-one setting, they said, he hadn't observed Blaze in the classroom and so hadn't witnessed his odd behaviors. They felt the evaluation wasn't very thorough and besides, Dr. F. hadn't really delineated any concrete strategies for helping Blaze succeed in a school situation, had he?

My interpretation of their reaction was that they were simply pissed off because they couldn't admit that they'd been wrong about Blaze. Yes, he was unusual, I would admit that, but nobody would be able to convince me that there was anything wrong with him. Of that, I was sure.

By the time his first year of school drew to a close, Dr. F.'s report had been buried in the recesses of Blaze's file and was not referred to at all when, at a year-end meeting, Sally and Dr. Roberts recommended that Blaze repeat kindergarten.

"Are you telling me that he's failed kindergarten?" I asked. "He's failed *special-ed* kindergarten?"

They assured me that this wasn't the case. In their opinion, this first year had been the sort of practice run he would have gotten if he'd gone to preschool. Many kids repeated kindergarten, they hastened to tell me, especially boys. It was a question of social maturity, not intellectual capability. In addition, kindergarten was only three hours long and they didn't feel that Blaze was ready yet for a full academic day. Reluctantly, because I still thought of this as a failure, I agreed with their decision. For kindergarten part two, they placed Blaze once again with Ice Princess. I thought this was a bad idea and I said so.

"Wouldn't it be better if he had a fresh start?" I asked. "Maybe he'd work better if he were with somebody new?"

My question was followed by simultaneous head shaking. No, no, they said, Blaze finds comfort in familiarity. It would be disruptive to make him adapt to another teacher. We've seen this before, we know. It had been a long and confusing year of adjustment for me and I was tired of constantly being on the defensive. I allowed myself the hope that, perhaps, they were right this time. Maybe a redo of this year would be exactly what Blaze needed to pull himself together. Fine, I said, let's try it again.

Blaze's second year of kindergarten (or "K2," as I liked to call it, since getting Blaze through school seemed very much like climbing that formidable peak) was less than stellar. Although he spent more time in her classroom than before, Blaze didn't warm to the Ice Princess nor she to him. There was the problem with the letter books, for one thing. All the kindergartners were given large, soft books wherein they could practice drawing things that started with *A, B, C* and so on and out-lining the letters in capitals and lowercase. Blaze rejected the letter books out of hand. "I hate the stupid *F!*" he'd say and that was it. Ice Princess was not pleased. "In first grade, the children will need to know how to write their letters," she said more than once.

Then there was the issue of coloring. Blaze would not even approx-imate staying inside the lines.

"Why do we have to have lines?" he'd ask.

"So you can make a picture that looks like something," I told him.

"Why can't I make a picture without lines?"

Ice Princess was really a stickler for staying in the lines and Blaze's "drawings" messed up the neat symmetry of her classroom walls. Even I could see that. Blaze's attempts at cutting and pasting were also still quite rudimentary. "He really needs help with this," Ice Princess would say, holding up a tattered piece of construction paper that was sup-posed to be a house, bird or fish. "Unfortunately, I'm just not able to give him the kind of one-on-one attention he could use."

There was also trouble with the monkey bars. Blaze couldn't hold himself up on them, couldn't swing from bar to bar and ended up dropping in a heap on the sand below. Other kids played on the mon-key bars with no problem. Blaze needed assistance. "I wish I could help him," Ice Princess said, "but I'm just not able to be out there all the time when he needs me." The monkey-bar debate got so hot that an occupational therapist was added to the IEP team. Together, she and Blaze worked on eye tracking, walking a balance beam, outlining letters in the hated letter books, and holding on to the monkey bars.

Blaze still couldn't tie his shoelaces, either. Almost every day, he'd come home with his shoes falling off, the laces straggling and dirtied from monkey-bar sand. "I do help him with his shoes," Ice Princess said, "but, at this point, he should know how to tie his laces. Perhaps you could work on this with him at home? Unfortunately, I can't always be there to tie them for him and he could trip on them."

What made all of these little failings worse was that Blaze was experiencing them for the second time. During the first part of the morning, Blaze still spent time with Sally and I knew that he was doing some work that was at the same academic level as what Ice Princess was doing with her class. Yet, when he had to perform with the regular kindergarten class, Blaze persisted in doing things his own way or not at all. Ice Princess was not optimistic about his chances in a regular first-grade classroom.

"First grade is so difficult," she said. "The academic expectations are very high."

"What are they studying, Sophocles?" I asked. "I mean, how hard can it be?"

Every time I protested that Blaze was capable of doing something Ice Princess said he couldn't do, my son made a liar out of me by either mangling the project or flatly refusing to do it. I was convinced that Ice Princess—indeed, the whole school staff—thought I was a blindly incompetent mother.

This feeling came to a crescendo, appropriately enough, on Mother's Day. Blaze brought home a yellow stapled booklet with his handprints stamped on the cover in blue paint. Inside, were all the children's recollections of what their favorite meals were that their mothers made for them and how these dishes were prepared. For good measure, Ice Princess had also asked the kids how much they thought these meals cost. All the responses were copied and typed verbatim, Ice Princess said in her introduction. I flipped through the book, smiling. One little girl said spaghetti was her favorite food and her mother prepared it by putting it in a bucket. Another described her mother putting artichokes in a pot and then dipping them in mayonnaise. There was a complicated description of mom cooking "chicken with salad" complete with tomatoes, bread, and "little white things called salt." Most of the kids described June Cleaver–ish mothers whipping up sweets, whether these were brownies, cake, or cookies, but many of them went into detail about main dishes. They were adorable. Then I read Blaze's entry and stopped smiling. He listed pizza as his favorite food that I made for him.

She takes it from a box and puts it in the oven and cooks it on the rack for a short time and then she takes it out and cuts it with the pizza cutter and then she puts it on a plate for me to eat.

A box. She takes it from a box! I was now officially the mother from hell; a non-nurturing, uncaring shrew whose child's most comforting food memories involved frozen pizza. Godammit, Blaze, I thought. Ice Princess must be getting a good laugh out of this one. I scanned the rest of the book. There was not one other child who mentioned his or her mother making food out of a box, which was good news for all the other mothers, every one of whom was now going to be reading about my son's lousy eating habits.

There was more to the story, of course, than what was on those damning pages. Blaze wouldn't have thought to tell Ice Princess that the reason I took pizza "from a box" was because it was one of very few things he would deign to eat in the first place. And it was Wolfgang Puck frozen pizza, thank you very much, and therefore not cheap, either. Still, why couldn't he have chosen one of the other things I made for him, like pasta with olive oil and garlic or sauteed tofu?

"Pizza from a box?" I asked him. "That's your favorite food?"

"I like it, Mom," he said.

"Yes, well, you're going to have to start eating some different foods. You can't live on frozen pizza."

Spurred by my shame over the Mother's Day book, I decided it was time for a change in the way I dealt with Blaze and I was going to start with the food first. After all, who was the parent here? He had to eat and so he'd have to eat what I made him. To make it easier, I created a food game to win Blaze over to my way of thinking. I made seven colored cards with drawings of different foods on each. One card had a drawing of a carrot, one had a sandwich, one a banana, and so on. I told Blaze that every day, he'd have to select a card and eat whatever was on it. He was in charge of which card he picked and he could eat whatever else he wanted as long as it included that particular food. Blaze seemed up for the game and we started well. I had included some foods that were already on Blaze's menu, so for the first couple of days he chose those. We argued about every other card.

"Why do I have to eat a carrot? I hate carrots!"

"Just eat a little."

"No."

"A little."

"No."

"One bite."

"No."

If I got him to eat even a fraction of the food in question, I considered it a victory and moved on. I was sure that eventually he'd come around but I had doubts about my own stamina. These kitchen arguments could go on and on. Blaze had a will of iron and never backed down. We finally reached a point where the only card left was the one bearing a sandwich. After discussing a variety of options, we settled on a very simple cheese sandwich, no condiments. As soon as it was ready, Blaze stomped out of the kitchen. "I'm not eating that," he declared.

"You will eat it," I said.

"I don't want a sandwich."

"Why not?"

"I don't like it."

"How do you know if you don't try it?"

"I don't want to try it."

"If you don't at least have a bite of this sandwich, I'm not making you anything else. You can be hungry."

"I'm not hungry," he said and threw himself onto the couch.

Although I had my moments of irritation, I very rarely got angry at Blaze. But seeing him sitting there, resolute, without the slightest regard for my authority sent me into a spin.

"You *will* eat it!" I snapped at him. "Whether you like it or not." I marched over with the sandwich and broke off a piece. Blaze turned his head away and started to yell. I stuck the sandwich in front of his face but he kept moving away from me. This episode was turning into a major power struggle and I told myself that if I let Blaze win it, I would never be able to convince him of anything again. There was more dodging and yelling from him, more feinting with the piece of sandwich from me. Finally, I held him down with one arm while I forced a piece of cheese sandwich into his mouth with my free hand. He cried, gagged, choked, and finally spit out the wad of bread and cheese. If he had screamed at me then, even hit me, I would have maintained my angry indignation, but he merely looked up at me, his eyes brimming full with tears and a terrible look of betrayal. This is me feeding my child, I thought, and I had to cover my eyes with my hand so that he wouldn't see the enormity of my mistake reflected there.

"Why did you do that, Mom?" His voice was trembly and small.

"I'm sorry," I said and I was. "I just wanted you to eat a sandwich."

"I don't like sandwiches," he said, and tears spilled onto his cheeks.

"I know," I said. "Forget the sandwich. I'm sorry."

I took him in my arms and stroked his head, soothing him while he sobbed it out. I was now very angry with myself. How long would it take me to realize that none of the usual rules applied to Blaze? He wasn't like other kids who would eventually eat if they were hungry enough. Blaze, I now knew, would rather starve before eating something that offended him in some way. It wasn't my job to change him, to mold him to any kind of standard, whether that standard came from a kindergarten classroom or my own imagination. My job was to feed him, in every sense of the word, to nurture him, and to understand him. If, for him, that nurturing came out of a box, then fine. It wasn't his judgment that was passed on the frozen pizza, it was mine.

I threw the food cards away and gradually stopped trying to cajole Blaze into trying new foods. In his own time, he added enough to maintain a balanced, if somewhat monotonous, diet. Blaze never went near a sandwich again, and later I came to a full understanding of the strength of his will and how deeply the sandwich incident had affected him.

"I want to go on a hot-air balloon ride," he told me one day.

"No way," I said.

"Why not?"

"I'm not going to ride around in a laundry basket hundreds of feet in the air," I told him. "Plus, it's really expensive. And loud."

"It'll be fun," he said. "C'mon, Mom, please."

"No."

"Please."

"I tell you what," I said, "I'll make you a deal. I'll go in a hot-air balloon with you if you eat a sandwich. Any sandwich with anything on it."

"No, Mom, not that deal. That's not fair. Give me another deal."

"All you have to do is eat a sandwich," I said. "That's all."

"I can't do it," he said.

"You'll go up in a hot-air balloon but you won't try a sandwich?"

"I'm not eating a sandwich."

"Okay, it's up to you. Let me know when you're ready to eat a sandwich and then we'll go in a hot-air balloon."

To this day, the sandwich remains unmade and uneaten.

Blaze only gets up early on the weekends. On weekdays, when he has to get up for school, I have to haul him out of bed. This morning is no different.

"Blaze, time to get up," I tell him for the third time. I bend over his bed and kiss his cheek. "Come on, honey, you've got to eat breakfast."

"I'm stuck," he says, voice muffled by covers. "With tape."

I sigh in relief. Blaze often finds himself "stuck" in bed. When he says he's stuck with glue, I know it's going to be a while before I can get him moving. However, stuck with tape means less resistance. When he's stuck with glue and tape together, I know we're going to be late for school.

"Tape's not so bad. Here, let me help rip it off." I make tape-tearing sounds and Blaze laughs, gets out of bed.

It's a warm May morning. First grade is almost over. Blaze has done really well this year. So well, in fact, that I wish it could go on forever like this. He's had a great teacher this year. Unlike Ice Princess, Ms. Lamb has eschewed strict curricula in favor of a more creative approach, letting the kids draw what they want or write stories off the tops of their heads. She gives spelling tests once a week and Blaze has scored 100 percent on almost every one of them. He is so proud of himself every Friday when he comes out of the classroom to meet me holding a perfect score in his hand.

Blaze no longer spends time in the special-ed class. Ms. Lamb doesn't have a problem with his behavior and he's doing grade-level work so there's no need. I see Sally sometimes when I go to pick Blaze up from school. "He's doing so well," she says. "I miss him." I tell Sally that Ms. Lamb is like a gift and that, were it not for her own skills, Blaze wouldn't be doing as well. I'm quite sincere about this too. Now that Blaze is flourishing in a regular classroom, I love everybody.

Blaze hops down the stairs to eat breakfast. It may take him a while to get out of bed, but once he's awake, Blaze stays in first gear, rushing full speed into his day.

Along with Blaze's academic triumph, there is something else that has changed this year. Blaze seems to have finally found his voice, which is to say, he talks now. He talks all the time. He questions, he postulates, he explores literal meanings and makes his own metaphors.

He rambles. Occasionally he talks nonsense, stringing words together for effect. When he does this, I stop him, tell him that he can't be understood and that people will think he's weird. Sometimes he tries to brake himself, but, more often, he goes on, having fallen in love with words, their meanings, the sounds they make as they roll around in his mouth. I've had to make some rules; things he can talk about at school and things that have to stay at home. For instance, two of his favorite topics over the last couple of months, death and God, have been consigned to the discussion-at-home-only category while racial discrimination (which he really is having a tough time wrapping his mind around) can be discussed at school, since his class's unit on Martin Luther King Jr. was what started the dialogue in the first place. He is not to discuss the fact that days of the week have colors for him at school, but it is all right to tell Ms. Lamb that the noise of the fire alarm scares him. This morning, Blaze wants to get in some discussion on the nonschool topics before we head out. He crunches dry cereal and talks between bites.

"Mom, who put salt in the ocean?"

"Nobody put salt in, it's just there."

"How did it get there?"

"It's always been there."

"Did God put salt in the ocean?"

"You could say that."

"Why did God make the ocean salty?"

"I don't know, Blaze."

He takes a very brief breather. There's more. There always is.

"Where's God, Mom?"

"God is everywhere," I tell him. "In everything."

"I thought God was in heaven."

"He is."

"Then where's heaven?"

"Where God is."

"Mom!"

"Okay, that's it, time for school, let's go."

Blaze struggles with his shoes and I help him. He still can't tie his laces. I don't know if he'll ever be able to tie his laces. Nothing I've shown him seems to work. I put his lunch box in his backpack (juice, granola bar, trail mix, fruit roll; the same things every day, according to his wishes) and we head out the door. A few steps away from the door and he's at it again.

"Is God inside me too?"

"Yes, in everything and everybody."

"Is God in heaven?"

"Yes, no, I don't know; please, Blaze, enough. I can't explain heaven to you this morning. Heaven is a state of mind. Everybody has a different concept of what heaven is, you know? Theologians and philosophers have debated the existence of God and heaven forever. It's too complicated to get into right now, you're just going to have to take my word for it." I do this sometimes, just ramble off on my own, knowing that somewhere in there a few words or the quality of my tone will make sense to Blaze.

"No more on God and heaven now, okay? Remember what I told you, no talking about this at school."

"Okay, Mom."

He's quiet for a bit and we walk the rest of the way to school in peace. Once we hit the campus, I tell him to have a great day and give him a kiss good-bye. "Be a good boy," I say.

"Mom?" he says in a half-whisper.

"What?"

He points to his forehead. "Heaven is here," he says.

"Blaze!"

"Okay, but is it? Is it, Mom?"

"Yes, all right. No more now."

"Bye, Mom."

I wave and smile at Ms. Lamb and watch Blaze disappear into her classroom. I wonder if he's going to continue thinking about this or if he's finally figured it out. God is in heaven. God is in everybody. Heaven is here. Well, I think as I turn around and head home, who's to say that he's wrong?

[*Chapter 5*]

BUTTERFLIES AND FIRE DRILLS

November 1996

$\mathcal{T}$hanksgiving has always been Blaze's favorite holiday. The Christmas-Hanukkah-winter solstice season is a bit too overwhelming for him, what with all the frenetic gift giving and year-end parties. Halloween is exciting for him, but it does involve some work and going door to door in search of candy is usually a solo effort. New Year's Eve is a bit of a bust because he can never make it up late enough for the new year to begin, and Independence Day, while beautiful with its fireworks, is too loud. With eight members in our family, there are many birthday celebrations throughout the year and Blaze loves these too, but Thanksgiving is the only time when we all get together without the expectations that come with gift giving and receiving. This is why Blaze, who often says, "I like my family to be together," loves this day so much.

Our Thanksgivings follow a predictable pattern. We all cook something within our own area of specialty and bring it to my parents' house. I make apple pie almost every year. This Thanksgiving, however, much to the derision of my entire family, I've expanded my range and made succotash. Maya makes a giant vegetarian pot pie and cinnamon rolls every year and my brother, Bo, makes two trays of lasagna. My father prepares an elaborate antipasto platter, a meal in itself, with marinated cheeses, vegetables, and olives. Lavander is usually in charge of beverages (which makes her a favorite with Blaze, who eschews all the delicacies in favor of frozen pizza or spaghetti, but will drink almost anything) and Déja brings bread. My mother cooks nothing, but lays the table with linen and flowers. There is always more food than anybody can eat. On the rare occasions when we are joined by nonfamily members (girlfriends, boyfriends, and lonely workmates with no family in town) who bring their own dishes, there are leftovers for a week.

We don't often have outsiders at our Thanksgivings. For one thing, our vegetarian feasts don't appeal to the majority of people who can't see celebrating this holiday without eating turkey. For another, our family gatherings are fairly loud, competitive, and intense, and it's a hardy soul indeed who can stand a full six hours of this atmosphere without having grown up in it. So far, we haven't found many return customers for Thanksgiving and generally that suits everyone fine, because the pressure to be on one's best behavior in front of a potential mate or friend is often too much for us anyway.

This year, there are no visitors, just the eight of us gathered around the table watching my brother as he ceremoniously "carves" the lasagna. Blaze circles the table recording the scene with a video camera, producing sliding images of the floor, ceiling, plates, and mouths. Midway through dinner, my father asks the same question he has asked for as long as any of us can remember.

"What is everybody thankful for?" he queries. "Who wants to go first?" Everybody groans with the weight of having to come up with either a smart-ass answer that is witty enough or one that sounds sincere and interesting at the same time. There is a mix of both this year; some of us making remarks about the food, not having to go hungry, being thankful for stretch pants, and so on. When it's Blaze's turn, he doesn't protest. "I'm thankful for the family," he says.

After we've eaten dinner but before we've stuffed ourselves with dessert, we break out the board games. This is another family tradition that lives on despite the fact that it almost always ends badly. By badly, I mean that there is almost no board game invented that doesn't lead to a raging argument among the various members of my family.

(Unlike the old days when the three youngest siblings were too little to play and went to bed early. Then, it was only the four of us, my parents, Maya and I, huddled around a good game of Clue or Masterpiece, now defunct. Now there are simply too many competing personalities for civility.)

Gradually, we've run through almost all of the available standbys. Trivial Pursuit was the first to go, hurled unceremoniously into the fireplace one year after this question was heard several times: "You think you're smarter than me, don't you?"

Pictionary bit the dust a couple of years later when various players accused other players of wanting to play the game only to show off their superior drawing skills. Monopoly is too long and too boring (although my brother makes interesting side deals—"I'll sell you Park Place if I don't ever have to pay when I land on it"—that piss off the players not in on said deals). With most of the old standbys gone, we try the new, faddish games that come out every year. Hardly any of them make it to a second Thanksgiving and usually end up in toy-drive boxes by Christmas. Still, we maintain this annual ritual with all of its histrionics. The biggest proponent of the game playing is Blaze, who has yet to participate as an active player.

This year we play a game, in teams, that has something to do with shouting out as many answers as possible within a certain category. We really don't need any encouragement to start yelling and soon it's a free-for-all:

"What's the matter with you, why can't you get any of the answers?"

"I got all of them in the last category, what about you?"

"Why are you helping their team? Don't you want to be on my team, is that it?"

"You think I'm stupid, don't you?"

"They're cheating!"

"I don't want to play on your team!"

By unanimous decision, the game ends before anyone can win. This way, we can avoid the usual door-slamming exits that follow a Thanksgiving board game.

"Why do we keep playing these stupid games?" my mother asks.

"Because it's fun," Déja says.

"So certain people can show off how smart they are," Lavander says.

"Is that directed at me?" Maya asks.

"Come on now," my father says. "Break out the cinnamon rolls."

Blaze is sitting at the table now, waiting for dessert (of which he always partakes), and has started playing with the small green chips that have come with the now-abandoned game.

"I've got a game," he says, suddenly. "Everybody plays." He deals the green chips until we all have at least two. "Okay," he says, "everybody look at your cards." We all pick up our chips and stare at them.

"Who's got the radio cassette?" Blaze asks.

"I do," I say.

"Okay, who's got the horse?"

"I do," my father says.

"Nana, have you got the jackal?" Blaze asks.

"Yes, I've got the jackal and I've got an elevator," says my mother.

"I have the zebra," Lavander says.

"I've got the metal iron," Blaze says. "What have you got, Bo?"

"I've got the . . . um, it starts with a *J. JL.*"

"Jail?" my father asks.

"Jell-O," Blaze says.

"I've got the CD," Maya says.

"I've got a cave and a vacuum cleaner," Blaze says. "The cave trades with the zebra." He exchanges one of his chips for one of Lavander's.

"Hey," Bo says, "I want the metal iron. I'm trading my Jell-O for a metal iron."

"I'm not trading," Blaze says. "You have to steal it."

"A steal! Excellent," Bo says.

It goes on like this for a few minutes, all of us trading, stealing and exchanging the plain green chips, enchanted by the fact that we're able to play this game that, for all intents and purposes, makes no sense at all. Finally, Blaze says, "All right, everybody has to add up their points." While we're all trying to come up with a number that might work, my father yells triumphantly, "I've got it! I win!"

"He wins!" we all cheer and break into hysterical laughter. We laugh so hard it takes several minutes to calm down enough to talk.

"That's a good game, Blaze," my mother says, wiping tears from her eyes. "What's it called?"

"Card Gazetteer," he says without hesitation and this sends us off into fresh gales. Blaze is glowing and wants to play again. It's the first game we've played for many years that hasn't ended in a row.

After the second game (which follows much the same pattern as the first), we break it up. Maya and my mother go to the kitchen to make coffee and tea.

"Blaze is so creative," I tell my father. "Look at that game. He just came up with that off the top of his head. And we all managed to play it."

"We could play it because we know him," my father says.

"But isn't that the essence of creativity?" I ask. "It's not because we all know him but because we're all willing. That's how a game gets made—somebody thinks up a premise and rules and then you just play."

"Yes, but it would be difficult for anybody else to play that game with him, that's what I'm saying," my father tells me. "Like somebody his own age, for example."

"So, does it make us weird because we can play his game?" I ask.

"What do *you* think?" my father says and shrugs.

"Maybe we should tell them about this game at the next IEP meeting," I tell him. "Then they'd really think we were all crazy."

•   •   •

By the time that Blaze finished first grade, I was convinced that his school problems were a thing of the past. I believed that he had finally "straightened out," to use my father's words, and that, despite his differences, he would be able to integrate into a regular classroom. He had been taking growth hormone for several months and was starting to catch up to his peers in height. Even better, he had been very healthy for a whole year, with no asthma attacks or frantic visits to the ER. Academically, he had kept up with his class and had even excelled in some areas. It was difficult to argue with this success, so at our last meeting of that school year, the IEP team decided to enroll him in a regular-education second grade classroom and use Sally's special-ed class as a backup plan if that was needed.

That summer, Blaze spent every day swimming. He was never happier than when he was submerged in water, whether it was in the ocean or our condo community's swimming pool. He called the latter "the jewelry pool" because of the way the light sparkled off the blue water. I lay on a chaise near the water's edge and read books, newspapers, and magazines while I kept an eye on him, feeling chewed up and tired after a night spent running around the restaurant where I worked. I was ready for a change, I decided, and it had been a long time coming.

I had been waiting on tables for half my life and I was sick of my identity as a waitress–single mother. I was already thirty-three and felt that I had nothing to show for myself, except for the ability to survive comfortably. I'd spent a good portion of the last few years in one predicament or another with Blaze, whether these were physical or school related. Now that these crises had passed, I discovered a big void in my personal life. I didn't want to end up becoming "Alice": an old waitress, soaking my feet and wisecracking with my son, waiting for some man to come and rescue me. (And even if I had wanted such a scenario, I had serious doubts that it would ever pan out quite that way for me, anyway.)

One of the side jobs I had during this period was a position as a reader for a well-known literary agent. When one of her employees left to get married that summer I took over the position in her office. It was the first time in my life that I'd worked full-time with the rest of the working world. I loved the job and immersed myself in it fully. I spent much less time with Blaze and throughout August, Maya took my spot beside the pool. When school started in September, she agreed to pick Blaze up when she was at home, which was most of the week. For the other days, I enrolled him in an after-school child care program. Even then, I didn't pick him up, though. It was Maya who brought him home before I got there. We all saw much less of each other, but I was convinced it was all right. This was what everyone else did, wasn't it?

Second grade began inauspiciously. Because I wouldn't be able to pick Blaze up from school anymore, I made it a point to meet with his new teacher, Kimmi, on the first day and ask her if it was possible to set up some sort of schedule to talk every week so that I'd know how Blaze was faring. Kimmi was very busy sorting pencils and arranging kitty stickers and seemed a little baffled as to why I would want to talk to her personally on a regular basis.

"He had such a great year in first grade," I told her. "I really think he can do well again but I want to make sure that if there are any problems, I know about them right away and then I can work on it with him."

"Uh-huh," Kimmi said.

"I used to talk to Ms. Lamb every day," I continued, "because I came to pick Blaze up. But I'm working at a different job now and I can't be here when school gets out, but I think it's important . . ." I trailed off.

Kimmi had long hair the color of butter and large, round eyes that stared at me with a total lack of irony. To be honest, I didn't see much else in those eyes, either, but it was the absence of irony that bothered me the most. Nothing to be done, I thought. You can't exactly complain about a teacher because she's not ironic enough.

"I could call you at home," Kimmi said as if she'd suddenly come up with a cure for cancer. "If that would work for you."

"That would be fabulous," I said. "Maybe every Tuesday or Wednesday—something like that?"

"Sure," Kimmi said, showing me her lovely white teeth.

Kimmi and Blaze were a bad match from the very beginning. At home, he complained that he didn't like her but, when pressed, wouldn't or couldn't say why. He absolutely hated sitting cross-legged on the floor at the beginning of the day when Kimmi did "circle activities" with the class. Each child had a masking tape strip marked with his or her name that they were required to sit on for the duration of these morning activities. As if she were echoing the complaints from kindergarten, Kimmi reported that Blaze did everything to wiggle, squirm, and finagle his way off his name square and out of the circle every morning.

"He's really having difficulty attending," she said. "I think that the activities we're doing now may be too difficult for him."

Blaze *was* attending, it turned out, just not to what Kimmi was saying. He reported on what each child in the circle looked like, what noises they made, whether anybody cried, laughed, or was sent to a time-out.

"Guess what?" he told me excitedly one day. "Lee threw up today in class."

"Oh, that's terrible," I said. "Didn't he make it to the nurse's office?"

"No, Mom," Blaze said, "he threw up on his *name.*"

True to her word, Kimmi called me every Tuesday night. Blaze was having a hard time with math, she said. His reading comprehension wasn't very good. He left the circle and she couldn't get him to come back. After a few of these calls, it became apparent that she was calling me simply because she had told me she would. Our conversations were punctuated by long, awkward silences. I felt her annoyance and unspoken frustration. I also felt that she was an idiot. She had not one positive comment to make and not one suggestion as to how to reach Blaze.

"I'm a little concerned about his language," she said one Tuesday night after we'd exchanged the obligatory greetings.

"What kind of language?" I asked her.

"Well, he says things like, 'the floor hurts my feet.' I don't really understand what he's trying to say there."

"He's saying that the hard floor hurts his ankles. You know when you sit them in the circle? He doesn't like that, the ground is hard on his ankles. He's grown four inches in the last eight or nine months, sometimes his joints hurt from all that stretching."

"Oh, uh-huh," Kimmi said, sounding entirely unconvinced.

"He's really anxious about the fire drills," Kimmi went on. "I don't really know what to do when he gets upset about them. He seems to know when we're having them. I think he reads my schedule of events that I keep on my desk."

Hmm, I thought, the old reading comprehension can't be that bad if he can figure out where she keeps her schedule, then sneak a peek at it and commit the contents to memory. "He's very sensitive to loud noises," I told her. "He's been freaked out by the fire drills since kindergarten. Sally's had a lot experience with this; maybe you could ask her about it?"

"Yes, that would be a good idea," she agreed. There was a long pause. I had the feeling that this would probably be the last telephone conversation I'd have with Kimmi.

"I'm not really sure what's going on with him," she said, finally. "I think he might need more support."

"What kind of support?" I asked her.

"Well, you know, Sally has such a great program. Perhaps it would be better if Blaze spent the academic portion of his day in her class. She can provide so much more structure and support than I can in my class. You know, I have so many children in the class, it's difficult to give one-on-one—"

"Send him back to special ed? Is that what you mean?" I asked her. I didn't want to hear another diatribe about how many damn children were in her damn class and how she couldn't give personal attention to any of them, let alone a kid, *my* kid, who required *so much* damned attention.

"Just for the morning," Kimmi said. "In the afternoon, he could join my class for their rotations through music and art."

"Should I talk to Sally and Dr. Roberts about this?" I asked her.

"Oh, I've already brought it up and they think it would be a good idea."

Really, I thought, you don't say.

A few weeks later, at the next IEP meeting, Kimmi brought up Blaze's inappropriate language and, again, I explained what it was that he meant. I thought I detected a note of "I told you so" in the decision to send Blaze back to special ed, but I tried not to be paranoid. Everybody wanted what was best for Blaze, I told myself, but it was becoming less clear to me what that was.

With Blaze back in Sally's class, I let myself drift away from school issues. My job occupied almost all of the available space in my brain, so this was no big feat. Blaze had run off the beaten path before and had managed to get himself together, so I had every reason to believe that he would pull himself together again. Even Sally told me that, in her opinion, Blaze operated on a cyclical basis. This boy was seasonal and now we were having a bit of winter. At home, his language was anything but "inappropriate." He had started composing songs, accompanying himself by strumming along on a little thrift-store guitar. The sound of the guitar was fairly dissonant with no chords or changes, but it was obvious that he could hear the music in his head. Each song had verse, chorus, and bridge. In the evenings, instead of working on his homework, which had become anathema to him, he would regale me with, "Listen to this, Mom, it's a new song from my latest album." I listened, occasionally scribbling down the lyrics on whatever scrap of paper was handy.

"Deadland" was one such song. "It takes three tickets to get to Deadland," he sang. "When you're in Deadland you can never get out. Deadland, Deadland, Deadland."

"Who's in Deadland?" I asked him.

"Oh, just some people go there," he told me. "Like Martin Luther King Jr. and John Lennon and Marvin Gaye."

"Is it a nice place?" I asked. "Peaceful?"

"No," he said decisively. "It smells really bad there."

I preferred his song, "We All Shine Upon the Night," which described looking at the moon in a dark bedroom. Other songs captured some of the anxiety he felt at school. "Catch the Broken Timer," for example, described sitting in a chair waiting for the timer a teacher had set to go off and pierce the silence with its buzzing:

"I asked the teacher when it was going to go off and she said, 'Don't worry, it's not going to go off'—Catch the broken timer, catch the broken timer, I'm running away . . ."

I thought about telling Dr. Roberts about these songs, but I stopped myself. I remembered, only too well, that first day of kindergarten when everything I believed was unique and wonderful about Blaze became an indication of a troubled mind. Nor did I tell Dr. Roberts, or even Sally, about Blaze's new fear, butterflies, which had intensified and become a major phobia.

The butterfly problem started at the same time Blaze entered second grade. Thankfully, there weren't a large number of butterflies out and about in the fall and winter and Blaze was able to keep his fears largely at bay. But in the spring, there was a butterfly explosion and they were everywhere, flitting gold, orange, white, and red from the agapanthus to the honeysuckle and jasmine. Blaze put his hands over his ears and shrieked when he saw them, even when they were several feet away. If a butterfly flew too close to him, he'd go into a rigid terror and run in the opposite direction, even if that direction was into traffic. I tried everything I could think of to allay his fear; first admonishing him, then gently explaining that there was nothing to be afraid of, then, on our weekend walks, avoiding whole areas where butterflies were known to cluster. The butterfly issue became an endless topic of conversation between us.

"Butterflies are beautiful," I told him. "And they couldn't possibly hurt you. Look how fragile they are—they're the most fragile creatures on earth."

"No, no," he answered. "They'll bite me."

"They can't bite, they don't have any teeth."

"They don't? Are you sure?"

"They don't even have mouths."

"Yes, they do."

"No they don't. They just drink nectar from the flowers."

"I don't like the way they fly."

"Why not? They just go from flower to flower. They're not at all interested in you. You are a big, scary human and they have thin, delicate wings. Blaze, of all the insects in the world, butterflies are the most harmless, the most beautiful."

"They are not!" he insisted. "I don't want to look at them. Why do they have to exist? I hate butterflies!"

There was nothing I could say and no explanation I could give to relieve his dread. I couldn't comprehend it. That same spring, Blaze was stung twice at school, once by a bee and once by a yellow jacket. He had been stung only because he leapt into a bank of clover during recess to avoid any contact at all with butterflies on the playground. These stings didn't bother him in the slightest; in fact, he took pride in remaining stoic while the school nurse applied salve to his finger. When she called me at work to let me know about the sting ("Just in case he has some kind of allergic reaction"), Blaze got on the phone and proclaimed, "Mom, I got *stung*," as if it were the very definition of cool.

The demystification of bee stings had no effect on Blaze's fear of butterflies and, as the weeks went by, that fear only grew deeper.

"I can't deal with this butterfly thing," I told him, finally. "You're going to have to get over it. What is it about butterflies? Just tell me."

"Mom," he said miserably, looking right into my eyes, "you just can't understand."

I realized then that I really couldn't understand, that there was something about the butterflies, something about Blaze himself, that had its genesis so deep inside him that there was no way he could explain it to me and it was, perhaps, something that defied explanation in a traditional, verbal sense. I thought about the symbolic meanings of butterflies; transformation, transfiguration, the emergence of self from the chrysalis. In every movement, butterflies represented the fragility and beauty of life. On a more practical level, the flight of the butterfly was erratic, flitting this way and that. There was no way of predicting its exact direction. I could see how that could frighten Blaze, how, if I thought about it long enough, it could even frighten me. I wasn't going to come to an understanding greater than this, I realized, and, like Blaze it wasn't something I could find words for. It was nothing I could make clear for his teachers or anyone else who puzzled over such an odd phobia. We all have our butterflies in one form or other, I thought. I could only hope that Blaze would, in time, learn to conquer his.

• • •

Spring drifted into summer and then into fall again. For me, the seasons were marked mostly by Blaze's school schedule. Southern California had none of the pomp and flourish of the changing seasons elsewhere. It was warm, then hot, then not as hot. Occasionally, it was rainy and cool. I was glad when second grade came to an end and expected that the next would be a better year for Blaze.

I was busier than I'd ever been. Representing the agency I worked for, I traveled to several writer's conferences. I spoke in public about the function of a literary agency and what writers could do to improve their chances of getting published. I wrote notes for my talks. I bought a briefcase. At night, I read proposals and manuscripts. I spent my thirty-fourth birthday in Chicago at an international book fair, discussing foreign rights with people from all over the world. I'd never been to a book fair before. I'd never even been to Chicago.

When Blaze went back to school for third grade, I was in the midst of writing a novel. I didn't bother trying to register him in a regular-education classroom. He would be with Sally again for the first half of his day and then move into a "regular" classroom in the afternoons. I disliked his new third-grade teacher, Mrs. Noel, immediately, but fought not to show it for Blaze's sake. I reckoned that, no matter how professional a teacher might be, if a parent was a pain in the ass, there would have to be some resentment toward that parent's child. Blaze needed all the warmth he could get at school, I thought, and so I swallowed my belief that Mrs. Noel was utterly insincere and felt unfairly saddled with a problem kid from special ed who disrupted the harmony of her classroom and upended the perfect curve of her standardized test scores.

At the end of September, the IEP team met to discuss Blaze's progress. It was easily the most dismal meeting I'd yet attended. Sally had typed her report this time so as to fit a maximum amount of bad news on the page.

Blaze continues to feel stressed in response to academic and social expectations, she wrote. *He often reaffirms his schedule and well-being by questioning peers and adults. He has difficulty conforming to quiet time in either classroom and complains that the floor is hurting his feet or pretends to be a machine. He is sensitive to usage of common words such as fire, very, boss. Extreme difficulty relating past events continues. Blaze often uses phrases inappropriately or refuses to talk about subjects without an easy response. Continues to vocalize repetitive inappropriate language, currently exhibiting perseveration with vocalizing strings of numbers.*

Sally told us that Blaze's academic performance was slipping, that he wasn't tracking words on the page, he had no written output, and difficulty following directions. Mrs. Noel said very little, except to mention that she'd seen almost no evidence of any academic gains where Blaze was concerned and that his behavior in her classroom was disruptive. To me, she seemed mildly annoyed that she'd had to attend this 7:30 A.M. meeting at all.

Dr. Roberts asked how Blaze was faring at home. As usual, there was a great disparity between my report and the school's. My father, who usually just listened during these meetings, weighed in with some thoughts of his own.

"I spend a lot of time with Blaze," he said, "and it's true, he does say things that are difficult to understand at times. But when I'm with him, he's not allowed to speak nonsense and he knows it. He can't get away with that stuff around me so he doesn't. So if he says something like, I don't know, whatever you wrote here, I tell him, 'Stop talking nonsense,' and he does."

"My dad is the enforcer," I said, smiling. "Blaze really listens to him." I didn't mention that, at home, Blaze had recently created two lists of words: the good list and the bad list. Words on the bad list included *true, nonfiction, no, cute, shut up, never,* and *very.* The good list was much shorter and contained *Texaco* and *yes.* Whenever I mentioned a word on the bad list, Blaze would complain loudly. I would make deals with him to remove certain words I used all the time from the bad list if I promised to never utter some of the others. It had turned into a game, one he seemed to enjoy. Clearly, the game wasn't going over too well at school where nobody had a clue what the hell he was talking about.

Dr. Roberts smiled. "Blaze is very lucky to have you in his life," she told my father. I had no doubt she was completely genuine. "It's clear how much time and effort you and your family dedicate to Blaze. The school setting is much more stressful for him than his home environment, though. Sometimes it's difficult to gauge how best to deal with his anxieties here."

"He does seem stressed," Mrs. Noel piped in. "He doesn't really participate with the class. He makes sounds and he rocks—"

"What do you mean?" my father said sharply and turned to glare at her full on. I saw the gray snap of anger in his eyes that had always signaled for me and my siblings to get the hell out of his way when we were kids, and my heart started beating a little faster.

"He rocks, you know, in the back—"

"He's not a rocker!" my father snapped. "Listen, in addition to spending a lot of time with Blaze and raising five kids of my own, I've also got experience with disabled kids. I've got a degree in psychology. I've known kids who rock back and forth. I've never seen Blaze do that. He does not do that. That is not who he is. Blaze is not a rocker."

There was a small, tight silence in the room. I gave wordless thanks for my father who could state what I could not. I knew where Mrs. Noel wanted to go: he rocks, he hears noises, he makes sounds, he perseverates. Sure, I thought, if I believed her, I'd have to lock him up for good. I couldn't scream *fuck you!* at the top of my lungs as I dearly wanted to. But my father could—in his own, perfectly reasonable way. To my mind, it was nothing less than the verbal equivalent of a SWAT-style rescue.

Without missing a beat, Dr. Roberts guided the meeting back

around to the annual goals and objectives for Blaze, both academic and behavioral. Mrs. Noel signed the meeting notes and quietly excused herself to go back to her classroom. The occupational therapist, who had been added to Blaze's team back in kindergarten, weighed in with her report and, like the others, it was hardly a rosy picture.

"We seem to have reached a plateau," she said, "as far as how much Blaze is willing to do for me." She described what she'd been working on with Blaze. Instead of working on gross motor functions like the monkey bars and walking on a balance beam, she had been focusing primarily on writing. There had never been a time when writing or drawing had been easy for Blaze and not for lack of trying. Improvement was terribly slow and Blaze grew increasingly frustrated. The occupational therapist told us that Blaze's frustration impeded his progress so severely that she felt it was probably a good idea to give him "a break" from occupational therapy.

"You mean you're firing him?" my father asked, only half joking.

"No, no, of course not that," the OT said. "It's more like he's reached a point where it's not benefiting him."

"Reevaluate in January?" Dr. Roberts asked, all business.

"Yes," the OT said, signed the papers, and left.

Sally took her leave shortly afterward, leaving me, my father, and Dr. Roberts alone in the conference room. I'd never known Dr. Roberts to rush a meeting. She always remained in the room, calm and impeccably mannered, crossing every t and dotting every i. She would never cut a conversation short.

Now, preparing to write up the team meeting notes in her immaculate script, Dr. Roberts asked if we had given any thought at all to medications for Blaze. Both my father and I told her that we wouldn't even consider it. As she had before, Dr. Roberts urged me to "read the literature" on Ritalin and similar medications that were proving very successful with children like Blaze. I thought, Blaze has been in this school for over four years and all I've heard is how he's not like any other children. Dr. Roberts reiterated that she had plenty of material and I would always be welcome to peruse it at any time. She had the names of several doctors as well, she said, if we wanted to consider another evaluation.

I left the meeting feeling hostile and dispirited. At home, I begged Blaze to listen to his teachers at school.

"You have to try harder," I told him.

"You can't talk nonsense at school anymore," my father added, sharply. "They're going to think you're a nut. Do you understand? That teacher of yours—what's her name—Mrs. Something? She said you rock. I don't ever want to hear that kind of thing again, do you understand?"

"Yes, Papa," Blaze said.

"Blaze," my father said, "you've really got to make sense when you talk to people at school. You can't tell people not to say certain words and you can't make noises in class. This is important, Blaze."

"Okay, Papa," Blaze said.

I went back to work and I finished writing my novel. The days grew shorter. Blaze brought notes home from Sally. "Blaze has been holding his ears a lot in class and on the playground, but he says they don't hurt," one said. "You might want to take a look at them." Another note said, "Blaze ran off the playground today to look at the construction equipment on the other side of campus. We have discussed safety with him, but perhaps you can reinforce at home?"

I didn't ignore the notes, exactly. I addressed them all with Blaze. I told him I was disappointed, tired, annoyed. He promised to behave. A small part of me observed, from a distance, that I was out of touch with my son. My righteous indignation at the school had little to do with what was really going on inside his head. My talks with him were tiny Band-Aids on a gaping wound. But the part of me that saw these facts was not quite strong enough to acknowledge them fully. I carried on—working, reading, and doing laundry on weekends. I don't know how long we might have gone on like that or what the end result might have been. But early in November, Blaze forced me to pay attention to him. I'd been in a slumber of sorts for eighteen months and Blaze was about to give me a rude awakening.

It was a gray Wednesday afternoon, heavy with the threat of rain. The ocean looked angry and bleak through my office window. I was tired. My desk was covered with bits of paper, each one with a separate task attached to it, and I was losing an ongoing battle to keep my in-box clear. I was wearing nylons and they itched. Sighing, I picked up the phone and called home. I liked to check in with Maya on Wednesdays because this was the one day of the week that Blaze stayed in the on-site child care program after school. Maya would pick him up at four and give him an early dinner. I was usually home by five-thirty. Wednesdays were long days for Blaze and I knew he often came home tired and grumpy. I wanted to talk to him and ask him how his day was.

"Bad news," Maya said when I got her on the phone.

"What? What is it?" I was immediately shaken out of my work lethargy. "What's wrong with Blaze?"

"Nothing's wrong with him," Maya said. "But when I went to pick him up today, they told me at the child care that he decided to just leave school today. Just took off across the field with some girl. Didn't go to child care at all."

"Where is he?" I had managed to work myself into a quiet little hysteria.

"He's here. At home." She sounded irritated. "The guys at child care saw him leaving and one of them ran to get him. It's a good thing they pay such careful attention over there. This is definitely no good. You've got to talk to him. You've got to tell him how dangerous it is to take off like that."

She continued on about how he could have gotten lost or kidnapped and where did he think he was going, and did I realize how serious it was, but I heard only the sound and pitch of her words. The flooding sense of relief I felt when she told me that he was safe at home had given way to something much darker. I knew that Blaze didn't have the maturity or enough fear of the unknown to protect himself. My mind went to the edges of what could have happened to him had the school staff not been as vigilant in tracking him down and then shut off. All I could see was a fleeting vision of my son vanishing into the horizon, slipping away from me forever. My whole body was stiff with fear and I felt as if I were suffocating. It was *my* responsibility to watch out for my son, not the school's, not Maya's. Who knew better than I that he was different from any other kid, that his leaving the school in the middle of the day was a much bigger deal than it would have been with any other nine-year-old in the school? It was I who needed to educate him about danger, make sure he understood it was not all right just to disappear—into the world or into himself. Clearly, I hadn't done any of this. I'd lost the thread that connected me to my son.

I was such an idiot. I'd spent the last year and a half thinking I was doing such a great job as a single parent, a supermom with a burgeoning literary career, a good provider who received no outside financial assistance from anyone. My son lacked nothing on the material level and was doted on by everyone in my large family. But I was failing, I thought bitterly, in my most important responsibility as his mother. I was not keeping him safe, something even the wildest of animals did for her young. If I couldn't do that, the rest was all a big joke.

We'd been limping along like this for a long time. I'd known that school wasn't going well, but I'd convinced myself that it was nothing serious. So, he'd gone back to special ed in second grade, big deal, I'd told myself. So he didn't seem as excited as school as he had in first grade, he'd work it out. So he was afraid of butterflies, so what? Blaze hadn't been able to tell me about the space that was starting to gape between us, but his actions that afternoon were much clearer than words. You are not here, he was telling me, and I am going my own way.

I hung up the phone, telling Maya that I was too upset to talk to Blaze and that I'd deal with him when I got home. I put my head in my hands, twin feelings of fear and shame running unchecked through my heart.

"What is it?" My coworker, Laura, had turned around in her chair and was looking over at me, concern on her face. My conversation with Maya had been quiet and I hadn't made a sound since I hung up, but Laura could hear what was going on in my head. She had spent many years as a single mother herself.

"Blaze left school today," I told her. "He just walked off the campus. The guys from child care got hold of him before he got too far." Tears started welling in my eyes. "We're pretty lucky if you think about it," I said and the tears spilled.

"I'm so sorry," Laura said.

"I have to do something about this," I said.

"I know," Laura said, with understanding for everything I couldn't explain in her voice.

I turned back around to my desk and stared blankly at its cluttered surface. I felt my life spinning out of control, taking Blaze along with it. In that moment, I realized that I would not be able to carry on a career in any traditional sense of the word. I certainly wouldn't be able to continue working eight to five, snatching a couple of hours with Blaze in the evenings before I fell into the couch with a stack of manuscripts to read. Yes, I could and would talk to him about what had happened today. I could make him promise that he'd never do it again, but that just wasn't going to be enough. I needed to give up the idea—for good this time—that I was going to have anything that resembled what I'd thought of as a conventional life. I had to get inside

Blaze's head. I needed to understand him. Blaze needed me to be more than his mother, I had to be his translator. In order to do that, I had to learn his language.

Sometimes the events that change the course of one's life don't announce themselves loudly. Sometimes the seismic shift is so far below the surface you can't feel the effects until everything comes tumbling down. This is how it was on that Wednesday in November. I went home and I asked Blaze why he had left school without telling anybody. He told me he wanted to visit Natalie's house, the girl he had started to follow home. "She said it was okay," he told me. I tried to explain to him that it was very dangerous to simply wander off when he was supposed to be somewhere else.

"Natalie walks home by herself," he said.

"Natalie's house is right near the school," I said. "Her mother can see her when she walks home. Anyway, it doesn't matter what Natalie does. It matters what *you* do."

He looked at me, amazed that I was so upset by his behavior. He simply couldn't understand what I was going on about. I felt like someone who had been away on a long trip and had just come home to find the place completely redecorated and filled with new inhabitants. How could it have been that I had drifted so far away from this boy? What had I been thinking? There was no hesitation about the decisions I knew I had to make next, just a renewed sense of determination. Looking down into Blaze's eyes, I hoped that I hadn't been gone too long.

When I gave notice two days later, my boss asked me if there was anything she could offer that would make me reconsider. I told her that I didn't really think that there was. She sensed that it wasn't about money (although if she had offered me a big spike in salary, it certainly would have made leaving more difficult) so she offered me flextime. I told her that even with flextime I wouldn't be able to dedicate the amount of time to Blaze that he needed. She warned me about tossing away my career out of a sense of guilt. She said I'd be sorry. She told me I would waste my talents working as a waitress, which is what I told her I'd probably be going back to. She was angry. She was disappointed. I agreed with her about almost everything. But she didn't have children. More important, she didn't have *Blaze*. I wasn't martyring myself out of a misguided sense of guilt. Blaze was my real job. What the hell did it matter that I did a great job for her if I couldn't get my own son together? What did that say about me as a person? It was difficult for my boss to understand this, but she came to an acceptance of it. Two weeks after Blaze walked away from school, I left my job. When I told Blaze that I wouldn't be going to the office anymore and that I was going to spend more time with him and try to help him with school, he gave me an uncharacteristically short response.

"Good," he said, and that was all.

[*Chapter 6*]

SHRINKING

January 1997

J am in Blaze's classroom, ensconced in what Sally euphemistically calls "the quiet room." This is a new incarnation for me—parent volunteer. As part of my plan to understand what is really happening with Blaze, I've decided to come here, to ground zero, and learn what I can. I discussed this with Sally a few weeks ago and she was all for it.

"We can always use the help," she said.

The quiet room is small and stuffy. The air in here is moist and heavy with the scents of childhood: peanut butter and jelly, glue sticks, and playground sweat. I sit in a tiny blue plastic chair at a low table, grateful that I can fit my thirty-four-year-old behind onto a seat designed for grade-schoolers. I'm waiting for my first student on my first official day. Sally's left me a note that I read, then tuck into my shirt pocket.

Today you'll read with kids one at a time, it says. *They get to choose a story to bring to you for five to ten minutes. If a child makes a mistake or substitutes or deletes a word, but the story makes sense—let it go. If a child makes a mistake that doesn't make sense or changes the story significantly, ask that child to try that part again.* At the end of the note, Sally says, *Please don't take it personally if a child initially resists reading to you. Transitions are hard, but the kids will get used to you quickly.*

Sally has included a list of twelve children who will come read to me in the little, glassed-off quiet room. Blaze is one of them. This should be interesting, I think.

Jake enters the room first. He's a big fourth-grader, full of pouting attitude. Jake falls heavily into a chair beside me, slaps his paperback down on the table, and folds his arms across his chest.

"I don't wanna read," he tells me.

"Okay," I start. "What *do* you want to do?"

I've said the wrong thing. Jake gives me a confused smile. Rookie, his smile says, you're not supposed to make it this easy.

"I mean, is there another book you want to read?" I ask quickly, trying to cover.

"No," Jake says. "I want to go to sleep. I'm tired. I'm always tired in here." He puts his head down on the desk and begins mock snoring.

"Jake," I say a little more firmly. "You've only got ten minutes in here with me, so let's make the best of it. Sit up now, please, and let's read. This looks like a good book. What's it about?"

"I don't know," Jake says, his voice muffled by his sleeve.

"Then maybe we should read it," I say.

"I'm not gonna read," Jake says. "I'm too tired."

I wait a few beats. "Jake," I say, "should I tell Miss Sally that you're tired and maybe you need to spend *more* time in here with me?"

Jake lifts his head and glares at me. I've hit a nerve. He picks up the book and opens it but stares at me, sullenly. When he opens his mouth to speak, I expect him to defy me again, but he says, "Are you Blaze's mom?"

"Yes," I tell him.

"He's weird," Jake says.

"I suppose he is, a little," I tell Jake, thinking, weird by special-ed standards, that really takes doing. "But we're all a little weird in our own way," I add. "Let's get started on the reading."

Finally, Jake complies. I'm surprised by how good his reading seems. He's reading from a fourth-grade novel and he has no trouble pronouncing any of the words. I'm impressed until I realize that he isn't really reading, he's only saying the words on the page out loud. He has a complete lack of inflection in his voice and when I ask him to tell me what has happened in the last paragraph, he can't.

"I'm only supposed to read," he says. "I don't have to talk about it."

"Yes, but—" I start to tell him about understanding the story and how important that it, but he's out the door. Our time is up.

Katie is the next one in. She's in second grade and reading on a kindergarten level. She's brought me a picture book and struggles over *cat*, *the*, and *ball*. She rubs her eyes and pulls at her shirt.

"Are you Blaze's mom?" she asks me in a surprisingly husky voice.

"Yes."

"He's nice," Katie says. I wait for the other shoe to drop but it doesn't. Katie struggles through a few more three-letter words and then slides out. She sends Tommy in and Tommy is followed by Alex who can't read at all—not a word. He's memorized some portions of the book he brings me, but that's it. He seems pleased with his effort. Blaze is the next one on my list. He saunters in and takes a seat next to me. He hasn't brought a book to read.

"Hi, Mom," he says. "Do you like the quiet room? What are you doing in here?"

"I'm reading with the kids," I tell him. "Where's your book?"

"What book?"

"You're supposed to bring me a book to read."

Blaze looks at me, bemused, as if to ask why he would possibly need a book or anything else resembling schoolwork while he's in the quiet room with me. "So, Mom, what do you want to talk about with me?" he asks.

"I don't want to talk, Blaze, I want you to pick out a book and read it to me."

"I don't want to read," he says. He sounds almost insulted. We tango back and forth for a few minutes on the question of what book he will read and then I reach behind my chair and pull one out from a stash Sally keeps there, probably for this express purpose.

"I don't want to read *that* book," he says.

"You're going to stay in here until you read something to me," I tell him. "You can't get away with this kind of stuff with me."

We argue for almost the entire time that he's in the quiet room, but, finally, Blaze reads something to me. It's only a few sentences and he stops every third word for a non sequitur, but it's something. I've been in here for an hour and I'm completely exhausted.

I have no more kids after Blaze leaves. The rest on my list are absent or busy working with Sally or with one of her three aides. I crack open the door of the quiet room and peer out into the classroom, hoping to catch a glimpse of insight. I see a couple of kids working on computers, oblivious to everything around them. I see Sally teaching a lesson about what lives in the ocean. Jake still looks angry. Alex looks as if he's perfected the art of sleeping with his eyes open. Blaze is tapping his pencil on the desk, softly at first and then louder and louder until Sally tells him to stop.

The bell rings for recess and all the kids rise at once. Were it not for Sally's stern admonishments, they'd all try to press through the door at the same time.

"Bye, Mom," Blaze says perfunctorily and is out of there with the rest of them.

"Thanks so much for your help," Sally says brightly. "How'd it go?"

"I had the most trouble with Blaze," I tell her. "So, not bad, I guess. I'll be back tomorrow."

"Oh no, you don't have to come every day," Sally says.

"It's okay," I tell her. "I want to."

I follow Blaze out to the playground, trying to be as unobtrusive as possible. I scan the swings, jungle gym, sandpit, and blacktop. He's not in any of those places, not playing with any groups of kids, not even playing by himself among the others. I spy him, finally, walking the perimeter of the baseball field on the outer edge of the playground. He's just walking, head down, alone, deep into the recesses of his own mind. I feel angry seeing him like this—not at him or anyone at the school, but at myself for being so long away, for drifting to the other side of a great divide that has opened between us. I feel sadness too, and not the wistful, photogenic kind. This sadness constricts, closes my throat, forces my hands into fists at my side.

My tall shoes totter on the spongy grass as I walk over to Blaze. He sees me coming and stops.

"What are you doing?" I ask him.

"Nothing," he says guiltily.

"Why are you all the way over here by yourself?"

"I like it here," he says.

"Why don't you find somebody to play with?"

"I don't want to find somebody to play with."

"It looks weird, walking around by yourself."

"Mom, aren't you going home? Are you going to be here all day?"

"Yes, I'm going home. But, please, come back to the playground."

"In a minute," he says. "Okay, Mom? In a minute."

I kiss him good-bye and turn to leave. But with every step I take off the grass, through the playground and off the school grounds, I have to fight an almost uncontrollable urge to run back, grab my child and take him home with me where I know he will be safe.

Quitting my job was not the magic bullet I'd hoped for where Blaze was concerned. Although I could now see what was going on at school for myself, Blaze's problems there remained the same, regardless of the fact that I was physically present. In Sally's class, Blaze was openly defiant and most of the time he simply refused to work.

"He *is* learning," Sally told me, "but I can't tell you what he knows or how much. I can't even tell you how he's learned it. He can do basic math, but he must have sponged it because he never gives any indication that he's paying attention."

As I continued to volunteer in Sally's class, I became more familiar with her kids and their behaviors. Blaze had certainly been a quick study in this arena and had managed to mimic every inappropriate behavior he saw, whether this was pencil tapping, making odd noises, or banging his books together. He was a one-sided mirror of his class, reflecting only the negative. Added to this were his own quirks: fear of fire drills and loud noises, and difficulty writing. Despite the fact that he found imitating them so interesting, Blaze had formed no friendships with the children in Sally's class. He continued his solitary treks around the baseball field at recess and when I occasionally found myself on campus at midday, I noticed that he ate lunch by himself as well.

While these behaviors were bad enough, they paled in comparison to what was going on in Mrs. Noel's class in the afternoons. Now that I had no day job, I was able to pick Blaze up from school every day. I came a few minutes early and snuck around the side of the classroom to observe. Blaze seemed completely out of touch with the teacher and with his classmates. He was always in the back of the classroom, lost in his own world. I tried talking to Mrs. Noel, but I felt as if I was butting up against a brick wall. Blaze was completely unable to handle the academic demands of third grade, she told me, and therefore it was difficult to include him in her lessons. I asked her if there was anything to be done about the fact that Blaze didn't seem to have any friends and spent so much of his time alone in a crowd. Mrs. Noel assured me that Blaze's classmates were "very tolerant of him." She gave me several wide, fake smiles and used my first name often when she spoke to me: "Well, I'll tell you, Debra . . . My feeling is, Debra . . . Did you know, Debra . . ." I found this disconcerting and more than a little annoying.

At home, I pulled out the Yellow Pages and looked under the heading of *schools*. I had no idea what I was looking for and didn't see much to begin with. There were a couple of private schools named after famous people with learning disabilities, a Waldorf school on the other side of the county, and a smattering of Montessori schools, most of which only went through second or third grade. I called a few of the schools and discovered the monthly tuitions were double what I was paying for rent. It was clear that I wouldn't be able to pay for a private school on my waitress income. I knew that several school districts subsidized private-school education for special-education students whose needs were not being met in a public-school setting, but Blaze's school district prided itself on having one of the highest standards in the county for both academics and special education. They weren't about to finance a costly private school education when they felt that they were quite capable of doing it themselves, thank you. I could hire an educational advocate (essentially a lawyer versed in educational law) to argue a case for private school, but there was no guarantee that an advocate would succeed either. In any case, advocates charged an average of $100 per hour (I called a few just to be sure) and none of the advocates in my area worked on a pro bono basis.

Sally confirmed all of this for me when I raised the issue of alternative schools with her during recess one day.

"The only programs that this district has considered in the past are the ones that are more for kids with—kids who have—meet the criteria for severely emotionally disturbed," she said. "There's one a few miles from here, if you want to check it out."

"No, I don't," I told her. "Blaze is not emotionally disturbed."

"No, I don't think he'd do well there," Sally told me.

"Well, what if I hired an advocate?" I asked, knowing full well I couldn't, but wanting to gauge her reaction anyway.

"That's certainly your right," she said, "but before you got Blaze placed somewhere, he'd have to have a diagnosis. An advocate would have to present that diagnosis coming in."

"Do you have any suggestions for me, then?" I asked her. Although

I'd always liked Sally, I had developed a new respect for her since I'd started volunteering in her classroom. The sheer effort and emotional output she offered every day was staggering, yet I never saw her level of energy flag. Watching her teach was like watching a math genius work a dozen puzzles all at the same time. It was more than impressive. Although I was wary of teachers in general, I trusted her more than I trusted anybody else at the school.

Sally couldn't recommend any private schools, but she did say that it might be easier to develop a more effective educational plan for Blaze if it was clearer exactly what his problems were and how they could best be addressed. It couldn't hurt to have him reassessed, she said. The professionals were learning more each day and it could only help his teachers to have additional strategies for teaching him. So, despite the fact that I'd always disliked labels and wasn't entirely sure that it would benefit Blaze to have one, I went in search of a diagnosis.

Once again, I took Blaze to the center for school problems to visit the same psychologist we'd seen when Blaze was in kindergarten. My reasons were fairly simple; I'd been in total agreement with Dr. F.'s assessment of Blaze the first time around, for one thing, and for another, money was still an issue. I just couldn't afford to take Blaze anywhere else.

I was spared filling out another medical history form as Dr. F. decided to refer to his original notes. I felt much less optimistic than I had when I'd brought Blaze in four years before. I told Dr. F. about Blaze's success in first grade, decline the following year, and the mess he was in currently. I shared my fears about Blaze's social development and the fact that he didn't seem to have made any social connections, much less friends, in his peer group. I blamed his teachers. If they were better equipped or more empathetic, I said, they would be able to reach Blaze. It couldn't be that difficult, could it?

Dr. F. spent less time with Blaze than he had the first time around.

After half an hour, I was summoned into his office. Blaze was sitting in the doctor's chair, playing with the computer.

Dr. F smiled broadly as he spoke to me. In his opinion, he said, there was nothing really *wrong* with Blaze, although he was certainly unusual and had a unique angle on the world around him. My son, he told me, was also a gifted manipulator and had created several strategies to avoid performing tasks he felt were too difficult. Blaze had difficulty with his handwriting, Dr. F. said, and also showed some difficulty with complex addition and subtraction. Dr. F. believed that these difficulties were somehow related to Blaze's endocrine problems, but he couldn't tell me how. When I told him that Blaze's endocrinologist steadfastly maintained that there was no connection between the medical and learning problems, Dr. F. shrugged. "We doctors are not always in agreement," he said. I certainly agreed with this and with almost everything else that Dr. F. said, just as I had the first time. Dr. F. promised to write a helpful report for the school and offered one last opinion about our situation.

"You realize," he said, "that if you were very wealthy, Blaze would probably just be considered charmingly eccentric."

I thought that this was one of the most insightful observations I'd ever heard from a professional, but I didn't see how it would provide any concrete help unless I discovered a quick way to become rich.

I received Dr. F.'s written report a week later and, once again, I shared it with Dr. Roberts and Sally. This time, even the normally reserved Dr. Roberts had difficulty concealing her disdain, telling me that it was one of the most unprofessional reports she'd ever seen. For one thing, there was no mention of any tests, Dr. Roberts said. Did Dr. F. even administer any? The report was carelessly written and rife with spelling errors and incorrect dates. All of this showed a basic inattention to the assessment, she said, not to mention that the body of the report said nothing useful.

Blaze is a young boy of above average intelligence, the report said, *who presents with a moderate dysgraphia and mild dyscalculia the nature of which suggests these parts of his development "stopped" at roughly the same time his growth curve flattened. These deficits are not extraordinary, however, and in and of themselves should not pose a difficult remedial issue. Rather, it is this examiner's opinion it is Blaze's personality in combination with these difficulties that are proving confusing to his educators.*

Both Dr. Roberts and Sally felt that this was a vast understatement of Blaze's problems. Sally, especially, was irritated that Dr. F. had not interviewed her by phone as he had the first time and hadn't taken into account any of the school's evaluations. But it was Dr. F.'s final summary that irritated them the most.

Blaze's neuropsychological profile is that of a bright young boy who has profited from parts of his educational experience but remains "frozen" in other domains. It may be that this is related to the same factors affecting his growth curve but whatever the etiology, it is clear he has developed little in visual-integrative tasks or in specific areas of motor function.

In and of themselves, these academic problems should not prove overwhelming. It is this examiner's opinion that the consternation occurs in trying to tease out behavioral versus cognitive contributions to his academic problems. He is by personality a highly eccentric, idiosyncratic youngster whose approach to common problems is anything but common. While this creativity can be a gift, it is also used to hide from situations he finds uncomfortable, particularly those that highlight his weaknesses.

It is suggested to all concerned that Blaze's greatest need is in the area of self-esteem. He perceives himself only as a problem and has little but his imagination as proof of his competencies. He sees himself as inferior to those around him and is rapidly evolving into a school phobia unless the cycle is broken.

"I really think he's done you a disservice," Sally said. "This is an oversimplified report and gives us nothing to go on."

"What about the dyscalculia and dysgraphia that he talks about?" I asked Sally.

"All that means is that he has trouble with math and writing," Sally said. "We already know that. He hasn't said anything about what's really going on with Blaze."

In other words, I thought, there was still no definitive diagnosis and a diagnosis was what everybody seemed to want. I couldn't entirely disagree with Dr. Roberts's and Sally's assessment of the report. It was true that the report contained many errors, all of which led me to believe that it had been put together very quickly with little attention to detail. I also wondered if, in the absence of his own tests and evaluations, Dr. F. had relied too heavily on *my* reports of what was going on at school and the way I shaded descriptions of Blaze's behavior with my own interpretations. It was plain that Dr. F. had seen Blaze's native intelligence, I had no doubt of that. But I wondered if he just took me at my word for all the rest and "phoned in" his report without really delving deeply below the surface. It was this doubt, combined with the school's disgust at the report, that drove me to yet another psychologist.

This time, I obtained a referral to the psychiatric department of our HMO and made an appointment with Dr. C., a clinical psychologist. I decided that I would be as open and trusting of this new psychologist as possible. I would be completely honest about Blaze's behavior at home as well as delineating, impartially, his problems at school. I brought copies of Blaze's records and filled out yet another medical-history form. I brought Maya along to the interview so that the doctor could get a clear view of Blaze's family situation. I cautioned Dr. C. that Blaze was likely to be resistant to tests. He had seen so many different psychologists, I explained, that he was becoming hip to the game and was starting to offer up what he thought the examiner wanted to hear. Please take this into consideration, I begged. Don't let Blaze know that you are testing him or else you won't get accurate results. I fought to trust Dr. C. although I had many misgivings. We had two sessions. For the first, Dr. C. interviewed me and Maya for over an hour. For the second, he interviewed Blaze for forty minutes and all three of us for a half hour.

I heard nothing from Dr. C. for weeks. Frustrated, I called his office several times. When I finally reached him, he promised to send his report to the school.

"No," I told him, "I want a copy of the report. I don't want the school to see anything before I've had a chance to look at it."

It was two months before I received Dr. C.'s report. When I opened it, I was immediately startled by the heading. *Psychological Evaluation*, it stated. *This report was prepared as a professional-to-professional communication and is not for release to the patient or his family.* By the time I finished reading, I understood quite clearly why I would not be the intended recipient of this particular evaluation.

INTERVIEW DATA:

Blaze's mother was interviewed prior to testing. On a second date, she and her sister were again interviewed and they brought in some extremely interesting videotapes of Blaze singing his favorite songs, which he has written himself.

Blaze's mother says, "The chain of his logic, the way he thinks is different." She says Blaze will say things such as "The floor hurts me," when he means that sitting on his bottom hurts. She doesn't suspect that he hears voices, but he has often heard music in his head, and that he has even gone so far as to ask her to put her ear against his head, so that she could hear the songs inside his brain.

Blaze is described by his mother and aunt as being extremely inquisitive and wanting a great number of details about certain subjects. For example, he perseverated for several weeks on the death of a spider which has been living in his room. He asks "endless" questions about his mother's life as a little girl. He appears to perseverate, asking the same questions again and again and again.

Blaze has written a number of songs which he accompanies by rhythmically strumming a guitar. He has given these songs names, and he sings them in the same order each time. Songs include "Nerve Night," "Catch the Broken Timer," and "Give Me Back My Note." Many of his songs focus on disturbing events which have happened at school.

Blaze has been with the same teacher for years. She says that he "is a little stranger this year than he was before." [She] describes him as having a lot of perseveration, particularly being afraid that frightening noises might happen, that somebody might use a blender, or that some other frightening thing would occur.

When he first came to the classroom, he had no language whatsoever. It was extremely difficult to get him to engage in any type of classroom activity, and the present goals are to keep him in the social arena, to help him stay calm in class, and to help him stop screaming and throwing things.

When Blaze becomes agitated, he screams, runs around the room, and makes siren noises. His teacher says he cannot accept any change in school and becomes upset when there is any alteration in the pattern. He is extremely resistant to anything which he perceives as a demand. He sits in reading group but will not make any attempt to read, and indeed must be assured before reading group starts that reading will be expected. He will not do any work in a journal because "he's afraid of his journal and he throws it." He will do the same work on paper, but it needs to be plain white paper with blue lines.

When Blaze doesn't want to participate in class, he will say things like, "I'm making a video now and I'm on mute. It's about the United States of America." At this point, he will sit and talk to himself, but will not interact with anybody else.

Because of his social limitations, [his teacher] considers him one of the more disabled children in the classroom. She says, "He wouldn't think to find himself if he got lost."

TEST DATA:

Interviewing Blaze was an interesting experience. Mostly he appeared to be giving me stereotyped responses which he had included in many conversations before. His first comment on sitting down with me was, "My mom decided to name me Blaze. I like parties with balloons." There was nothing in the context on the interview which I was aware of which might have elicited this comment.

Asked about school, Blaze says, "I like to run and make siren noises, siren noises, *roo-oo-oo* . . ." He was unable to name any friends at school. I asked him if he had enemies and he said, "A little of them."

Later he said, "If there's any noise, loud noises, I'd have to run away, or scream really loud, or make a siren noise." It was quite evident that Blaze was simply describing his coping mechanisms. This was not an attempt at display. He was telling me what it is that he does.

TEST DATA:

Perhaps the most interesting test data came on the Rorschach, although the Rorschach was unscorable. Confronted with the first two cards, Blaze simply repeated, "I don't know," again and again and again. Finally, when presented with the third card, he said, "I'm on the phone, I can't talk now. I'm on the imaginary phone." This appeared to be the same behavior described by his teacher, in that he enters a role-play world in order to avoid complying with demands.

On the Peabody Picture Vocabulary Test, Blaze attained an IQ of 40, which is in the lowest one percentile of the population. I judge this to be an underestimate of his actual intelligence, because of the interference of his emotional disorder with his test performance.

Blaze's drawings were of extremely poor quality, showing the drawing level of a 4- or 5-year-old child. This is somewhat in line with the measured intelligence of the PPVT, but again I would be extremely reluctant to overinterpret any findings about his intelligence.

DIAGNOSTIC IMPRESSION:

Blaze meets the diagnostic criteria under DSM-IV for an autistic disorder. He has marked social impairment and stereotypical responses which interfere with his capacity to interact socially and gain academic skills. While he lacks the stereotypic movements often associated with autism, he certainly has stereotypic and repeated verbalizations which more than meet the criteria for this diagnosis.

RECOMMENDATIONS:

Blaze will no doubt continue to need to be in a sheltered classroom setting. For a child bearing this diagnosis, he is fairly high-functioning. Although it is quite evident that he has significant academic and social limitations which are likely to be continuing, it is unlikely that Blaze will respond to psychotherapeutic interventions. It may be helpful to assist his mother in managing his behavior at such points as it becomes difficult.

It is certainly worthy to note that Blaze's mother is extremely supportive, and Blaze appears to have a family which provides a warm and loving context.

My eyes were burning with tears by the time I finished reading and I had to resist a strong impulse to tear the report into tiny pieces. I was deeply disturbed by this damning document on many levels, but the worst feeling I had was that of betrayal. I had very little confidence in Dr. C. and felt that his assessment was largely a load of crap, but the account given by Sally, the person I had trusted the most, wounded me deeply. Dr. C. had clearly based much of his interpretations on Sally's information and I had to go through it all a second time to try to understand what she had told him. The words assaulted me like little daggers coming off the page.

He wouldn't think to find himself if he got lost.

He is a little stranger this year than he was before.

He is one of the most disabled children in the classroom.

If this was how Sally felt, why hadn't she told me? She had been Blaze's teacher for the better part of four years and I considered her an ally. This year, especially, I had opened up to her and shared my fears. I believed that she had been frank with me and had kept me informed. But her description of Blaze painted him as dangerously off-kilter and out of touch with reality. It was possible that Dr. C. had misinterpreted her words or taken them out of context (he certainly had with mine), but there were quotation marks around her most damaging comments. I couldn't imagine that he had made them up. I wondered if she had always thought of Blaze as one of the most disabled children in her classroom or if she'd only come to feel that way this year. I had no doubt that Blaze could sense her feelings. If she thought he was "strange," as she apparently did, I was sure that Blaze would act as strange as possible for her.

I felt like a wife who has just seen the lipstick on her husband's collar. I wanted to march into Sally's room immediately and confront her with Dr. C.'s report but I couldn't. I had absolutely no intention of sharing that document with anybody from the school—ever. I didn't just disagree with Dr. C., I felt he was dangerously off base. I had taken such great pains to explain to him why and how Blaze would react to a testing situation and he'd completely misconstrued what I'd said. He'd come up with a diagnosis of autism based on Sally's report of Blaze's classroom behavior, his own interpretations of what I'd told him, and Blaze's refusal to participate in any of the tests he'd given. What struck me as most ridiculous, though, was that in the space of two months, Dr. F. and Dr. C., colleagues at the same HMO, had come up with two completely opposing reports. I rejected both of them and decided that I would never set foot in the psychiatric department of that institution again. Nor was I particularly disposed to searching out another psychologist. I was finished, for the time being. I didn't believe that Blaze was autistic just because Dr. C. had managed to tweak reported data to match a few entries in *The Diagnostic and Statistical Manual.* Nor did I believe that he had dyslexia or ADD or any other disorder that would make him easy to classify. Yes, he was different. Yes, it was a challenge to understand him. Certainly, it was proving difficult to educate him. But if I were to believe the conflicting opinions of the professionals who had seen Blaze to this point, I would be convinced that my son was mentally retarded, intellectually gifted, autistic, and emotionally disturbed. This was why these doctors and reports, especially the most recent, were dangerous. I could only guess at what would happen if Blaze were saddled with an inappropriate label. Eventually, I felt sure, he would *become* his diagnosis.

I buried Dr. C.'s report in my own personal files. My doubts about Sally and her assessment of Blaze, however, refused to be as neatly dispatched. I no longer felt particularly comfortable around her, nor did I trust her reports of Blaze's behavior, good or bad, when she offered them. I began staying longer during my volunteer times, slinking out of the quiet room when I was finished with the reading, to sit at a desk in the back of the room and watch what was going on. I didn't hear any siren noises coming from my son, but I believed that he probably reserved his worst behavior for when I wasn't there. Still, I saw no evidence of the crazed child described in Dr. C.'s report. Rather, I saw a frustrated, isolated boy who was getting less and less positive reinforcement for being in school. I wondered if Blaze had been with Sally for too long, if, perhaps, they both needed a break from each other. But despite my new misgivings about Sally, I still hadn't met anyone more qualified to teach Blaze. It was a conundrum and I tried to imagine what would happen in fourth grade where the stakes would apparently be raised once again. Fourth-graders were considered well out of babyhood and into increased academic and social expectations. I wondered how Blaze would cope with being a veteran in Sally's class while negotiating another new teacher in the regular. As it turned out, I didn't have to wait long to find out.

Sally pulled me aside one recess shortly before the end of the school year and said, "I think you should know . . . It's not common knowledge yet, but you'll probably find out soon enough and I know you want to plan for next year. . . . "

"What is it?" I asked, alarmed.

"I won't be teaching this class next year," Sally told me. "This class isn't actually going to *exist* next year."

"What?"

"No more special day class here," Sally said. "The district has decided to combine the SDCs, so all the kids here can transfer over to the other elementary school for next year. Of course, that'll mean Blaze too."

A string of expletives formed in my mouth and I swallowed them quickly before they could tumble out. "There's no more special ed at this school? Is that what you're saying?" I asked, deliberately ignoring the acronyms that everybody in special ed seemed to be so fond of.

"Well, there will still be help from the resource specialist."

"Who's *that*?" I asked, my head spinning from this new information.

"It's a pull-out program. The kids go see her for an hour or so a day for help with their classwork. Nothing like what the kids would get in an SDC."

"So I'm supposed to just pull Blaze out of the school he's been in since kindergarten? Away from everything he knows? So he can be in a special-ed program I don't even know anything about?"

Sally said nothing, struck temporarily mute. I imagined she was searching for the right words. Something between empathy, professionalism, and reason, I guessed.

"And where are you going?" I asked her.

"I'm going to regular ed," she said, a smile bursting like sudden sunshine on her face. "I'm going to be teaching first grade."

"You want that?" I asked her.

"I asked for it. I'm burned out here," she said, and it was my turn to be mute. So she was sick of special ed. And why wouldn't she be, I thought, looking around. It didn't take a whole lot of insight to know that hers was probably a thankless job. Her considerable teaching skills would most likely produce shining, tangible results with a group of happy little six-year-olds.

"First grade is lucky to have you," I said, sincerely. "I hope they know that."

There was a brief silence between us and for one horrible moment, I was sure I was going to burst into tears and struggled to hold back the flow.

"What am I going to do with Blaze?" I asked her.

"It's a good program at the other school," Sally said weakly.

"No," I said, shaking my head. "No, I'm not going to send him there." I felt a sudden anger clutching at my throat. "When were they going to tell us parents about this?" I asked Sally sharply. "Were we just going to show up with our kids in September and have them shipped off to another school?"

"Oh no," Sally said. "They'll send a letter, you know, over the summer."

I gave her a hard look. It was pointless to continue the discussion with her. She had already checked out. I was on my own.

"I guess I'll go talk to Dr. Roberts," I told her.

Sally nodded and bent down to pick up some stray scraps of blue construction paper. I turned away from her and headed out to the playground.

Two days before the end of the school year, I met with Sally and Dr. Roberts. It was a quick meeting, resulting in only one paragraph of notes, not one word of which reflected the contentiousness of the preceding conversation.

The IEP Team met to discuss Blaze's placement for the 97–98 school year, Dr. Roberts wrote. *Blaze's mother requests that Blaze be withdrawn from the special day class starting in the fall of 1997, so that he can remain at his school for the 97–98 school year. The IEP Team discussed concerns related to Blaze's difficulty attending to reading activities and written work. Blaze fatigues quickly when engaged in reading and writing activities. Blaze is able to tell the information that he knows but has difficulty with completing worksheets. Blaze's special-education needs will be discussed in the fall prior to beginning the school year. Debra Ginsberg has offered to assist the general-education teacher during the next school year, if her schedule permits.*

If my schedule permitted. As if I had, or could have, a schedule that wasn't primarily dedicated to Blaze. I was sure of only one thing as I signed the form. In less than three months, Blaze and I would be starting fourth grade together.

For Blaze, fourth grade begins well. For me, it is a little rockier. Blaze is very pleased to be out of Sally's class. I've spent the summer explaining how important it is for him to be on his best behavior now, and I've underlined the need for a fresh start. I've told him that I will be coming to school with him. This will be to help him, I explain, but it will also mean that he won't be able to get away with anything while I'm there.

Blaze's new teacher, Grace, is wary, both about my involvement and Blaze's abilities to handle a regular-education classroom. She has doubtless been extensively briefed by Dr. Roberts, who has made it clear that she thinks this placement is a mistake. I can't say that I blame her entirely, but, instinctively, I feel that this is the only option. And instinct is all I've got to go on at this point.

Grace tells me that I can't start coming to class for at least a couple of weeks because she needs to establish a rapport with her class. "Fine," I tell her, "but I don't want to wait too long. I want him to get off to a good start."

Grace hesitates before she says, "I understand why you want Blaze in this class and I think it's great that you're going to come in here and help him, but you can't be with him all the time. I want him to learn.

I don't want him to just sit around all day doing nothing if the work is too hard for him."

I give her a long look and decide that she is sincere. "We have to try," I tell her and hear a hint of desperation in my own voice. "It's either this class or he's going to stay home."

Two weeks later, Grace lets me in and I take a seat next to Blaze at one of the half-dozen hexagonal tables in the room. She introduces me as "Blaze's mom" and tells her students that I will be "helping out in the classroom." The children give me confused looks at first, not knowing quite what to make of me (I am Blaze's mother, after all), but within a couple of days they absorb and accept my presence among them.

Blaze's fourth-grade classroom is nothing like the fourth-grade class-room I occupied two and a half decades ago, yet when I sit next to him now, a few weeks into the year, visceral memories of my own school experience come flooding back to me. Despite the fact that I have distinct recollections of my earliest childhood, fourth grade is the first clear memory of school that I have.

We had just moved, the summer before the school year started, from London, England, to Brooklyn, New York. It was something of a culture shock. The school building was old and seemed huge. Every sound echoed off the walls and floors. The lunchroom was loud and close with the smell of baloney and ketchup. I was vaguely nauseated at lunchtime for the entire year. The fact that my groovy parents packed my lunch with peach nectar (instead of chocolate milk) and cream cheese sandwiches (instead of something normal like baloney) didn't help matters.

Despite the fact that my mother had registered and introduced me as Debra, nobody managed to call me by my proper name. I was "Debbie" until I went to college, despite my best efforts to the con-trary. (Elementary schools are obsessed with diminutives. There's an almost pathological need to shorten the names of everybody in sight, both adults and children.)

Physically, I was small for my age and almost painfully shy. I had a British accent, which, added to the fact that I was a new girl, turned me into something of a curiosity. I tried not to speak too often because every time I did my classmates would demand I repeat the words. "Say *castle* again," they said. "Say *milk shake;* say *can't.*"

My classroom was dark and smelled ancient. To me, it seemed that my teacher was at least as old. She was often unwell and, in the sharpest memory I have of my childhood, I can still picture the way she leaned over the sink one afternoon and vomited into it.

Every Wednesday, we had a citizenship assembly and students were expected to wear the colors of the flag. Every Tuesday night, I went into a panic trying to search for clothes that were red, white, and blue. I wanted desperately to blend and to fit in and sensed, somehow, that this very desire marked me as an outsider.

It was the academics, however, that proved to be the most difficult adjustment. For the first time, I was unable to glide through class with all the right answers. Penmanship, something I'd never had to consider before, was taxing and I struggled to make my hand form what seemed like impossibly complex cursive letters. But my real downfall was math. Multiplication tables sent me into a sweaty panic and division was impossible. Numbers became such enemies to me that even learning to tell time was a hellish experience. My father, something of a math wizard, spent hours poring over homework sheets with me, expressing utter disbelief at my lack of the facility he possessed in spades. My fear of math precluded any real interest I might have developed in the subject. Every math class I took from then on was a phenomenal struggle. One of the happiest moments of my academic career was the day I passed the last math class I would ever have to take to satisfy the requirement for my college degree. Facetiously dubbed "math for poets," the class had given me at least as much anxiety as I'd had in fourth grade. When I finished, I offered silent thanks that I would never have to worry about math again.

That is, until now. As I watch Grace write her daily math puzzler (*What number added to the following number will create a number with the same digits in reverse order?*) on the blackboard, I am gripped by the same primal fear that held sway over me twenty-five years ago. Once again, I am small and scared, in a strange place where every noise jangles my nerves and sets my heart beating like crazy. In those days, the safest place to be was deep inside my own head where I could make up elaborate but quiet fantasies to sustain me. I look at Blaze with these sense memories dancing through my head and have a small moment of epiphany.

To be sure, Blaze is a separate entity and I am in no danger of exchanging my own identity with his. Yet, I wonder, couldn't it be similar for him? He is less capable than I was of quieting the sensory overload that is school and his coping mechanisms are less acceptable, even inappropriate. But for the first time since his school odyssey began, I can truly feel, in body and mind, what he must feel every day.

The recess bell rings and the class erupts into a flurry of eager activity as twenty-five nine- and ten-year-olds struggle to keep themselves in their chairs until Grace dismisses them.

"Table two, you may line up," Grace intones. "Table three, I see papers on your table, please put them away. Table four, you may line up. Table one . . ."

Blaze is soon surrounded by a cluster of little girls who talk all at once.

"Blaze, are you coming with us?"

"Blaze, do you want to go to the swings?"

"Blaze, will you sing us that song again that you made up?"

I watch as my son is enveloped in a swirl of pink-plastic barrettes and flowered stretch pants and I smile. Every day, without any prompting at all from me or their teacher, the same three or four girls collect Blaze at recess and lunch and include him in their circle. Between them, they make sure that he never eats alone and never drifts away from the playground. They make certain he copies his assignments and if he balks, they write it down for him. They also report to me. I leave school at lunchtime and when I come back to pick Blaze up a couple of hours later, "Blaze's girls" surround me and offer their impressions of his day.

"Blaze did a great job in art today," Sara will tell me.

"Blaze wouldn't clean up when the teacher told him to," Jenny offers.

"We have a reading assignment," Sierra says. "I put it in Blaze's notebook."

Blaze reacts to the attention with bemused detachment, but he goes with them, he talks to them, he *relates* to them. Without knowing it, they modify his behavior more effectively than the most skilled psychologist. When Blaze spouts a non sequitur or goes off on some metaphoric tangent, the girls give him a blank look and instantly redirect the conversation. They never treat him with condescension. I don't understand where this serendipity comes from, nor can I figure out what Blaze has done to deserve it, since he has never tried to elicit their friendship. But I am so grateful for these amazing little girls that I am often brought to tears.

I watch Blaze shuffle out to recess with his entourage now and smile again. Grace tidies her desk briefly and comes over to me.

"There are treats in the teachers' lounge," she says. "Let's go. Or are you still stuck on the math puzzler?"

"I can't help it," I tell her. "This is a particularly difficult one."

Over the last few weeks, Grace and I have become friends. I have enormous respect for her. Without ever raising her voice, she maintains total command over two-dozen boisterous fourth-graders. One withering look from her is enough to silence the most vociferous dissenter, but when she speaks, it is always with kindness. Unlike my own fourth-grade teacher, she is young and pretty with perfectly manicured nails and—despite the fact that she is expecting her first child—never throws up in the sink. It is her love of teaching, however, that wins her the most points with me. Grace is not afraid to try different approaches with kids who don't grasp basic concepts right off the bat. When a struggling student finally masters a subject, she becomes genuinely excited. For this reason, the third-grade teachers often recommend her for their tough cases. Indeed, this is how Blaze ended up in her class.

For her part, Grace likes the fact that I am realistic about Blaze's problems as well as my own. She is delighted that I've admitted my struggle with math and has taken it on herself to reeducate me at the same time as she teaches my son. We spend recess together, strategizing over how best to help Blaze with the academic workload and discussing her upcoming lesson plans.

Slowly, I've opened up to her. For the first time with a teacher, I've shared some of my fears and doubts about Blaze. I feel I can trust her.

"We've got to make sure that he gains some independence," Grace says. "He has to be able to take care of himself—that's the most important thing. What about sixth-grade camp? I don't see him being able to go at this point."

"Sixth-grade camp?" I ask, baffled.

"The sixth-graders all go away to camp for a week at the beginning of the year," Grace says. "It's sort of a rite of passage."

"Sleep-away camp? Without parents?"

Grace laughs. "Of course without parents. It would be terrible if Blaze missed that. It's such a great experience."

I shake my head. "I can't see him going away for a week by himself," I tell her honestly.

"Well, it's a couple of years off," Grace says. "We've got to get him ready."

I don't tell her that I'm not sure if Blaze will ever be ready to spend

a week away from home in the company of strangers, but I feel comforted that she wants to prepare him for it. She's taken a proprietary
interest in Blaze and I couldn't be happier. The only dark lining in this
silver cloud is the fact that Grace is due to deliver in December and
will be on maternity leave for the second half of the year. I plan to
learn as much from her as possible before this happens.

"I'm thinking of taking Blaze for another evaluation," I tell Grace.
I would never have shared this kind of tidbit with anyone at school
before, but I trust Grace enough to seek her opinion. "I'm not happy
with the report I got from the last psychologist I took him to." This
isn't entirely true—I'm actually still furious, albeit quietly, about what
I feel was a complete misinterpretation by Dr. C.

"What are you hoping to get out of it?" Grace asks me.

"Maybe I can get a real diagnosis this time," I tell her. "I want to go
to somebody who's seen a lot of children. Somebody who might have
seen somebody like Blaze before. I guess I'm looking for someone to
tell me what to do about school. . . ."

"Because you can't come to school with him forever," Grace says,
reading my thoughts.

"Yes," I tell her. "But I would if I could. You know I would."

Blaze paces back and forth in the waiting room. My father and I don't
bother telling him to stop this time. We are, after all, in the office of
Dr. S., a child *psychiatrist,* an actual M.D. as opposed to the psychologists we've seen to this point. Let Blaze act as nutty as he wants, we
think. This is why we're here. Maybe, I think, if Blaze *really* acts
strange, I'll feel justified in bringing him here in the first place. I
haven't coached Blaze at all for this meeting. I want him to act as true
to himself as possible. I don't care if he talks nonsense or asks Dr. S.
the same question ten times. I won't mind if he covers his ears with his
hands or asks the doctor to place the phone in the desk drawer because
he can't stand the thought that it might ring unexpectedly and loudly.

If Dr. S. is worth his salt, he'll understand just who Blaze is and he'll be able to tell me, in practical terms, how I can best help my son navigate a path through the complicated avenues "out there," beyond the confines of home.

Blaze interrupts my thoughts as he begins obsessing about two lights on the wall. What do they mean? Why are they on the wall? I tell him that the red one lights up when you first enter and summons the doctor. The green one flashes when he comes out to see you. My father and I have to explain this to Blaze five times and still he wants to know why they are there.

Finally, the doctor emerges. I am relieved to see that he is relatively plain-looking—no disturbing physical features like crooked teeth, a too-shiny bald head, a speck of food somewhere on his face. This would drive Blaze to distraction, I think, and then stop myself short, realizing that it would actually drive *me* to distraction. I wonder, fleetingly, how many times I project like this on a daily basis and why it takes a visit to a psychiatrist to draw my attention to it.

"Blaze and I will go inside and have a little chat," Dr. S. says, "and then we'll all meet together afterward."

"Hi, Dr. S.," Blaze says, marching happily into the inner sanctum. "Are we going to fight the visitors?"

Dr. S. looks at me and raises his eyebrows. I cover my face with my hands in a gesture of mock exasperation. My father barks out a laugh. "Good luck," he tells Dr. S.

"Oh, not to worry," Dr. S. says, completely missing my father's ironic undertone, "we'll be fine."

As they head into the office, I hear Dr. S. asking Blaze, "Did you think the visitors were in my office? Could you hear them?"

I wait until the door is shut behind them and then I ask my father, "Can you believe that kid? The *visitors*?"

My father just sighs and opens the newspaper in front of him.

Blaze is alone with Dr. S. for forty minutes. Through the wall, I can hear peals of delighted laughter coming from my son. "What could possibly be going on in there?" I ask my father.

"Not a clue," he responds.

"Well, at least he's having a good time," I say.

Blaze is still laughing when, later, Dr. S. ushers us into his office.

"Sounds like fun in here," I tell Dr. S., giving him a tentative smile.

"Oh yes, we've been having a good time," Dr. S. says and shakes my father's hand. "Blaze," he says, "why don't you go play in that room over there for a bit so I can talk to your mother and your grandfather."

Blaze willingly—surprisingly—acquiesces and bounces off to a small room filled with toys off the main office.

"I hope he finds something in there to amuse him," Dr. S. says. "He didn't seem to be interested in any of those toys when I was talking to him. He was focused on the balloon I had. I was making noises with it and he just thought that was hilarious. That's what all the laughing was about."

"I'm not surprised," I say, too eagerly. "He's always been interested in more . . . mundane kinds of things. Rolls of tape and things like that. You know, when he was a baby . . ."

"Yes," Dr. S. says gently and I feel my cheeks flush. My father shoots me a warning look that says *Don't talk so much.*

"Well, I've had a chance to look this over," Dr. S. says, referring to the detailed medical-history form I filled out and sent to him several days ago. "It's very interesting. History of birth trauma . . . oxygen deprivation . . ."

"*Major* birth trauma," my father says. "He wasn't breathing."

"Yes, I see that," Dr. S. continues. "Any history of mental illness in the family?"

"None at all," my father says.

"What about Mommy's side of the family?" I ask my father.

"What about them?" my father says, slightly irritated.

"You know," I whisper, "how *strange* they are?"

"What are you talking about?" my father says.

"What kind of strange?" Dr. S. pipes in, glancing at my father and smiling.

I review all I know about my family. I'm sure that it's because I'm sitting here with a psychiatrist (who, it appears, even has a *couch* in his office) that I'm suddenly sure that I'm just part of a long line of crazy people. Perhaps it's not a random twist that makes Blaze the way he is, I think. Perhaps he's merely the product or distillation of generations of weirdos who've managed, one way or another, to get through life without major exposure. My mother's family certainly fits this profile. Her parents gave odd nicknames to all the neighbors. Her uncle Eric lived with his married brother his whole life, and some fifty years after his brother had married her, he still referred to my grandmother as "my brother's wife." Uncle Eric was a bona fide eccentric if ever there was one. He witnessed bees praying and claimed to have met the devil. He never married nor even had a girlfriend that anyone knew about. He put on a hat to hand out chunks of fudge to his great-nephews and then replaced it carefully on the hat rack when he was finished. His brother, my grandfather, was no straight arrow himself. He was given to fits of pique and attacks of weeping. He didn't want my grandmother to drive a car and she never did. I don't drive, either, and that is perhaps the most damning sign of the lot. It's not that I haven't tried and it's not for lack of desire. Every time I get behind the wheel of a car, I am clutched by a nameless, blackout-inducing panic. Like my grandmother, I have no problem being a passenger, but just the thought of driving myself induces a sickening terror. I break into a sweat thinking about it now and notice that Dr. S. is looking at me quizzically, still waiting for an answer about why I think my family is strange.

"Well," I say, "none of them were actually committed."

I detect a low hiss coming from my father.

"I think what Debra means is they're a little eccentric in some ways," my father says. "My wife's father threw his tea into the fireplace when he didn't like it—that kind of thing. Nothing big—no mental illness."

"Yes, yes, of course. Every family has its eccentrics," Dr. S. says. I wonder what the doctor thinks. Does he often encounter families whose members argue about whether or not they are insane? Is this very argument a mark of insanity—and denial of it? I hate trying to second-guess professionals in the field of human psychology. I'm too suspicious to trust any of them completely. And yet, here I am, almost begging one of them for his expert opinion on my son.

"Well, Blaze and I had a good conversation," Dr. S. says. "He was very cooperative. He certainly is different, there's no question about that. He has a . . . unique way of filtering information. I can see why this would hinder him in the classroom."

"Yes," I say, leaning forward in my chair, "that's exactly right."

"He has a great sense of humor," Dr. S. adds, smiling. "I would even say an advanced sense of humor. But then there are the other things that you've noted on the medical-history form and that I saw evidence of when I was talking to him. The perseveration, hypersensitivity to noise, anxiety . . ."

"What do you think caused these . . . *things*," I say, lacking a better word.

"In my opinion," Dr. S. says, "Blaze's birth trauma is probably to blame for some of his developmental anomalies. Oxygen deprivation at birth can have serious effects that sometimes won't appear until later. And in Blaze's case, we don't know how long the cord was around his neck *before* he was delivered."

"Nobody ever mentioned that to me when Blaze was born," I tell Dr. S. "None of the doctors said anything about oxygen deprivation."

"Sometimes it's a liability issue, unfortunately," Dr. S. says. "Was Blaze born at an HMO?"

"No," I say distractedly. "It was a teaching hospital."

"Oh, uh-huh?" Dr. S. adjusts his position in his large leather chair.

"So, is there a diagnosis for this kind of thing?" my father asks. "We've heard a few different ones."

"The last psychologist I took him to said that he was clearly autistic," I say indignantly, still angry about Dr. C.'s report.

"Blaze is definitely not autistic," Dr. S. says with authority. "I would gladly stake my reputation on that. And I've been around a while."

"What is it, then?" I ask.

"My diagnosis for Blaze would be PDD-NOS," Dr. S. says, "which stands for pervasive developmental disorder, not otherwise specified."

"Not otherwise specified?" I ask, bewildered. "What does that mean?"

"Well, for example, autism is considered a pervasive developmental disorder as is Rett's Syndrome—have you heard of that? No? Well, regardless, the 'not otherwise specified' add-on means that the child has some of the behaviors or issues of other pervasive developmental disorders, especially problems in communication and in the social arena, but doesn't fit the profile of any of those disorders."

"So, basically, that diagnosis includes a whole bunch of random stuff thrown together. It could be anything and it includes everything." I give a short laugh at the ridiculousness of it. "It tells me nothing."

"Yes," Dr. S. says. "Unfortunately, we in the psychiatric profession feel compelled to label everything, even that which we don't understand."

"This isn't even much of a label," I say. I appreciate his candor, but I'm frustrated by what seems like a *non*-diagnosis.

"What do we do about this?" my father asks. "What's the treatment, if there is a treatment?"

"Well, he doesn't need psychiatric therapy," Dr. S. says. "Although I suspect that Blaze is becoming more aware of his differences. There's a possibility that he'll get depressed when he realizes fully that he isn't on the same academic or social level as his peers. It might be helpful then to have him see somebody—a counselor or somebody similar—who could help him with those feelings."

"Is there a special school for kids like Blaze?" my father asks. "Maybe if he were in a better school, one that was designed for kids like him?"

Dr. S. shakes his head. "There really aren't any schools specifically for kids like Blaze," he says. "There aren't really very many kids *like* Blaze."

My father and I both nod assent at this. From the small toy room, we can hear the sound of things crashing to the floor. I make an instinctive move to stand and Dr. S. motions for me to sit. "It's okay," he says, smiling, "that's what that room is for."

"What do you think about medication?" I ask him. "I keep hearing that I should give Blaze drugs."

"Like I said, Blaze might experience depression or anxiety when he becomes fully aware of his differences. In that case, you might want to try some of the newer antidepressant medications that are available now, like Prozac, but you'd be experimenting. There isn't much data available on how helpful these drugs are in cases like this." Dr. S. shrugs. "But we're learning more all the time."

"Forget it," I tell him. "I would never experiment with my child. Do you have any suggestions for what I can do to help him?"

"Behavior modification," Dr. S. says. "More of what you've already been doing with him. You might want to consider having him evaluated by an educational specialist. We're somewhat out of my area of expertise there, but I know of somebody who's quite good." He mentions the same woman that Dr. Roberts has been recommending for some time. I have a moment of utter paranoia, wondering how it can be possible that both Dr. S. and Dr. Roberts have come up with the same person. Is it possible that there is only one educational specialist in the county or are they in cahoots? I decide on the former and realize that Dr. S. isn't going to be able to give me any sweeping, miraculous answers. I am convinced, however, that he has come closer to the genesis of Blaze's differences than anybody else. My father gives voice to this very thought as it passes through my mind.

"I really think you're right about the birth trauma," my father says. "It's so important. Maybe if he hadn't been rushed out of the womb . . ." He gives me a vaguely accusatory glance, but I shrug it off. This isn't anything I haven't heard before, after all.

"Dad," I say, "I'd still be pregnant if I hadn't had labor induced. He didn't want to come out. He'd have stayed in there forever."

After a few more minutes, our session is finished and we take our leave. Dr. S. doesn't think that it's necessary to see Blaze again, but he says he'll be happy to share his thoughts with the school staff if I feel it would be helpful.

In the car, on the way home, my father asks Blaze what Dr. S. talked to him about when they were alone together.

"He asked me what I was afraid of," Blaze says. "He asked me about my friends at school and my teacher."

"What else?" my father prods.

"I don't know," Blaze says with finality, signaling that he won't be giving up any more information. The three of us are silent for a while, digesting our own thoughts as we glide through the lovely scenery of palm trees, ocean, and blue sky. My father adjusts the rearview mirror, giving Blaze a long look in the process.

"I'm not giving him drugs," I say quietly. "Why would I want to experiment with him. *That* would be insanity."

"Absolutely," my father says. "And we don't want to change him, anyway. Why would we want to make Blaze a different person than he is?"

I look back at Blaze who returns my gaze with a steady one of his own. It's true, I don't want to change Blaze. But I do want to help him. As I turn away from Blaze and stare out the window once more, my one hope is that these two desires won't collide, conflict, and cancel each other out.

Sunday begins with seeds. Sesame and poppy.

Blaze sits in the living room watching TV and eating bagels, scattering seeds into the carpet. He has an unusual method of consuming the bagels, first peeling them and then eating the outer, seeded crust.

When I emerge from my bedroom to join him, I see the doughy carcasses of at least three skinned bagels lying on his plate. The smell of onion flakes is in the air.

"I had a bad dream last night," he tells me.

"What was it?" I ask.

"I dreamed there were a whole bunch of garbage trucks lined up at the school and they were all making a very loud noise and I had to cover my ears. How loud was it, Mom?"

"I don't know, Blaze, it was *your* dream."

He considers this briefly before he says, "Just tell me how loud it was. Give me a number."

"I can't give you a number for how loud something was that you dreamed about."

"Okay, then how loud do you think it would be?"

"How loud what would be?"

"How loud if a whole bunch of garbage trucks were lined up in front of my school?"

"I don't know. And I told you I don't want to keep doing this thing with assigning numbers for every noise, remember?"

"Okay, this is the last time."

"No, I'm not doing it."

"Just give me a number."

"Blaze . . ."

"Any number how loud it would be."

"Okay, twenty-five, but that's the last time—"

"Only twenty-five? Don't you think it would be louder?"

"Blaze, that's enough."

Blaze gives the questioning a rest for a moment, but he's still processing my responses. I hear him mumbling something about trucks, school, loudness. After a while, he says, "Mom, that couldn't really happen, could it? There couldn't be so many garbage trucks lined up at my school, could there?"

"Yes, technically it could happen," I tell him, "but it won't. I really don't think you'll ever see a whole bunch of garbage trucks lined up at the school. The school doesn't make that much garbage."

"Was it only a dream?"

"Yes, it was only a dream."

We drift off into our own silent reveries for a while after this and I attempt to make it through the Sunday paper. I hear Blaze call my mother on the phone.

"Nana," he says, "how loud would it be if there was a whole bunch of garbage trucks outside my school? Give me a number."

There is a pause and then I hear him chuckling. My mother and Blaze are constantly finding ways to make each other laugh. Each one thinks the other is tremendously amusing.

"Get dressed, Blaze," I tell him, "we're going out for a walk."

Blaze protests, as he usually does. "I don't want to walk, walk, walkery-walk," he says. We begin the series of negotiations I know so well. He will get dressed, but only in twenty minutes. He will go for a walk, but only if we can stop for a soda. It's all right to visit Vons, but Ralph's is out of the question. I tell him we'll go to Starbucks and we settle that but he refuses to go to Barnes & Noble so I have to argue with him. He has to read a biography and write a report on it for school and we're going to look for a suitable book today. Grace went into labor a month before she was due to deliver and there is now a new teacher, Mr. B., in her classroom. I like Mr. B., who comes from a special-education background, but I feel somewhat adrift without Grace's counsel. I feel that Grace could give me some much-needed pointers on how to get Blaze interested in this project.

"I don't want to do the stupid biography," Blaze says, confirming my suspicion that getting him interested in working will be much like extracting impacted molars.

"Too bad," I tell him.

Once we are out of the house, I feel liberated. Blaze too is happy to be out and he links his arm into mine. I have always loved these outings with him. Since he was an infant, I've been taking him on brisk walks to the beach, to the movies, any place where there was a coffee shop where we could stop and rest before turning around. When he was younger, first fitted into a front pack and later strapped into a stroller, we seldom spoke. Now that he walks beside me, our Sunday strolls are times when we discuss everything.

Blaze has much to talk about these days. Since our visit to Dr. S., he's developed a strong interest in the circumstances of his birth. He's come up with the request that we restage this event so that this time he will have "enough breath to cry." He has also been producing some very interesting drawings lately.

I've paid careful attention to this because Blaze has never enjoyed drawing or art of any kind, for that matter. He lacks the fine motor control and patience necessary to color for any length of time and finds it impossible to stay within any lines, real or imagined. So it was intriguing to me that, for a period of several days, he chose to do the same drawing over and over again. Each time he'd tear up the finished product, declaring that it wasn't quite right. Finally, he came up with a version that seemed to satisfy him and he presented it to me for my appraisal.

The drawing consisted of five rows of different brightly colored circles of more or less the same size. He had used every marker in the house so that no one color was repeated. Below the circles was a stick figure lying on its side. I looked at it carefully, searching for clues—

something, perhaps, like the characters in *Close Encounters of the Third Kind* who heard the same five notes again and again until they finally made sense. I couldn't really figure it out until I turned the paper over and saw what Blaze had written in his big, awkwardly shaped letters: *July 23, 1987, 1:15 A.M., Portland, Oregon.*

"What is this?" I asked him.

"That's what it looked like when I was born," Blaze said. I stared at him, dumbfounded, for a few moments and he attempted to help me. He pointed to the small stick figure and said, "See, that's me and that—" he pointed to the circles, "is what it looked like."

I'm mulling over what these drawings could mean as we pass a construction site where a new block of town houses is going up. Blaze asks me how the electricity gets into the buildings. He wants to know why there is a fence erected in front of the development and can we go behind it and walk around? A car with obvious muffler trouble roars by and Blaze ignores our earlier discussion and ask me to give the noise a number.

"I don't want to keep giving the noises a number," I tell him.

"Well, why are there so many loud noises in the world?" he asks.

"Why do you let them all bother you?" I question back.

"I can't help it," he says, "my yellow wire is broken."

"What do you mean, yellow wire?" I ask, baffled.

"When I was born, they didn't put the yellow wire in right so it got broken and now I'm so sensitive to loud noises."

"Honey, you need to explain this to me," I tell him. "Do you have other wires too or just the yellow one?"

"No, there's other wires," he says, pleased that I'm taking an interest. "There's a blue one and a red one. The blue one is for feelings. The red one controls butterflies and dogs and all flying things. The red one is also for talking and playing. The yellow one is for hearing. There's a girl in my class who has problems with her blue wire. That's why she cries all the time."

"And so you figure your yellow wire is broken?"

"Yes, it was too short when they put it in so it snapped."

"Who put it in?"

"I don't know. Somebody."

"So tell me," I go on, "is there any way of fixing a broken wire? You know, so that the loud noises wouldn't bother you so much."

"Yes," Blaze says, thoughtfully. "You have to find a white wire and patch it together."

"Where can we get the white wire?" I ask him.

"I don't know," Blaze says. "I guess we have to look for it."

By then we are at Starbucks and so the conversation shifts abruptly to what kind of snack we will be having. As Blaze sits and chews on a scone, the topic turns back to the biography.

"I don't know who to do it on," he tells me. "Nobody. I want to read a biography of nobody."

I think about this for a minute and remember last week when each student in Blaze's class was given a letter of the alphabet and asked to choose a word beginning with the letter and then draw a picture of that word. The idea was to create a sign-language book as a class project. Blaze was assigned the letter *N*. After thinking for a while, he turned in his assignment. He had chosen the word *nothing* and left the space for the picture completely blank. I am beginning to think the biography might go the same way.

"Blaze, you can choose anyone for this biography," I tell him. "Think about all the famous people you've heard about."

"Do they have to be alive?"

"No. You can do it on somebody who's died, like a musician or a composer. How about Beethoven or Mozart?"

"How about Marvin Gaye?" he asks. "That's who I want to do for my biography." I ponder this for a minute. It's a great idea, I think, because he's come up with it by himself, but now I'm torn as to whether or not to shoot it down. I sincerely doubt that I'll find a kid's biography on the life of Marvin Gaye and how could I possibly read him an adult biography on this man? I have a moment picturing Blaze presenting this biography to his class, telling them about Gaye's drug problem, singing "Sexual Healing," telling them that Gaye was killed by his own father. No, this is not going to work.

"Maybe Marvin Gaye's not such a good idea," I tell him. "There aren't any kids' books on him."

Blaze is irritated by this information and refuses to discuss the biography question any further. When we finally get to the bookstore, I have to convince him to consider someone else to read about. We finally settle on Thomas Edison, but Blaze is not finished with the Marvin Gaye issue.

"Mom," he says, "did someone kill Marvin Gaye?"

"Yes."

"Who killed him?"

"Some crazy guy," I say, unwilling to go into detail. Blaze senses I am not telling him the whole truth.

"I think it was one of his backup singers," he says.

We take the walk back home slowly, passing a small canyon along the way. Blaze dances along its lip, a little ahead of me. I watch the way his boyish body cuts the space of blue sky and sandy earth and the unbridled joy in his movements. When we are approaching home, he asks me a question he's been pondering for the last few minutes.

"Remember that frog that was stuck in the drain that one time?"

I do remember. Two years ago we came across a frog trapped in a swimming-pool drain, struggling vainly to get out. "Yes," I tell him, "I remember."

"We didn't rescue it, did we?"

"I asked you to put your hand in there and get it out, remember? You didn't want to do it." I don't remind him that *I* didn't want to do it, either. The thought of grasping a slippery frog in my hand was a bit too much for me.

"Well, I thought we should just turn him into a prince."

This is the piece of the story I'd forgotten. Blaze had been adamant. He wasn't going to put his hand in there to get the frog. The solution was simple; we could just turn him into a prince and then all his worries would be over.

"Well, that didn't work, did it?" I say. "It's not so easy to turn a frog into a prince. It would've been easier just to pull him out."

"Whatever happened to him?" Blaze wants to know.

"I think someone else rescued him," I say, although I'm not sure of this at all. "Why are you thinking about this now?"

"I don't think we tried hard enough," Blaze says. "We should have turned him into a prince."

The rest of the afternoon unfolds lazily and turns into darkness. We follow our established routines, eating dinner, cajoling Blaze into the shower and, finally, I tell him it's time for bed. He complains, saying he's not tired, he doesn't like his sheets, his bed's too small, his room is the wrong shape, but finally he yields and allows me to tuck him in. I kiss his cheek and he tells me, "Mom, do you think that frog got out of the pool? He didn't die, did he?"

"No," I tell him, "I don't think so."

I make sure that he's looking at me and then I tell him, "I love you."

This is one of my obsessions. I have little compulsions too. Blaze isn't the only one around here who perseverates. As we both get older, I find more of them cropping up, not so funny now, sometimes ever-so-mildly debilitating. Would I notice them if Blaze didn't have a pathological aversion to salad, a fear of butterflies, a moratorium on certain words? Maybe not. But I notice them more now than I have before. I have a box that I keep near my desk. In it I keep a small plastic frog, a stamp, a red plastic pyramid puzzle that comes in two pieces (the pieces must form a pyramid in the box or it's not right and will bother me), and a glass fish from Italy. These things have to be standing up in the box. The box has to be in a certain place. If it's at the wrong angle to my desk, I can't work.

There are other things too. Patterns on sheets have to be facing up. Can't have upside down sheep on the bed, for example. Throw rugs have to have straight corners. I have gotten out of bed late at night to fix corners. I have also gotten out of bed to check my purse. Is my wallet still there? I don't know why it wouldn't be—it was there an hour ago—but still, I can't fall asleep until I check. Oddly, I don't ever feel compelled to check door locks.

I can occasionally talk myself out of needing to feed these compulsions, but, others—the ones that involve Blaze—can never be swept aside. I have to tell him I love him before he goes to sleep, before either of us goes anywhere. That has to be the last thing he hears from me always. I want Blaze to always know how much I love him. If I don't tell him, I am convinced, I will suffer. My house will burn. I will lose all that is precious to me. I sense that Blaze has always understood and accepted this. So when I lean over him again and whisper those words, he replies right away.

"I love you too, Mom," he says, and I turn off the light.

Chapter 8

DANGEROUS BORDERS

In April of 1973, I was ten years old. We had just moved to Los Angeles and I was attending an elementary school in West Hollywood. My new classroom was large and sunny and sometimes I had trouble concentrating on the teacher's words. I created elaborate fantasies in my head and used my hands as puppets to act them out. Usually one hand played the part of a damsel in distress and the other played the part of a handsome prince who had come to save her. I amused myself like this quite often until, one day, a male classmate noticed me and said, "Hey, what are you doing with your hands? Are you weird or something?" I was gravely embarrassed and never made the mistake of letting myself be seen again. From then on, I was much more subtle. Sometimes I only used my fingers.

I had one good friend, Andrea, who had short, feathery hair, a pug nose, and a freckled face. Andrea was fearless. She was also very confident and never at a loss for words. We spent recess together, walking around the playground, chewing SweeTarts and sucking the sugary liquid from the molded wax lips and bottles that were all the rage then.

Sometime that spring, I found myself in possession of certain facts concerning reproduction. Since I knew only the bare minimum, however, I discussed my newfound knowledge with Andrea to see if she could offer greater insight.

"Oh, I knew all of that," Andrea said, unruffled.

"Well, how does it work?" I asked her. "Do the man and the woman stand up?"

"They lie down," Andrea said knowingly. "The man lies on top of the woman."

I was disturbed by this piece of information. "That doesn't make any sense," I told her.

"Why not?" she countered.

"Because the man's heavier. The woman should lie on top of him, don't you think? Are you sure you've got it right?"

Andrea was miffed that I would doubt the authenticity of her information and haughtily assured me that she was correct.

"Well, then what happens? How do they know when it's over?"

I had too many questions even for an authority like Andrea. She had to concede ignorance and the two of us spent that recess, and a few more, trying to work out the answers. I was still puzzled by what I perceived to be major design flaws in the act of sexual intercourse as I knew it, but it didn't matter because Andrea and I dissolved into giggles and moved on to other topics. Neither of us ever thought to question our parents on the matter. We had each other and that was a much safer alternative.

Shortly after I turned eleven, my family moved again—this time to the other side of the country. There was no more Andrea or anyone like her for me. I started getting my information from novels. By the time my twelfth birthday rolled around, I couldn't imagine sharing the kind of information Andrea and I shared with anybody. I would be in my thirties before I had that kind of conversation with a girlfriend again.

Blaze does not have the equivalent of an Andrea in his life. What's more, the ten-year-old world he inhabits is vastly different from the one I passed through. The borders, I am learning, are drawn in wider circles. Innocence has become something of a packaged concept. Blaze's peers are exposed to the kind of information I didn't have until I was in my teens. Everything about the way these kids interact with one another and the thoughts they share is more sophisticated and complicated than I remember. I am sometimes plainly astonished by what they know and how they express themselves.

One day, Mr. B. decides to give the class an assignment he feels will stimulate some creative thought.

"I want you all to imagine that you could go anywhere in the world for fifteen minutes," Mr. B. says, "at any moment in time. That means you could go back in history if you wanted or into the future. But you only have fifteen minutes to spend there. So, I want you all to write a paragraph explaining where you would go and why you would want to go there."

Twelve hands shoot up immediately.

"What?" Mr. B. says.

"Can we go somewhere *out* of the world? Like another planet?"

"Can we stay here, I mean, like in this time? Do we have to go into the future?"

"How long does the paragraph have to be?"

"Can I stay longer than fifteen minutes?"

Mr. B. sighs and establishes that other planets are acceptable, he doesn't care how long the paragraph is, and that when he says *any time*, he means the present as well. "Now, get to it!" he commands. "We're going to read these out loud." There is a collective groan in the class-room, but the kids start scribbling furiously. As usual, Blaze merely looks around.

"Come on," I tell him. "Do the assignment."

"What?" he says.

"If you could go anywhere in the world, at any time, where would you go? You're supposed to write that down." I am whispering so that

I won't bother anyone else, but Blaze says, "What?" again loudly and everybody looks up. I hand him the pencil and explain it once more. "Now, write," I tell him.

"Time!" Mr. B. calls. "Okay, who wants to go first? What, no volunteers? All right, Maria, you're first."

Maria stands up and blushes. "Um, if I could go anywhere, I would, um, go to, um . . . I would go to heaven? To see my grandmother? I would go to heaven because my grandma died last year. She had cancer. I know she's in heaven and I miss her. That's all I wrote down because I didn't have enough time to finish."

"That's just fine, Maria," Mr. B. says and I can swear I hear a tremor in his voice. I'm glad I don't have to speak because I know I'd be too choked up.

"Scott, why don't you go next?"

Scott says, "I'd like to go into the future, into the year 2050. I want to see what cars will be like in the future. So, if I had fifteen minutes, I'd go into a car dealership of the future and test-drive a car. Then I could come back here to the present and design a car just like it and make a fortune."

"Very entrepreneurial," Mr. B. says dryly. "Ravi, what about you?"

Ravi stands, a deeply serious look on his face. "If I could go anywhere," he says, reading from his immaculately printed composition paper, "I would go back in time to when the India-Pakistan conflict began and try to persuade the two governments not to begin a war. This way, I could help prevent all the bloodshed that has occurred over all the years."

"Well, that's very interesting," Mr. B. says. "Thank you for sharing that. Denny, your turn."

Denny stands up so fast that he almost knocks his chair over. "I would spend my fifteen minutes at the White House," he says. "And I'd tell the president not to have an affair so that we would have a leader to look up to. And—"

"Denny!" Mr. B. cuts in, after shooting me a pleading look to say, *what can I do about* this? "We want to try to keep our essays about appropriate topics. This is not an appropriate topic for the class."

"Why not?" Denny says. "He's the president. My father says—"

"Denny, have a seat," Mr. B. says quickly. "We're running out of time." Mr. B. wheels around, looking for a student, I assume, who might break the tension. "Blaze!" he says. "Where would *you* like to go?"

There is a moment of silence in the classroom as everyone waits for Blaze's response. I offer up a quick, wordless prayer that he'll say something that makes sense.

"Ace Hardware," Blaze says without standing up. "I'd like to go to Ace Hardware."

The class erupts in laughter, but I sense it is not the cruel kind. I am laughing myself, as is Mr. B. "And why would you want to go there?" Mr. B. says.

"It's good there," Blaze deadpans. "They have good tools there. And there's a train that goes around a track at the top of the store. I like it there."

Mercifully, the bell rings for recess and the class files out. Well, I think to myself, at least I don't have to worry about my child being jaded before his time. I can rest comfortably in the knowledge that I won't have to explain war and presidential dalliances any time soon.

I don't maintain this level of comfort for too long, however. Some time later, as fourth grade marches to its end, certain events dictate that I must explain the facts of life to my son. When this happens, I am distressed. Compared to what his peers know, asking this boy to integrate the "facts" as I can present them seems comparable to asking him to reproduce the Sistine Chapel with a package of crayons.

If there's one thing I've learned this year, it's that Blaze's classmates will use any opportunity to discuss topics other than those with an academic slant. By the spring of 1998, I've been sitting beside them for eight months, so I know this to be true. In September, I was "Mrs. Blaze's mom," my son's personal aide and some sort of strange, not-very-tall adult. By the Christmas holidays, I had become "Mrs. Ginsberg," their teacher's friend and part-time helper. By the time spring break rolled around, I'd morphed into "Ms. Ginsberg" and sometimes, "Debra," a blend of all the above with the addition of confidante thrown in for good measure.

They now have no qualms talking to me about anything that comes into their heads. I am clearly an adult and an authority figure, but I also sit at the table with them and go through lessons with them as if I am another student. I help with homework, but I still complain when I feel the math is too hard. I offer dictionary definitions and vocabulary words. I listen to stories of baby sisters and read from the giant book of Beanie Babies. I am also Blaze's mother and I believe that status has granted me some special favors because, while he often inspires a cross of bewilderment and amusement from his classmates, Blaze is genuinely liked. My position in this classroom is one I cherish. Even better, I am privy to many unedited moments of ten-year-old life, providing me with a priceless education of my own.

This is how it comes to pass that, one Monday morning, the barely ten-year-old Jimmy asks me, "Ms. Ginsberg, do you like *South Park?*"

I weigh all the possible answers before giving one. I don't particularly like what I know of the TV show he is referring to. Its constant desire to be as politically incorrect as possible doesn't seem that funny to me, but I figure I am probably too old and out of the loop to appreciate it. I definitely don't think it is appropriate for kids Jimmy's age. Should I tell him that I've seen it and don't think it's so great or should I just act like a grown-up and tell him he shouldn't be watching it at all?

"Does your mother let you watch that show?" I ask after a moment or two of this internal debate.

"Well, she doesn't want me to watch it," he says, "but I complain that all my friends get to watch it so she says that if I have to watch it, she doesn't want to know about it."

"Well, in my opinion, I don't think that it's an appropriate show for kids your age," I tell him, feeling stuffy and aged. "I don't even think it's appropriate for *me* and I'm an adult."

"But why?" he asks me. "It's the best show on television. It's really funny."

This sounds like parroting to me, so I ask him, "What makes it so funny? Tell me about one of the shows and explain to me why you think it's funny."

There is just the vaguest hint of embarrassment on Jimmy's face when he says, "Well, there is one thing, but I can't tell you about it."

"Why not?"

"Because it's inappropriate for school."

"Aha, so what does that tell you about the show?" I ask him.

Jimmy shrugs, seemingly glad that I'm not going to press him to explain. At this point, however, our conversation has attracted the attention of our other tablemates who are waiting, curious, for the other shoe to drop.

Steffi, a petite blonde with a cherubic face, pipes up. "I'll tell you," she volunteers and proceeds to describe a complex scene, high in sexual content, that ends with a character licking a length of carpet for several hours. The word *lesbian* is bandied about at the table as the rest of the kids chuckle self-consciously. For a moment or two, I am too shocked to respond. When I manage to lift my dropped jaw from the tabletop, I ask Steffi and Jimmy, who are both blushing, "Do you understand what all of this means?"

"Oh, yes," they both assure me, but I have to believe that they do not. It is completely beyond my ken that two ten-year-olds can find this scene funny unless they are aware only of its literal elements. I debate pressing them further, but I am clearly out of my depth, so I turn to Maria and Ali, who are looking at us as if we were speaking

Greek and ask, "Your mothers don't let you watch this show, do they?"

"Hmpf," Maria snorts. "My mother doesn't even *know* about that show." Ali merely shakes his head.

As usual, Blaze contributes nothing to the conversation, preferring to watch and listen. He enjoys watching me interact with his peers for many reasons. For one, I am less likely to be demanding any academic output from him if I am concentrating on other kids in the class. For another, he is often able to get a clearer view on their thoughts and feelings if they are filtered through me. He doesn't pay careful attention to the actual words spoken during these conversations but rather takes note of the emotional current of our interactions. He will often remark later that when I was talking to Maria, she was happy or that when I was discussing homework with Jimmy, he was frustrated. He always notices distress in his classmates, even when nobody else does. It is for this reason that I'm not worried that he'll start asking uncomfortable questions about the content of this particular conversation.

The *South Park* discussion sparks a debate at the following Tuesday-night dinner with my family.

"These kids can't possibly understand what the show means," I tell my father. "They just know it's supposed to be dirty and that's why they're laughing."

"You're wrong," my father says. "They *do* know. They're getting all this stuff from their parents."

My mother agrees with him and then Maya jumps in to agree with me. I find it ironic that, in this case, the younger generation is clinging to old-fashioned notions of innocence.

"If it's true that these ten-year-olds can understand the content of that show and then be able to laugh at it, then I'm afraid there's no hope for society," I say.

My father laughs and counters in kind. "There isn't any hope for society," he says. "Get used to it."

• • •

I am not allowed the luxury of filtering these debates internally and trying to apply them to my own child because, shortly after our dinner discussion, Blaze starts getting into trouble at school for using "inappropriate" language. The first warning comes shortly after Grace takes her maternity leave and is replaced by Mr. B. One day, after I leave the classroom, Blaze calls his new teacher a "dick."

I am mortified when Mr. B. whispers this in my ear so that the other children won't hear and get any ideas. Mr. B, who can barely control his own laughter, understands that Blaze doesn't comprehend the meaning of what he is saying. But he certainly knows it is rude, I argue. As for the rest of it, I decide to call in my father to have a little chat with my son.

"Do you know what a *dick* is?" my father asks Blaze in a rather strident tone.

"No," Blaze admits, honestly.

"Well, I'll tell you. A *dick* is a rude term for a penis. So, basically, you called your teacher a penis. Do you understand how disrespectful that is?"

Blaze struggles to contain his laughter and maintain an appropriate level of chagrin, but I can tell that he finds the whole thing very funny. My father is masterful, never betraying his own amusement. He continues on, telling Blaze how important it is for him to have respect for his teacher—and everyone else, for that matter—and how he shouldn't throw words around that he doesn't understand just because he's heard other people use them because then he'd really seem like an idiot, wouldn't he? Blaze agrees, but I'm not entirely convinced that his contrition outweighs his amusement. My uneasiness is soon justified.

I arrive to pick Blaze up from school one day shortly after my father's discussion with him, only to be greeted by a confused and troubled Steffi.

"Blaze said something very bad to me," she says. I have to kneel down beside her to hear what she whispers in my ear. "He said he was going to stick a knife in my wiener," she breathes. From the corner of my eye, I can see Blaze cowering in the classroom, a very guilty look on his face. I give him a fierce glance to indicate he is in big trouble, but my first duty is to reassure Steffi. I pull her aside from the little crowd of girls surrounding her and put my arm around her shoulders.

"Steffi," I begin, "what Blaze said was totally inappropriate and I am going to speak to him about that, but I hope you know that he doesn't really understand what he's saying. Do you know that?" She nods, shyly. "He probably heard somebody say something like that and he's just repeating it. But I am so sorry he said it and he will apologize. He doesn't mean anything by it and he would never want to hurt your feelings. Do you understand?"

Steffi nods again and, before she runs off to catch her bus, she gives me a sweet little smile. "I know," she says. "I know he doesn't know . . . I know he didn't mean it."

When I walked into the classroom, Mr. B. gestures toward Blaze and says, "You heard what he said?" I shake my head in assent. Mr. B. is also of the mind that Blaze is merely repeating words he's heard in the classroom without the slightest comprehension of meaning or context. Together, we demand an explanation from Blaze and, after considerable prodding, Blaze reveals that he's heard an almost identical sentence from another boy in the class.

When we get home, I have it out with Blaze. I tell him how disappointed I am that he would say such a rude, hurtful thing to one of his friends. I remind him what my father told him about not repeating things he's heard, especially if he doesn't understand what those things mean. I explain what *wiener* is slang for, and Blaze is painfully embarrassed. The worst part of this whole episode, I tell him, is that what he said had violent overtones. How could he say such a terrible thing to a little girl?

Ultimately, I come to the understanding that Blaze is venturing into territory that, until now, he's left uncharted. He is learning that throwing out certain words and phrases will get him some attention from the boys in his class. He is still receiving plenty of help and mothering from the girls, but for the first time in his life, he is trying to go beyond them, to reach for acceptance from his male peers. I realize that this is a huge milestone for a boy who has spent most of his days watching his social milieu from within the confines of his own shell. But if the Steffi episode is any indication, I think, it is obvious that Blaze still doesn't have a map or compass to navigate this new landscape. I can't tell Blaze how to be a boy—nor do I want to. What I can do, I decide, is give him some information.

As I knew it would, this decision generates both internal and external debates.

"I have to have a 'facts of life' discussion with Blaze," I tell my father and we discuss how, when, and why. My father offers to have the talk with Blaze and, at first, I think that this is a splendid idea. After all, I am no authority on becoming a man. But when my father says that there is no time like the present and offers to have his talk with Blaze immediately, I go into a state of panic. I remember the confusion *I* felt when I stumbled onto the facts of life at ten years of age and I fear that Blaze would be totally lost. I doubt that he has the emotional maturity to digest it all. I decide, finally, that, rather than passing the buck to my father, I will explain the whole thing to Blaze myself.

I reckon I need to find a completely unbiased book, preferably with illustrations, to read to Blaze so that my own interpretations won't color our discussion. Besides, I reason with my father, wouldn't it be better if he heard it from me first? Perhaps then he wouldn't feel it was a topic he could never raise in my presence.

The first task, finding a book that explains the facts of life, proves to be much more challenging than I imagined. I roam the aisles at my local bookstore with Blaze trailing behind me, finding everything

except what I am looking for. There are several books about menstru-
ation for girls and an overabundance of books on potty training. I see
books for teens about coming to terms with homosexuality, AIDS,
suicide, and a new baby in the family. There is nothing I can read to
Blaze. I solicit the help of a bookstore employee, finally, and explain
what I am looking for. She is a young woman who seems sensitive to
my plight. "There must be something here," she murmurs and begins
pulling books off the shelf and leafing through them. Judging by the
look of astonishment on her face, I feel safe assuming she's never
perused this particular section of the bookstore before.

"I just need something very basic," I tell her. "I need a book that
lays out the simple, physical facts. I don't want any of this stuff about
masturbation or sexually transmitted diseases. It's definitely too soon
to tell him about all of that."

She takes a look at Blaze, who is walking around the store singing a
tune of his own creation, and raises her eyebrows as if to ask, *This* is the
kid you want the book for?

After a long search, I settle on a book that has a section devoted to
sexual intercourse and a few pages explaining inappropriate language,
illustrated with nonthreatening cartoons. I am not convinced that it is
the best text to use, though, and my trip to the bookstore only reinforces my belief that this subject matter is filled with potential mine-
fields. I often feel that there are few second chances with Blaze and
that if I explain a concept (or, in this case, a physical reality) incorrectly, it will take years to reconstruct and change my words in his
mind. This also means that I will have to think very carefully about
the moral overtones of what I tell him. I want him to respect women,
but I also want him to respect himself. More than anything else, I
want him to feel safe and comfortable. There is no book or pamphlet
that can aid me in achieving that goal. I decide to bide my time a little and think very carefully about what I want to tell my son.

Blaze has been very quiet about the whole Steffi incident after my initial lecture and watches my bookstore machinations with interest. I suspect he knows something is up and that he is in for a serious conversation very soon. I know Blaze has wisdom beyond what he is credited for and it isn't a huge leap of faith for me to believe that he will use this wisdom to see us both safely across this crossroad.

A few days after my initial visit to the bookstore, Blaze's class goes on a field trip to see a historic section of the city as part of their social studies unit. Since I am a permanent fixture in the class, I get to go along as well. I sit at Blaze's table, as Mr. B. reads off his expectations for the class's behavior, and wait for the arrival of the other parent volunteers who will be coming along to help. Jimmy, of the *South Park* discussion, sits next to me and complains that he is tired, having spent a wild time at another boy's birthday party over the weekend. He relates the events eagerly: ice-skating, pizza, and lots of girls.

"There were some really hot chicks there," he says. I raise my eyebrows and he continues. "There was this one chick, she was a real babe. Scott thought so too," he adds, referring to another boy in the class. "The only problem is that she's nineteen years old," he says, chagrined, and waits for my response. I can't help smiling; although, once again, I am amazed at his precocity.

"Maybe," I tell him, "you and Scott can double-date."

"That might be a good idea," Jimmy says. "If you put both our ages together, we're the same age as her. . . ."

"Jimmy," I sigh, "you are definitely something else."

It turns out that Jimmy's mother is one of the parent volunteers. She is wearing a tight blue T-shirt and jeans and her hair is a dark waterfall down her back. I introduce myself to her but she doesn't seem at all interested in starting up a conversation. I can't even approximate how old she is. (I stopped being able to guess at women's ages when Blaze started school. All the other mothers seemed so much older than I was, yet I knew they couldn't be so I was completely thrown off.)

The two other parent volunteers for the field trip are the mothers of the most boisterous, outspoken boys in the class. When, several hours later, we all eat lunch together in a park, I watch these boys interact with their mothers. Jimmy leans over his mother, his arms around her shoulders. The other boys ditch their too-cool attitudes completely and beg their mothers to take them to the gift shop, to watch them play on the grass, to take their hands as they cross the street. By contrast, my child, standing apart from the group and listening for the sound of trains in the distance, seems positively detached.

For a few minutes, these boys are just that—little boys—clamoring for their mothers. I feel a stab of sentiment and find my eyes blurring with tears as I watch this interplay, but I don't want to blink them away. I am afraid to miss any part of this brief time in Blaze's childhood and I believe a blink is as long as it will take for Blaze and the rest of those boys to cross over from being the children they are to the adolescents they are becoming. I suspect that Blaze's crossing will be unconventional, but perhaps, I hope, not so different from those of his peers.

I am saddened by what I feel is the beginning of the end of innocence for all of these children, including my own. It is both foolish and dangerous to maintain a stance of happy ignorance, I decide. The best I can do is to impart my own values to Blaze with gentleness and conviction and hope that he will mark his passage across this border with courage and strength.

An entire year passes before I break out my little facts-of-life book and sit down with Blaze for the discussion. I've been equivocating this long about whether or not he's ready and, I admit, struggling with my own cowardice.

When we finally do sit down to talk, it is because Blaze insists on understanding the biology behind conception. Again, it seems, everything cycles back to birth. I tell him, nervously, that I'm going to explain everything to him and that he must listen very carefully and ask me any questions he might have.

"It's okay, Mom," Blaze says as if to reassure me and I wonder, briefly, which one of us is the adult. Miraculously, I get through the specifics without losing my composure. The book, with its dispassionate objectivity, helps a great deal. Blaze listens attentively. There are no giggles, no looks of alarm, no blank stares of incomprehension. When I finish, the book closed in my lap, there is a moment of silence between us. I ask Blaze if he has any questions. He has just one.

"Doesn't it hurt the woman?" he wants to know.

How, I wonder, could I ever have doubted Blaze's unlimited capacity for fundamental understanding? His question allows me to launch into a discussion about intimacy, respect, and physical expressions of love. For a moment, we live in a perfect world where everything is beautiful and pure. I don't know what will happen down the line with my son's attitudes toward women, men, or himself. But I do know that I got there first, before *South Park,* a jaded classmate, or even the daily news. For that, I am very grateful.

[*Chapter 9*]

TEA AND EMPATHY

I viewed Blaze's fourth-grade year as something of an idyll for both of us. There had been a few bumps in the road, but, on the whole, it had been a very successful time. I wasn't sure how much of this success had to do with Grace (who began coming over to our house for tea and tutoring in the spring), Blaze's peers, or the fact that I had come to school with him every day.

I kept thinking that a large part of Blaze's readjustment at school came from within himself. This was the year that he'd started thinking and talking about his birth. It was also the first time that I'd ever seen him take any steps, however tentative, toward forming some relationships with children his own age. But I often felt that trying to understand Blaze was like trying to understand the ocean. To me, he seemed just as deep, changeable, and unfathomable. So much of what I learned about him came from a purely instinctual level. I knew that coming to school with him was the right thing to do at the time but I couldn't have said why, exactly, or what else I could have done. I also knew that I wouldn't be able to give a repeat performance the following year. A fifth-grader couldn't have his mother tagging along with him to class every day. Aside from the fact that it probably wouldn't do him any good on a purely social level, I doubted that I'd find another teacher as sympathetic as Grace. So, as the year drew to a close, I was faced with the dilemma of where to place Blaze for the following year. My thoughts were cloudy and uncertain. Should I place him in another regular-education classroom for fifth grade and just hope for the best, or should I transfer him to the other school in the district that had a special-education class?

Dr. Roberts made a valiant attempt to sway me toward the latter option, even going so far as taking me for a visit to the special-ed class in question. We rode up to the school early one misty morning as Dr. Roberts meted out bits of information about the school, the program, and the teacher.

"Mr. Davidson has been teaching this class for years and years," Dr. Roberts said. "He's a terrific teacher. We're lucky to have him."

"Yes," I said. "Yes, I'm sure."

Once in the classroom, I sat next to Dr. Roberts and watched as Mr. Davidson gave instruction to a class of about fifteen fifth- and sixth-graders who were mostly boys. The atmosphere was casual but hummed with precise organization. Mr. Davidson was a big, bearded man with a rumbling, deep voice. He wore jeans and a Hawaiian shirt. My immediate impression of him was that, unlike most of the teachers I'd met, he wasn't afraid to get his hands dirty, literally or metaphorically.

I was impressed with Mr. Davidson's control over the kids. I was also a little startled by how old the kids looked. The boys were big, much bigger than the kids in Blaze's class. I recognized a couple of them from Sally's class so long ago. They looked almost like adults now.

"Don't you think Blaze would be lost in here?" I whispered to Dr. Roberts. "These kids look huge."

"That's because there are some sixth-graders in here," Dr. Roberts said. "They are a little older, but I can tell you that Mr. Davidson is a gifted teacher. He does really well with these children."

I was inclined to believe her, mostly because I was struck by how overwhelmingly normal all the kids looked. Nobody spoke out of turn, made siren noises, or rocked in a chair. Hands were raised, questions were answered, papers were pulled out. I would have been hard pressed to identify any "handicapping conditions," from this brief visit.

Dr. Roberts sat next to me, emitting a sort of proud special-education glow, watching the proceedings with a small smile on her face. She was clearly in favor of this class. But I had my own glow going and that had to do with how well I felt Blaze had done in a regular class. I wasn't sure that Dr. Roberts was giving him enough credit for that. I was also loathe to take him away from the classmates he'd just started getting to know.

"I think I've seen enough," I told Dr. Roberts. "Thanks for bringing me here."

Back in her office, I told Dr. Roberts that I wanted to keep Blaze at his "home" school in a regular fifth-grade class.

"Will you think about Mr. Davidson's class over the summer?" she asked. "You can always change your mind."

I assured her that I would, but also extracted a promise from her that Blaze would have help in the classroom from an aide come September. Dr. Roberts wrote this into her notes. And, as I was learning, once something was written down in the notes, it had to be done.

As I made these arrangements with Dr. Roberts, I marveled at how my relationship with her had changed over the last five years. I had gone from a fearful hostility toward her to a warm respect. A good portion of this transition had taken place during fourth grade. My position as über-mom allowed me to drop by her office at various times during the day on an unofficial basis to let her know how things were going and I did this quite often. She had listened with interest when I told her about Dr. S. and his verdict of pervasive developmental disorder, not otherwise specified, saying that she'd thought the same about Blaze. When I told her that Dr. S. had said that giving

Blaze medication would only be an exercise in experimentation, she disagreed, but didn't push the issue. Again, she recommended taking Blaze to the educational specialist she knew.

"It's something I might do at some point," I told her, "but it's too expensive for me at this point." I told her that Dr. S. had recommended the same person and I was relaxed enough by then to tell her about the conversation my father and I had had with the good doctor. For reasons I couldn't understand, I then told Dr. Roberts that I didn't drive and that if anyone needed psychological counseling, it was probably me. I laughed a little at the end of this statement, but to my surprise, Dr. Roberts took it very seriously.

"Yes," she said. "That would be money well spent. You should see somebody first, before you think about getting Blaze evaluated. It's just as important to take care of yourself, you know."

"Hmm, yes, well, maybe . . . ," I said.

I didn't give Dr. Roberts's proposal much more thought as I became wrapped up in the year-end frenzy that seemed to consume the school staff and students alike. One of the last events of the school year was the much-lauded "authors' tea." For this effort, the entire student body was instructed to produce a piece of free writing and turn it in to the teacher. Of these submissions, every teacher would select two or three students from each class to read their work in front of parents, staff, and students at an evening tea. There was much scribbling and pencil chewing going on in our class as we prepared for the event. As usual, Blaze was quite lackadaisical about the whole thing, preferring to study the machinations of his classmates rather than produce something of his own, even though he'd recently been scratching out some poems and songs at home.

I'd more or less given up on him submitting anything to Mr. B. and was busy helping his classmates with their work when he insisted on telling me about Breanna, one of his tablemates, and what had happened to her.

"Breanna was crying yesterday, Mom," he told me. "She was really upset."

"Oh, uh-huh?" I said, distractedly editing a poem about the color red.

"Mom, really," Blaze went on. "She cried and it was like a storm. Her face was all dark and light and quiet. She didn't make any sound but there were all these clouds and rain in her face."

This I paid attention to. "Blaze," I told him, "why don't you write that down? Write down what happened to Breanna yesterday. Just like you told me."

"Oh, okay," he said, as if this was a good idea that hadn't occurred to him. Blaze's difficulty with the physical act of writing inclined him toward brevity, so he was finished very soon after he started. He handed me his paper and when I read it, I had the same surge of joy that I felt whenever I read anything particularly good.

When Breanna cried it looked like a storm
She didn't make any sound
but there was rain
and clouds
and sun
and darkness in her face

Blaze hadn't used any punctuation, so I added a couple of commas and periods. That was the extent of my edit.

"That's a great poem, Blaze," I told him. "I love it."

"Really?" he said, disbelieving.

"Yes," I said. "The only thing it needs is a title. You have to call it something. What do you want to call your poem?" I waited for his answer while a few lofty titles floated through my head. "The Quiet Storm," maybe? Or perhaps, "Raining Tears?"

"'Breanna Crying,'" Blaze said, simply. "That's what it's called."

Yes, I thought. Yes, indeed.

Blaze turned in the Breanna poem after I scribbled down a copy to keep for myself. I didn't think about it again until the next day when Mr. B. took me aside and said, "I love Blaze's poem. It's so different. I want to put him in the authors' tea. What do you think? Do you think he'd mind reading it out loud?"

Blaze didn't mind the idea of the authors' tea at all and seemed even a little excited at the prospect. We had a dry run in front of the class where Blaze and the other two children who Mr. B. had selected stood up and recited their work. Blaze had nary a problem. However, Breanna, the subject of Blaze's poem, blushed several shades of carmine and crimson when he read it out loud. She had an amazingly expressive little face. Blaze had captured it perfectly.

Mr. B. was possibly more excited than either me or Blaze. He got a tremendous kick out of Blaze, who always said exactly what was on his mind, even if this meant spouting less than politically correct statements about other teachers he didn't particularly care for. For Mr. B., a first-year teacher looking for a permanent position, this must have been both amusing and enlightening. But Mr. B. also genuinely liked Blaze's poem and wanted to share it. He wasn't recommending Blaze out of what my mother would have called *rachmones* (which translates to something between *pity* and *compassion*, but since it's a Yiddish word, there is a slightly ironic edge to it) because Blaze was a special-ed kid.

I discovered, only later, that had it *not* been Mr. B.'s first year teaching, he would most likely not have chosen Blaze as one of his readers. It turned out that the authors' tea was quite a political event. The teachers got to show off their kids here and show up their colleagues who may not have produced as great works of literature. The event was heavily choreographed with the earlier grades reading first and everybody sitting in a particular spot on the stage. There were rehearsals. Semiformal dress was required. The children were required to write brief introductions for their writing and a bound program was distributed to all the parents and staff. The last thing anyone needed was an awkward kid who needed extra prodding or who might screw up at the podium. In other words, a kid like Blaze.

When I discovered all of this, I went into a bit of a panic. Blaze had never stood up in front of an audience in any capacity and he had certainly never displayed any desire to follow the kinds of directions and choreography required for this event. My unleashed imagination ran wild with possible scenarios. What if he walked onto the stage before he was supposed to? What if he got stagestruck, didn't read his poem, talked out while someone else was reading? He hated loud noises. What if the clapping and cheering freaked him out and he ran screaming from the room? I began to think the whole thing was a terrible idea, and I struggled to keep these thoughts from Blaze, who seemed remarkably relaxed. But despite my misgivings, it was a done deal. Blaze was in the program and that was it. My parents were attending. And as if all this wasn't enough, Dr. Roberts informed me that she was planning to stay at school late so that she could see Blaze as well.

When the evening of the authors' tea finally arrived, I was too anxious to sit next to my parents in the audience. I cowered in the standing-room-only section of the library. From my vantage point, I could see the holding room where the kids waited for their turn to read. I noticed that Blaze was making a bit of a stir, walking around the room, not sitting perfectly quietly like he was supposed to. I broke out in a cold sweat, adrenaline pumping unchecked through my body. Never doing this again, I told myself. Never, never. Can't take the stress.

My nervousness precluded any enjoyment I might have gotten listening to the poems and stories from the lower grades, even though, from some far distant corner of my brain, I noticed how cute the little ones were as they stumbled through their rhyming couplets. When it was finally time for Blaze's class, I was on the verge of hyperventilating and thought I might very well pass out where I stood. A thin little girl read a passage she had written comparing popularity at school to chasing butterflies. Then it was Blaze's turn. I saw Dr. Roberts emerge from her office and stand quietly on the periphery.

There seemed to be an almost unnatural silence in the room as Blaze walked up to the podium. He bumped into the microphone and it crackled. I swore I could hear the indrawn breaths of every staff member who had ever worked with my child in that school. Blaze cleared his throat.

"Ahem, excuse me," he said and smiled. He paused in front of the audience for a few seconds, just long enough to convince me that his performance was going to be an epic disaster. Finally, he spoke.

"A girl in my class became upset and started crying," he said. "When I looked at her, it reminded me of a storm so I wrote about it."

He read his poem then, in a perfectly assured cadence. He didn't rush or go too slowly. He didn't stumble or waver. He looked born to this, as if he'd been performing in front of crowds his entire life. It was over in a matter of seconds.

"Thank you," he said and the room erupted into a thunderous applause. He took his place next to his classmates with a huge grin on his face, wide enough to swallow my ocean of doubts forever.

I was a mess— tears everywhere, throat closing up, hiccups. I could hardly breathe. I was so proud of him, so relieved, so drenched with emotion, that I thought I would suffocate. Through the blur, I wondered if I was alone or if other parents felt the same way I did—that everything involving our children was painful in some way. The emotions, whether they were joy, sorrow, love, or pride, were so deep and sharp that in the end they left you raw, exposed and, yes, in pain. The human heart was not designed to beat outside the human body and yet, each child represented just that—a parent's heart bared, beating forever outside its chest.

Blaze received much praise before I could even get to him. As he filed out with the rest of his class, several adults patted him on the back, gave him a high five, or told him what a great job he'd done. I only knew half of these people. Some of them were teachers, but as for the rest, I had no idea.

"Are you Blaze's mom?" I heard through my daze and turned to see one of the sixth-grade teachers I barely recognized.

"Yes," I said.

"What a wonderful poem that was," the teacher said. "Totally original. I'm very impressed. Most of this stuff was cookie-cutter writing. Blaze has a real voice."

"Yes," I said. "Yes, he does."

Mr. B. came up from behind me and squeezed my shoulder.

"He was great," Mr. B. said. I didn't trust my own voice to stay steady, so I nodded and moved away quickly, before I could embarrass myself by bursting into tears.

A couple of days after Blaze's performance, Mr. B. told me that Dr. Roberts would be resigning her position at the end of the school year. I felt an unexpected wave of disappointment. When I stopped by her office (which was always open to me) to chat, she was full of congratulations.

"Blaze did such a fine job at the authors' tea," she said. "He has come such a long way. A couple of years ago, it wouldn't have seemed possible."

"I had my doubts," I confessed. "But Blaze always surprises me."

"Well, he has a wonderful support system," Dr. Roberts said.

"Yes," I countered, "but I actually came here this morning to talk about you. I heard a rumor that you're going to be leaving us."

"Yes, I'll be leaving at the end of June," she said. "I know the person who'll be replacing me as administrator and she's terrific. I'm sure everything will be fine in the transition."

"It's not that so much," I told her. "We'll . . . we'll miss you." I couldn't imagine having said such a thing to Dr. Roberts a few years earlier. I was frankly amazed that I was saying it now, but it was true, I *would* miss her. For all my internal raging and disagreements with her, she had remained a steady presence in Blaze's school career. Although it had taken me a while to believe it, she cared about Blaze and wanted what was best for him.

"And I'll miss all of you too," Dr. Roberts said and smiled. Never one to talk much about herself, she moved right along. "I was thinking about all that you've done in the classroom this year," she said, "and I was wondering if you'd be interested in working in our preschool program as an aide."

"What?"

Dr. Roberts went on to describe the class, which was an early-intervention program for severely handicapped three- and four-year-olds ("Sometimes a little older," she said). The children had a wide range of disabilities, Dr. Roberts told me, and the program was designed to help them learn skills for use in the classroom. The idea was that, when these children reached kindergarten age, they would be able to spend some, if not all, of their time in a regular kindergarten class.

"I really think you'd enjoy it," Dr. Roberts said. "There's such a wide range of modalities in that classroom. And you'd be wonderful with the children."

Before I had the chance to ask too many questions, Dr. Roberts whisked me off to the classroom in question to have a look. The class was in Sally's old room, I noted, and was now filled with several very small children and a multitude of aides and teachers, none of whom looked older than high school age. The atmosphere was one of tightly controlled chaos. Everyone seemed to be moving and speaking at once, although there was clearly a method to the madness.

"Show me blue, Vincent."

"Oops, no, try again!"

"Do you need to go potty, Jake?"

"Show me green."

"Good job!"

"Jake, do you need to go potty?"

"It's circle time, Steven. Go to circle."

"Show me red. Nope, try again! Show me red."

"Circle time, Steven."

"Jake?"

"Yay! Red! Good job!"

"Everybody out of the way! Jake needs to go potty!"

An aide rushed by, holding a tiny boy by the hand. His feet barely brushed the floor as they hustled into the bathroom.

Dr. Roberts looked at me somewhat apologetically. "There would be a little toileting involved," she said.

"You mean taking kids to the bathroom?" I asked.

"Well, yes, some of these little guys have a harder time with potty training, so we help them out with that."

"That doesn't sound too bad," I said like the novice I was.

"Oh, good," Dr. Roberts said.

Back in her office, Dr. Roberts had me fill out the necessary forms for employment and rounded up the principal for an impromptu interview. Slightly baffled, the principal asked me a few perfunctory questions, stressed the need for confidentiality in special education, shook my hand and said, "Welcome aboard."

I felt slightly as if I was being rushed into the job before I might have the chance to change my mind, but this trepidation was tempered by the thought that this was a job I ought to take. One didn't get that many opportunities to perform real service, I thought, and here I was being offered the chance without even trying. It seemed like a sign of some sort.

"When would you want me to start?" I asked Dr. Roberts.

"Oh, we, um, need people for the summer session," she said. "So that would be in about three weeks."

"Oh."

As if to sweeten the deal, Dr. Roberts added, "You'd be working next to Blaze's classroom this summer and you'd have the same hours. And I've just found a summer school aide for Blaze. She's a psychology intern and very bright. I think it will be a great match." Dr. Roberts gave me a small, enigmatic smile. "She's also quite lovely to look at."

"Oh," I said. "Well, that will certainly appeal to Blaze."

During the last week of school, I gave Dr. Roberts an understated but elegant pin that reminded me of her and a letter thanking her for all she'd done for me and Blaze. A couple of weeks later, I received a card from her in the mail.

It has been a real pleasure to know you and Blaze, she wrote. *I have appreciated the benefits of the positive approach your entire family takes, as each person helps Blaze to grow while making it clear that he is well-loved. You have done a great job of supporting him this year. He is in good hands as a member of your family.*

Coming from Dr. Roberts, I thought, these words of praise meant more than the sum of their parts. I only wished it hadn't taken quite so long for me to realize it.

[*Chapter 10*]

LOST AT SEA

$\mathcal{E}$very inch of progress Blaze had made in fourth grade was lost by
the end of the first month of fifth grade. It was astonishing how rapidly
everything fell apart. I had been so sure that placing Blaze in a regular
fifth-grade classroom was the right thing to do, but it turned out to be
one of the worst decisions I'd ever made where my son was concerned.

Blaze's success in fourth grade had convinced me that he'd be all
right in a regular class and this was reinforced by how well he'd done
in summer school. Mr. Davidson was the teacher for that summer-
school class, along with the aide that Dr. Roberts had hired, and Blaze
had accomplished quite a bit. As I reacquainted myself with "Ring
Around the Rosie" and the joys of pudding snacks with my preschoolers, Blaze produced a folder's worth of written work and learned some
basic math facts in his classroom two doors down.

Some time in July, Mr. Davidson took me aside and reiterated what
Dr. Roberts had told me a few months earlier.

"I think Blaze would do really well in my class in the fall," Mr.
Davidson told me. "Kids like him make my class successful."

"I don't know," I said. "I really think it's important for him to be
around the kids he's come up with through the grades."

Mr. Davidson gave me a look that said he didn't think this was nearly as important as I did, but what he said was, "I'm not trying to sell you on anything, you understand. Just something to think about."

"I will," I said and I did, but only briefly. Dr. Roberts had promised that Blaze would have an aide in the fall and I would be working at the school, able to keep an eye on Blaze, but still allow him the independence he needed. This was my plan and I thought it was a good one.

Unfortunately, there were a couple of key people missing from this plan. One was Grace or even a teacher *like* Grace. The other was Dr. Roberts.

Blaze's fifth-grade teacher was pleasant, but she was definitely not in line to be my buddy. Like most of her colleagues, she suffered from the big-class syndrome and was clearly under pressure to produce kids with high test scores and winning essays in strictly defined categories. Blaze didn't come close to fitting her model student. This pressure wasn't necessarily coming from her, but from the other parents.

Since having Blaze in the "mainstream" environment of fourth grade, I'd come to know some of these parents, although not in a social sense. I got to know the moms and dads as we stood outside class waiting for our kids to be released for the day. I heard their complaints about the homework (too much, too little, not academically challenging enough), the classes (What do they need to take art for? They should have more sports here), and the teachers (too distant, played favorites, didn't challenge the kids, didn't produce high grades, and so on). But one of the biggest complaints I heard was that the "lower" kids were mixed in with the "higher" kids and therefore dragged everyone down. *Lower* was a euphemism for *special* (which in itself was a euphemism) and *higher* was a politically correct way of saying *my kid.*

Special-education law springs from the Individual with Disabilities Education Act, enacted in the 1970s with endless addenda ever since. The law states (and any parent with a child receiving any special services whatsoever will have seen this at least once) that every child has the right to a "free and appropriate" public education in "the least restrictive environment possible." *Least restrictive* is interpreted in many different ways, but most commonly means that the child should be "included" in regular classes as much as possible with as few adults shadowing him as possible. Just like everybody else, in other words. The theory behind this is actually a very good one. It assumes that a special-needs child will learn practical social and academic skills from her "normal" peers while the normal kids will learn compassion, tolerance, outside-the-box thinking, and other qualities not normally fostered in a regular classroom. In some early-education programs (the one I worked in was one example), there was even "reverse mainstreaming," where kids from the regular-ed classes would spend time in special ed for those very reasons.

The concept of mainstreaming was anathema to most of the regular-ed parents I met. Not wanting to seem terribly politically incorrect, most of them wouldn't come right out and say, "I don't want *those* kids in class with mine," but the implication was there.

"It's ridiculous to hold the whole class up because one child is reading on a third-grade level . . ."

"They've got those special-ed kids in there now and you know what *that* means. . . ."

"I'm not saying they shouldn't be in school, you understand, but shouldn't they be in their *own* class?"

Without knowing that I was a parent of a special-ed kid, parents bitched and moaned to me all the time. If I felt compelled to tell them that my son was in special ed, I often got looks of dismay, embarrassment, even irritation, as if I shouldn't have been listening and by doing so, I had violated some sort of code.

All this is to say that in fourth grade and in the beginning of fifth, while Blaze was "passing" as a regular-ed kid and I as his "normal" parent, I finally understood the kind of pressure most of these teachers faced. No doubt it would have been different if I'd been living in an area with a lower average income and a different demographic. In that case, poverty and disadvantage would have created their own pressures. This was why my area was one that was regarded as highly desirable by most teachers, even though most of them couldn't afford to live where they worked and had long commutes. Ultimately, I think, many of these teachers were caught between administrative directives and parental pressures, leaving them very little time or inclination for special-needs kids.

Blaze's fifth-grade teacher certainly fit this profile. She seemed a nice enough woman and I believe that she tried to integrate Blaze into her class as much as possible, but she simply didn't have the tools or the time. This translated into an odd sense of helplessness that hovered in the air between us every time I spoke to her. Nor was there any of the camaraderie I'd had with Grace or even Mr. B.

Because Blaze's teacher couldn't provide the academic support he needed in her class, he spent almost the entire morning with Mary, the resource specialist. Mary's job was to provide one-on-one tutoring and extra study time for the aforementioned "lower" kids who were struggling with a regular academic load. Most kids came to see her for twenty- or thirty-minute blocks of time but Blaze spent hours there at a stretch.

Mary and Blaze had gotten along well enough the year before when I'd gone with him on his visits to her small office, but without me there (and because they spent much more time in a small space together than they should have), deep fissures began to appear in their relationship. Mary prided herself on her take-no-prisoners style of instruction ("You think *I* like reading?" she'd tell a recalcitrant sixth-grader. "Well, I don't, but it doesn't matter, I have to read, and so do you. So just do it already."), which was amusing for about five minutes, but then became very depressing.

I held open the possibility that Mary might once have been a talented educator, but by the time Blaze got to her, she seemed burned out and resentful. Blaze was intimidated by her and complained about her almost constantly. She was mean, he said, and she yelled at him. Don't exaggerate, I told him, just do your work for her. She made him write the same sentence over and over, he said, until it looked right. He resisted looking up a word in the dictionary so she made him sit for an hour until he produced the definition of *navigation*. She sent him outside, made him sit on the bench, wouldn't let him go to recess. And it wasn't just him, Blaze said, she was mean to everybody, especially Matt, who often worked alongside him in her office. Matt was frequently in tears, Blaze reported.

Don't make trouble, I said.

Sometimes Blaze would stop by my classroom on his way to Mary's office and gaze longingly at the preschoolers. He wanted so badly to just chuck it all and go back to the joys of circle time.

"Can't I stay here with you, Mom?" he'd ask.

"Blaze, you've got to go to Mary. Go on, now."

"I can't go there, Mom. She's evil."

"She is not! Don't say that."

"She is. She's an evil beast," he said, but off he would go, looking miserable and defiant at the same time.

Mary demanded that Blaze spend part of the morning writing in his journal. When I read his entries, I was disturbed by how sad they seemed.

9/14/98

Devin sometimes plays with me at recess. Sometimes we play ball with a soft ball. At class time I think about her.

9/17/98

I wish I could fly, but I can't. I can only fly on an airplane and go to San Francisco. I don't think it's fair that I can't fly. But I don't have wings.

9/18/98

When I was three years old, I had pajamas that looked like they had a hood and they had a zipper. They went all around my body. I had two pairs. One was light blue. Another was dark green. The zipper on my light blue pair broke and my aunt said, "What a bummer." I remember this story but my mom does not.

9/19/98

I am such an idiot. Just a cow. I belong at America's Dairy Farm.

9/21/98

One time I was at the beach. There was a high tide. It came in like crazy and splashed the road.

9/23/98

When Matt was upset, it felt like there was loud music in my head. When he cried, it felt like drums went off. I wonder if Mary felt that too. When we work quietly, it feels like Für Elise by Beethoven.

Blaze's afternoons weren't much better than his mornings. The aide Dr. Roberts had promised worked with Blaze for less than three hours at the end of the day and there wasn't much love lost between him and Blaze from the start. Blaze mostly acted out in the afternoons, tossing books around, stomping out of class, and refusing to do work of any kind. His new aide, a young man with a distracted air about him, had no clue how to reach Blaze and didn't make much of an attempt, besides. Slowly but steadily, Blaze began to spin out of control at school and I didn't know what to do to help him.

And of course, Dr. Roberts was now gone as well. The scope and complexity of Dr. Roberts's job finally became clear to me when I found that she'd been replaced by two people: a special-education administrator and a school psychologist. Dr. Roberts had been pulling double duty all those years and it became apparent to me why she'd finally called it quits.

Helen, the administrator, was all business and began her tenure by brandishing the motto, "Things are going to change around here." I found myself in the awkward position of being this woman's employee *and* a parent of one of her special-ed students. It was difficult to talk to her about Blaze. I didn't feel that she understood him or his school history. Helen was also a big believer in zoning and thought every attempt should be made to keep Blaze at his home school. This was a complete reversal of Dr. Roberts's feeling that Blaze should move to Mr. Davidson's class. But after only a few weeks of fifth grade, I knew that Blaze wasn't going to be able to stay where he was. By the end of September, he was spending his afternoons circling the classrooms with his shoes off, muttering, "I hate the evil beast. The evil beast must be destroyed."

Clearly, things were not working out.

I scheduled an IEP meeting with Helen, Mary (a.k.a. "the Evil Beast"), and Mr. Davidson to arrange for Blaze to spend the first half of his day in Mr. Davidson's class. While brief, this meeting was easily the most entertaining I'd yet attended, because it consisted mostly of Mary and Helen sniping at each other. Such a lack of decorum would never have occurred on Dr. Roberts's watch.

Mary complained that she didn't have the resources for a kid like Blaze. Helen warned her that resources weren't the issue here. Mary then said that Blaze's aide was "useless."

"Personnel issues will be dealt with outside of this room," Helen snapped. "This is neither the time nor place." I kept my eyes fixed somewhere between Helen and Mr. Davidson, afraid that if I looked at my father, who was in his usual position next to me, I would start laughing uncontrollably.

But Mary was only just beginning. She yanked out some of Blaze's "work samples," consisting mostly of angry-looking scrawls, and thrust them across the table. "There," she said. "That's all he's capable of."

Mr. Davidson, who had also quite obviously been enjoying the interplay between the two women, suddenly stopped smiling and picked up the papers with an expression of extreme distaste.

"This isn't right," he said in his rumbling baritone. "I worked with Blaze in summer school and I've seen him do much better than this. *Much* better. I don't even know what this is." He then gave Mary what I could only describe as a ferocious stare. There was an intense silence in the room for a few seconds and then Helen picked up her pen and said, "All right, let's wrap this up, shall we? I don't think anybody disagrees that Blaze should move to Mr. Davidson's class for the mornings."

There were immediate and simultaneous murmurs of assent from everybody in the room.

The director feels very strongly about Blaze remaining for the afternoons to maintain contact with the peers at [his home school], Helen wrote in her notes. I signed the form and passed it to my father. Dr. Roberts would never have referred to herself on an IEP form, I thought to myself and, for some unknown reason, this made me smile.

When we left the meeting, Mr. Davidson walked out with me and my father.

"I know we agreed to mornings," he said, "but I'd really like to have the kid for the whole day."

"You sure about that?" my father said.

"Yes," I said, in an attempt at levity, "you should be careful what you wish for; you might get it."

"I'm serious," Mr. Davidson said. "He's a good kid. I know he's capable of much more than he's doing. That work she showed us in there was ridiculous. You know that, right?"

"I do," I said. "It hasn't exactly been going well with Mary."

"I can tell," Mr. Davidson said.

"Let's see how it goes," I said, finally.

"Okay. You folks have a good evening," Mr. Davidson said and took his leave.

"What do you think?" I asked my father.

"I like him," my father said. "He's different, isn't he?"

"Bit of an iconoclast, I think," I said.

"That's good," my father said. "That's good for Blaze."

Before I had a chance to even think about transferring Blaze, however, there was another bit of torture to endure: Blaze's three-year review. The triennial review was basically a mega-IEP meeting that produced a blizzard of paperwork. Psychological tests were performed and evaluated, current levels of academic performance were assessed based on various educational tests and class work, and levels of social development were discussed. I had been through one of these marathons in second grade when Blaze was starting to have big trouble in Kimmi's class. I couldn't remember the specifics of that meeting. It had become a long blur of bad news in my memory.

I was determined to be better prepared for this meeting. The new school psychologist had an office next to the preschool classroom where I worked. At lunchtime and during any break I got during the day, I went over to talk to her and discuss Blaze. I knew that she was planning to give him a battery of tests, so I explained Blaze's history with tests, how, in my opinion, they'd never produced valid results and how anxious I was to make sure that we had an accurate reading. I was more forthright and objective with her about Blaze's school problems than I had been with anyone who was not an immediate family member. I told her about my concerns, my fears and my hopes for Blaze. I was so honest, I almost sickened myself with my own sincerity. I offered to help her administer the tests. Blaze, I told her, was highly resistant to any kind of testing situation.

The psych listened to me, said she appreciated my help, discussed various developmental disorders with me, and even gave me some research literature to read. We started having some spirited discussions about psychotropic medications for children. The psych was a big proponent of medication whenever possible, which didn't surprise me, but our disagreement on this issue was a friendly one. Our whole relationship was a friendly one, in fact. I was glad that I was now working within the system, learning the procedures and acronyms of special ed. I felt that this afforded me a distinct advantage.

Predictably, Blaze proved difficult to test. He was cooperative but distracted. He gave the psych the answers he thought she wanted, rather than trying to solve any problems himself. He refused to do anything that he perceived as difficult. I was disappointed, as usual, that Blaze refused to show his real abilities, but not particularly worried. I had an understanding with the psych and I felt she'd be able to tease out the real Blaze in her assessment.

The meeting to go over her evaluations started in the early afternoon and would last for over three hours. The school psychologist, with whom I had established such rapport, led the discussion by passing out copies of her nine-page report and explaining its contents. Every test she had administered, the psych explained, had shown Blaze to be performing in the mentally retarded range. Although Blaze's distractibility was a factor, she said, she felt that these results were fairly accurate. She didn't feel that Blaze met the criteria for autism, although she wrote in her report that *Ms. Ginsberg tended to see Blaze's behavior as more appropriate at home than has been observed at school.* Blaze's anxiety level at school was very high, the psych said, and had significant impact on his social and academic performance. Therefore, she felt that Blaze could also be considered severely emotionally disturbed.

"You think Blaze is *mentally retarded*?" I said when she finished speaking.

"Well, his test scores do indicate functioning within the mentally retarded range," the psych said.

My immediate impulse was to lean over the table and shove the nine-page report down her throat, but I just stared at her in horror. I felt completely blindsided. My face grew hot and my throat constricted. I looked over at my father, who was reading the report and shaking his head. I'd never seen my father look so sad and this affected me more than my own indignation. I felt a huge chasm of hurt open inside me. I couldn't stand to witness my father's pain so I turned away and my eyes met Mr. Davidson's. Mr. Davidson was not reading the report, but was watching me. I saw concern in his face and I saw real, unfettered empathy. This undid me more than anything else and my eyes filled with hot, angry tears. I couldn't respond to the psych, couldn't speak a single word because, once again, I was crying in an IEP meeting and struggling mightily not to let it show.

Mr. Davidson took over, presenting his own evaluations, which were decidedly more positive than those of the psychologist. Had I not been so completely unsettled by the psychologist's report, I would have been pleased that Mr. Davidson had noted Blaze's academic strengths and had accurately pinpointed the areas where he needed the most help. As it was, though, I was unable to muster much enthusiasm for the rest of the meeting.

It was dark outside by the time Helen began writing her summary. Once again, the psychologist's report raised its ugly head.

"Based on what we have here," Helen said, "we can consider changing Blaze's handicapping condition to either mentally retarded or severely emotionally disturbed."

"There's no way—" I began, but Helen cut me off.

"Now, hear me out," she said. "If you decide to go with mentally retarded, Blaze could qualify for services through the regional center."

"What kind of services?" my father asked.

"Respite care, and that kind of thing."

"You mean, like, baby-sitting?" my father said.

"In a sense, yes," Helen said. "They provide trained aides who relieve parents and provide support."

"We don't need that," my father spit out. "We've got plenty of qualified baby-sitters in our family."

"But that's not even the point," I broke in, finally finding my voice. "Blaze is *not* retarded. Why would I say that he is?"

"It's just a matter of qualification," Helen said.

"No, it isn't," I said. "I would never give Blaze a false label just to get services that I don't even need. What happens when he reads these reports down the line and finds out that his mother thought he was retarded? And he *isn't* retarded." I shot a searing look at the psychologist. "And he is *not* disturbed in any way."

"Fine," Helen said, irritated, "we'll keep the handicapping condition as speech and language impaired. Transition to Mr. Davidson's class full time after the holidays? Does that work for everybody?"

Nothing was working for me at that point, but I agreed, signed the forms, and walked out with my father. I felt like I'd aged twenty years.

"What do you think?" I asked my father. This was the obligatory question after every IEP meeting. My father was usually steady and could be counted on to give me an objective summary of the meeting to counterbalance my own roiling emotions. But this time he was fresh out of optimism.

"The shrink thinks he's retarded," my father said. "What else is there to say?"

"But Mr. Davidson—"

"Yes," my father said. "He's Blaze's best bet. You're not going to get anywhere with those women. Nowhere."

February 1999

They call this boat a "floating marine lab." On board, there is what seems to be an inordinate amount of rope, several buckets filled with various sea creatures, and a tiny galley, which I look to lovingly every time I pass it on our endless loops around the boat. Inside is warmth and possibly a cup of coffee. At this point, I could easily be convinced to trade some of my teeth for a cup of hot coffee, even bad coffee.

I can't imagine—no, don't want to imagine—what's below deck. It wouldn't matter anyway; the upper deck is all that concerns me. I glance ruefully at the rows of life vests around us. I can visualize strapping one on and diving into the bay. I'm not at all sure that I'd be less comfortable than I am now. This is the first time I've been on a boat since I was a kid and too young to remember now (the SS *France,* the ship my family sailed from London to New York in 1972 on one of our many moves across continents, doesn't count, because that was the size of the *Titanic*). And now here I am on a swaying vessel (the fishing boat from *Jaws* comes to mind) in the middle of the San Diego Bay, on what must surely be the coldest day in the history of this fair city. I am in no way dressed appropriately and as a result I've more or less lost feeling in my freezing hands, but my sad state of attire is only one of the ways in which I am inadequately prepared for this adventure.

It strikes me that I've taken quite a chance coming out here today. What if I got seasick? How embarrassing would it be to have to puke over the side rail? I don't see any kind of bathroom, although surely there must be one somewhere. Surprisingly, the pitching and rolling doesn't bother me, just the cold. This is because of Blaze, I am convinced. I have no time to be concerned about my own discomforts because I am too busy worrying about him. He's having a meltdown and this is a state of emergency.

To be even more specific: this boat effort is actually a field trip and I am a tagalong parent helper with Blaze and his class. Actually, there are two classes here—a "regular" fifth-grade class and Blaze's class of special-ed fifth-graders, helmed by the highly capable Mr. Davidson. Blaze has now been in his class full-time for two months. This is the first time I've had a chance to watch my son in his new classroom environment, although I am aware that a field trip on a pitching boat hardly counts as an average situation.

I haven't paid much attention to the other class here. For all I'm concerned, they might not even be here at all. I can focus only my own son, who is redefining bad behavior, even by special-ed standards. In fact, the other special-ed kids are remarkably quiet and well behaved, making Blaze's antics stand out even more.

Blaze won't sit quietly on the deck when instructed. He won't even stand where he's supposed to. He insists on drifting around to the side of the boat, perilously close to the railing. He's not even making an attempt at pretending that he's listening to the captain (or skipper, or whatever she's called) describe marine life and the wonders of the ocean. He's whining that he wants to buy chips and soda in the galley. He's hungry. I couldn't get him to eat his lunch in the classroom before we left and now his blood sugar is low and he's flipping out. He'd been looking forward to this trip, but he's been out of synch all day.

First it was, "When are we leaving? Why aren't the buses here yet?"

Then it was, "Why can't we get on the bus yet?"

Once we were on the bus it was, "When are we going to get there?"

"Why can't we get on the boat yet?"

"When are we going to get a soda?"

He's been stuck on the last one like the proverbial broken record. Of course, as soon as we are allowed into the galley, if that blessed moment should ever come, he will attach immediately to the next thing, whatever that is. But Blaze is not just whining, he's whining *loudly*. He's running off. Before we even boarded, I had a moment on the dock when I thought we were going to have to turn around altogether and go home. There were a couple of large dogs roaming around and Blaze did an enhanced version of his usual dog freak-out by running willy-nilly down the dock, screaming wildly. None of my threats or enticements could reel him back in. It was Mr. Davidson, speaking in measured but rumbling bass tones, who finally got through to him. This brought a simultaneous sense of relief and inadequacy. Can't even control my own child, I thought.

Things only got worse once we were on board. It's taken both me *and* Mr. Davidson (a former marine, I might add) to hold Blaze to one spot on this rocking boat. When my son is finally silent for a few torturously short minutes, I am conscious only of the bitter wind and cold.

"Not really one of the nicest days to come out here, weather-wise," Mr. Davidson says, reading my thoughts.

"It's not too bad," I say, smiling, trying to be the perky parent helper I'm pretending to be as opposed to the wretched mother I am. "A little chilly, maybe."

Mr. Davidson laughs. I'm not fooling him, even slightly. "They'll let us in to the snack bar pretty soon," he says.

"Well, there's always that to look forward to," I answer stiffly. I have a feeling that my lips are blue, but I can't be sure.

"You know, he's going to be okay," Mr. Davidson says, nodding his head toward Blaze, who looks like he's getting ready to start up the chorus of "when are we going to get a soda?" any second now.

"I'm not so sure," I say. "I've never seen him quite this bad before. I don't know if it's because I'm here. But what if I wasn't? He might have been even worse."

Mr. Davidson ponders this for a moment. "I am a little surprised," he says slowly. "I thought he was looking forward to this trip."

"He *was*," I say. "Only it took so long. The anticipation . . . Now he's in a spin and it's hard for him to get out of it."

"We usually leave earlier, but there was another class ahead of us today," Mr. Davidson says. "It makes for a real long day. I'm sorry about that."

"Not your fault."

Blaze is up again and is leaning over the railing, a cardinal sin on this boat.

"Excuse me, young man," calls the captain. "You need to be sitting down here please. Young man?"

"I'll get him," Mr. Davidson says. "Keep an eye on the other kiddies, will you?"

Nobody else needs monitoring, as it turns out. They're all sitting there, docile as cold little lambs. I watch Mr. Davidson grasp Blaze's arm gently but firmly and steer him back to the fold while speaking into his ear, and turn my head back out to face the gray, choppy water. I sense that this is going to be one of those days without end.

At last, the snack bar break comes. I get my coffee and Blaze eats a bag of chips and drinks a soda. These items are barely past his gullet when he queries, "When are we going home?"

"Listen," I say sotto voce, through gritted teeth, "I don't want to hear one more demand out of you, do you hear me? You've already shown me your worst behavior today as it is. You wanted to come on this damn boat and you've done nothing but complain all day. I've seen better behavior from two-year-olds. You are embarrassing me and you are embarrassing yourself. This is a nightmare!"

"I want to go home," Blaze says. "I've had enough."

"We'll go home when it's time to go home."

"I want to go home now."

I hiss at him and grab his arm in a grip much less gentle than Mr. Davidson's. "Quiet!"

"I won't be silent."

"Just wait until I tell Papa about this." I don't like to bring my father in as the bad guy, but this is an emergency situation. It works too. For a few moments, Blaze stops complaining. He refuses, however, to participate in the planned activities aboard the boat.

If I were less miserable, I think I would admire this field trip. The kids form groups and rotate along a series of stations on deck, learning a variety of ocean facts, from how to tell a sea star from a starfish to examining the water for algae. I follow along helplessly, stopping periodically to pull Blaze aside and tell him to cooperate. Mr. Davidson watches my machinations with bemused interest and remains entirely unruffled.

"I don't know how you do this every year," I tell Mr. Davidson.

"Just lucky, I guess," Mr. Davidson answers. "I've got the sixth-graders too, so I get to go on this boat trip *and* go away to sixth-grade camp every year." He follows this statement with a chuckle.

"I don't . . ." I trail off for a moment, unsure how to finish my sentence. "I don't think Blaze will be able to go to sixth-grade camp," I say, finally. "I know it's not until next year, but if this is any indication . . . I just can't see him going away by himself for a whole week."

Mr. Davidson eyes me carefully. I don't know him very well, but I can already tell that he's not a man who admits defeat easily. If he were, he couldn't possibly have spent twenty years teaching special education. He looks at me now a little sadly and says, "Maybe not. It doesn't seem like something he'd enjoy. It's pointless to force camp on a kid who isn't ready. But we'll see."

It's after five P.M. when we arrive back at the dock. My gratitude at being on terra firma once more is matched only by a sense of penetrating exhaustion. Blaze seems to have gotten some sort of bizarre second wind and he sits opposite me on the bus that will take us back to school, chattering and annoying his seatmate, a small boy who just wants to pass out peacefully where he sits. I'm too pissed off at Blaze's shocking behavior today even to talk to him.

It's dark when we arrive back at the school. My father is waiting in the parking lot to give us a ride home.

"Well, how was it?" my father asks as we climb into the car.

"Aside from the hypothermia?" I ask and shake my head. I spout my litany of complaints about Blaze's behavior. How he was out of control. How he wouldn't listen to me. How embarrassed I felt for both of us. How he didn't deserve to go on any more field trips. My father's face grows stormy and he turns around to look at Blaze.

"How could you do that to your mother?" he asks. Blaze says nothing.

Once we are home, I tell Blaze, "I want you to take a shower, get into your pajamas, and go to bed. I'm finished talking to you today."

"I'm sorry about my behavior, Mom," Blaze says.

"Why be sorry now?" I say. "What's the good of that?" I choose my words carefully, consciously trying to elicit true remorse from my son. He has to understand the consequences of his actions. I don't want him to be sorry because my disappointment in him makes him feel uncomfortable. I want him to be sorry because he doesn't want *me*, or anyone else, to feel sad, disappointed, or pained.

I collapse into the darkness of my own bed shortly after Blaze, but despite my fatigue, I can't sleep. The day spins itself around and around in my head. I keep seeing Blaze run away, out of control, listening to nobody. My thoughts are black. Is this the way it's going to be forever? Blaze is growing. In height, he has almost caught up with me. He is no longer a small boy to be lifted up and away from trouble by his mother. What will happen if he continues on in this way? I can barely control him physically now. I have more faith in Mr. Davidson than I've had in any of Blaze's teachers, but I wonder now if that will be enough. And if it isn't? Where do we go from here?

Chapter 11

MAGIC AND APPROPRIATE LAUGHTER

June 1999

There are two days left until the end of the school year. In my classroom, as well as in all the others, the kids seem to sense the anticipation of the exhausted adults around them. We're all tired for good reason. This has been a tough year in the preschool. One of our kids stopped showing up in February, her emotionally unstable mother claiming that "she's sick." Another child barely made it through surgery in March and spent several weeks on life support. Still another was in a major car accident that severely injured her sister. The school nurse asked the child's father for a medical release, but he hasn't produced one. She hasn't been back to school since then. Our teacher went to their house, but the doors were all locked, shades drawn, and weeks' worth of mail was crammed in the mailbox.

The "light toileting" Dr. Roberts had so euphemistically described when she offered me this job turned out to be a vast understatement. There have been between eight and ten children in our classroom this year and, at any given time, only one or two are able to use the bathroom by themselves. Some children arrive every morning with a full diaper. "He did it on the way over here," the mothers always say. "So sorry."

Our children often come to school sick. "He was fine this morning," the mothers say when we point out fevers, coughing, streaming noses. As a result, our classroom has become a veritable petri dish of infectious diseases. We had an outbreak of strep throat in April, which sent three adults in the classroom (myself included) to urgent-care facilities. We've battled pinkeye, bronchitis, and pneumonia. I've already had all three this spring.

Of course, there have been high notes as well. Most of the kids have made good progress. Little things, like successfully potty training a child who, mere months ago, shrieked in terror at the very thought of the bathroom, send us into a state of euphoria. I started a rudimentary, but very successful, yoga program with the kids a few months ago. The sight of eight severely handicapped preschoolers in perfect "downward dog" position, alone, was worth the price of admission. Still, I understand now, like never before, why teachers start looking so very happy come June. In the staff lounge, there is a calendar with a running countdown of the days left (complete with a red X through the days we've survived). It's as if we're all soon to be paroled.

Today, one of our parents has scheduled a magician to come by the class and perform his act. We speculate: Will it freak the kids out—rabbits jumping out of hats and the like? Loud noises? Crowds? These are all things that are way out of the comfort zone for our kids and we are nervous. What's more, we've invited the two other special-ed classes to join us, so the room will be full of special-needs kids from the ages of three to eight years old.

At the appointed time, we gather on the floor: kids, teachers, and aides. I've got one child on my lap and one directly in front of me within arm's reach. The little one in front of me is a sweet towhead from another class named Jill who I've worked with a few times over the course of the year.

"Hi, Miss Debra," she says through the space her front teeth have recently vacated. She grabs one of my hands and holds on to it tightly while I pat her softly on the back with the other. I have learned the power of touch this year. We are always in physical contact with our kids. We stroke their heads and their backs. We clean their faces and brush their cheeks with our fingers. We hold them on our laps, our arms creating a ring of safety around their bodies. We hug them tightly when they are sad. We squeeze their hands and dance with them. Touch is our primary form of communication in this classroom, a wordless language that everybody understands. When I look around now, I can see this language spoken clearly.

The magician, who looks somewhat daunted by the task ahead of him (I can hear him asking himself, *What was I thinking?*), introduces himself and performs a little physical comedy with a chair. He fakes falling down a few times and the kids, including our little ones, laugh uproariously. He asks for volunteers. These kids, who often won't even acknowledge the presence of other humans, willingly and eagerly jump up to "help" him.

The magician does the old ring trick first, sliding large metal rings in and out of each other.

All the adults say, "How does he *do* that?" but the kids look back at us like we're all crazy. Of course the rings disconnect, their glances seem to say. Why wouldn't they?

The magician chooses Sam, a six-year-old diagnosed with autism, to hold a set of rings and tells him to try to pull them apart. Of course, Sam can't do it and his face reddens with the strain of trying. Then the magician effortlessly separates his own rings. Sam doesn't waste any time pondering how the magician is able to do this, promptly handing over his own rings with an expression that clearly says, *Fix these.* Sam doesn't seem mystified, merely relieved, when the magician pulls the rings apart.

The other tricks follow suit. None of the children are surprised or amazed when the magician pulls brightly colored paper out of a little girl's shoe or lifts a pair of red silk shorts from a previously empty bag, or wads up tissue in his hand and throws it back out as thin white streamers that cover the whole audience. As I watch their faces, I realize that none of these things are out of the natural order for these kids. This is not to say that they don't like the magician—they love him and they love his brightly colored objects, his collapsible wand. They laugh, they applaud. They pay *full* attention. The real magic, it occurs to me, is in their understanding that there *exists* real magic. If not magic per se, then certainly belief of some kind. And pure belief or faith seems to defy the presence of rationality. Can one really explain why one believes? And isn't there real magic in pure faith? This is what I see in the faces of the children and what makes me unsure, for a moment, if I have any right to be instructing *them*. They are so clearly providing lessons for me.

It is this magic, I know now, which often sustains Blaze. His ongoing fascination and belief in the tooth fairy is just one example. Blaze has always been tickled by the whole concept and has written her long notes explaining what has happened to his teeth, where they fell out, and so on. Once he stopped losing his teeth, he wrote her a note pleading with her to leave something anyway, explaining that he couldn't do anything about the timing of this frustrating tooth business. He quizzed me repeatedly about the particulars of the tooth fairy. How did she get around? What did she do with all the teeth? How big was she? What did she look like? When these discussions started getting really involved, I tried to subtly imply that the tooth fairy might not actually exist. Blaze's reaction was equally subtle.

"I know that, Mom," he said. "But she *does* come."

I could just as easily *give* him a few quarters or a packet of M&M's (the usual tooth fairy treats), but he doesn't want that—he wants the magic of a tooth vanishing in the middle of the night, replaced by sweet rewards.

I don't blame him for believing. I too believed in the tooth fairy even after she "forgot" to take a tooth of mine one night and, after I complained bitterly the next day, left me a note (in my mother's handwriting, oddly enough) about how busy she'd been. Still, I held fast to my illusions. I lost more teeth and they were traded for strange, magical gifts in deepest night. A silver tiepin with a diamond stud, a plastic ring, a miniature book.

When Blaze started losing his teeth, I was less creative about what I put under his pillow—mostly candy he liked and quarters he could use to play video games. I felt strangely guilty about removing the envelopes in which he'd carefully placed his teeth and his name ("So she knows who it's from," he said) and replacing them with treats, as if I were doing somebody else's job.

I've kept almost all of Blaze's teeth and all of the notes he's written to the tooth fairy. I felt strange about this too. What if he found them? Would it rattle his faith? No, I think now as I watch the magician pull some other improbable item out of his bag. He would assume, I am sure, that the tooth fairy herself gave them to me for safekeeping.

I turn my attention back to the magician who, although sweating profusely, seems surprised and pleased at the warm reception he is getting and the high level of attention being fixed on him.

There are a few exceptions. Four-year-old Anna has an enormous fear of crowds and public events so she spends the entire session screaming at the top of her surprisingly capable lungs. A few of the kids turn to look at her with knowing looks on their faces. Each one of these children is intimately aware of the fact that, in some way, each is a square peg. When they look at Anna, they understand that whatever is behind her screaming defines her particular square shape. They don't let it distract them in the least.

There is also Jonah, who doesn't venture outside the confines of his own head very often and must have an aide assigned to him at all times. Jonah flails out and hits me first and then Sam, broadside, across his back.

"No, Jonah," his aide says, in a tone that implies this is by no means the first time he's spoken these words, "No hitting." I change my seat, but Sam just flinches a little and doesn't even turn around.

Anna's sobbing increases in volume and her body starts to go rigid, so the preschool teacher lifts her up and pats her back soothingly until Anna quiets ever so slightly. Jill's teacher, who is sitting next to me, sees this interchange and shakes her head. She clearly has other ideas as to how the Anna situation could be handled.

"See, if that were me," she whispers, "I'd just ignore that behavior and remove her from the group." She studies my expression and reads my reaction to this. "But I guess there's a long history with her, isn't there? You've probably tried a few things already, haven't you?"

"Definitely," I answer. "A few months ago, we couldn't even have kept her in the same room. This is actually an improvement."

"Right," says Jill's teacher. "You just can't tell."

A little later, when Jill laughs with unbridled glee, I turn back to her teacher and say, "I just love her, she's so sweet."

"You see, there it is," the teacher responds. "She *is* a darling, but she has a problem with appropriate laughter. We're working with her on that."

Appropriate laughter. This phrase suddenly depresses me. I am struck again by how difficult it is to navigate a world where we have to be mindful of when laughter is appropriate. The mechanism that allows these kids to accept the magician's tricks as natural and Blaze to continue believing in the tooth fairy is the same one that signals their need to be taught how to laugh appropriately. I sigh out loud. I wonder, as I have so many times before, how Blaze and all these children are going to survive with their own magic intact after going through the minefield of what is, today, normal and appropriate. The standards are always changing, it seems, and around here normal has become an arbitrary concept. Most days, the world seems completely mad to me anyway. Where is the line between normal and abnormal? Who is qualified to draw it?

The magician is a huge hit, much to his own delight. As he packs up, promising to come again, he is besieged by applause and thanks. After he and the other classes leave our classroom, we gather in a circle to have story time before our kids go home.

Just before they leave, the teacher takes a poll. "What was your favorite part of the magic show?" she asks and goes around the circle. Every child has a distinct, relatable memory. What makes this so astonishing is that these kids sometimes can't remember their own names and often have trouble answering yes or no questions, let alone those that ask why or what.

"The shoe," says one child.

"The red shorts," says another.

"The rings," says a third.

From her spot on the carpet, Anna, her face and eyes red and puffy from crying, says, "Paper in the sky."

This too is magic. And for a moment, it reinforces my own faith in magic, in these children, and my faith in Blaze. And, just now, a moment is all I need.

[Chapter 12]

APPROACHING THE TOWER

$\mathscr{I}$ take the pill early in the morning and begin to feel the effects almost immediately. First comes a sort of electrical buzzing that starts in my chest, works its way into my jaw, and settles at the base of my neck. My breath starts to come quicker and shorter. My fingers tingle a little. My heart starts doing some annoying little flips as if it misses a beat and goes back to make up for the loss with a double. I cough. The buzzing sensation moves into my head and my eyes start to feel tight. After an hour, a ragged headache claims a band around my head where it will remain for a long time. There is no real "rush" that I can distinguish, but about twenty minutes after I take the drug, I am talking faster and getting organized. Sure, I think, I can write on this stuff. I could also probably be talked into cleaning the bathtub with a toothbrush or organizing thirty years of loose photographs. I could write a term paper. The term paper seems a particularly appropriate task because the feeling I am experiencing reminds me very much of my college days where I and dozens of other hapless students would drink thick, black coffee until our bladders threatened to burst and when that no longer did the trick, scrounge around for stimulants the chemistry majors had been cooking up that week. We took whatever would keep us awake. Once I even saw a hardy soul snorting lines of espresso in the library.

My chest feels constricted and my head is alive with noise. I'm not enjoying myself. Those college days are long gone, to be sure. Inexplicably, I decide to make myself some coffee. I drink two cups and go over the edge. My heart starts to pound, I begin to sweat, and my eyes feel stabbed with pain. I am now useless, irritable, and uncomfortable.

When the drug wears off a few hours later, I feel sapped, disoriented, and tired. Much later, when according to all the literature the drug should have metabolized and passed out of my system, I lie awake in bed staring at the unforgiving blackness of the ceiling.

I am not the only one in my house who can't sleep. In the bent hours after midnight, the shape of my twelve-year-old son hovers next to my bed, outlined dimly in dark.

"I had another nightmare, Mom," he says. His voice is tremulous and still soaked with sleep.

"What was it?" I ask him.

"I dreamed I was a cartoon character. There were black lines drawn around me. I couldn't move off the paper."

"It's only a dream, honey," I tell him and take his hand. "See? You're not a cartoon. I couldn't hold your hand if you were a cartoon."

He doesn't seem particularly comforted. He wants to know if I'll walk him back to bed. Back in his bedroom, he puts on his headset and listens to music. He wants his door closed so that nothing can get in. Or out. I kiss him and assure him that he remains three-dimensional, but he's drifting away, still troubled.

Now in my own sleepless bed again, the tears start. I know how Blaze feels and I know why he can't sleep and why he's having nightmares. After all, today we have both been on the same drug. It's not speed, cocaine, or anything cooked up by college chemistry majors.

It's Ritalin.

After years of resisting the attempts of doctors, teachers, and special-education administrators to convince me to give my child some kind (any kind!) of psychotropic medication, I have arrived here, like so many others before me, at the house of Ritalin. And I didn't start Blaze on this course of drugs because I finally yielded to the pressure of all those professionals—in fact, they've backed off from the whole medication issue lately. No, I made this decision all by myself.

I toss around in my bed, imprisoning myself in the twisted sheets. It's ironic, I think, as I sit up and stare at the clock for the tenth time. I held off for so long and now I'm giving Blaze Ritalin, not because he's been failing at school or because his behavior has gotten worse, but because he's been doing so *well*. So what's wrong with this picture?

It took Blaze a couple of months to really settle into Mr. Davidson's class, but after he did, the transformation was quite impressive. Suddenly, out of nowhere and with no particular reason, my son knew his multiplication tables. I had tried every kind of strategy to get him to learn and memorize these before to no avail. Grace, the math wiz, had tried even harder, but Blaze seemed stuck where he was, mathematically. Then, after only a few weeks in Mr. Davidson's class, he knew all his math facts. What's more, they were lodged in his brain forever. I couldn't stump him.

Blaze was also reading, really reading, in class and answering comprehension questions about the material he'd read. Mr. Davidson's class split into groups and read from novels every day. Rather than choosing a few long novels, Mr. Davidson opted to teach many, shorter books. Blaze (and I assumed the other students as well) didn't have time to grow bored with any one particular novel and was exposed to many different styles and stories.

Blaze brought homework from school and we worked on it together. Every week, he carried home a packet of all his work from the week before, so I could see exactly what he'd been doing and the progress he'd been making. By the end of fifth grade, Blaze had jumped the academic equivalent of two grade levels.

But there were other, more important, signs of progress besides the academic gains. Blaze was starting to feel a measure of security at school—a sort of emotional safety—that had been lacking for so long. In Mr. Davidson's class, the boundaries of acceptable behavior were always very clearly drawn. There were rules to be followed and standards to be adhered to. Blaze pushed and strained at these boundaries in a mighty effort to see how far he could go before someone would reach out and pull him back.

I observed this struggle from a distance. Blaze took a bus to school in the morning and I didn't see him again until he returned home. Mr. Davidson communicated through notes and phone calls. Occasionally, we met for parent-teacher conferences. It was a far cry from my previous immersion in Blaze's school day, but I never felt out of the loop.

"He's been throwing his assignments away on his way out to recess," Mr. Davidson told me. "We've been retrieving them from the trash. He's discovering that just because he's made them disappear, doesn't mean they won't be coming back. It's only a temporary reprieve."

Blaze also found that his old response to fire drills and trucks didn't elicit the same response as it had before.

"He's only allowed to get out of his seat once," Mr. Davidson said. "After that, he starts losing privileges, like playing games during free time."

At home, Blaze would complain, "I hate Mr. Davidson, he's too strict. He's mean."

"You mean he won't let you throw your homework away?" I said. "What a terrible man."

"Yes, that's right," Blaze said indignantly and then stopped himself short. "Mom, are you being sarcastic?"

"Yes, Blaze. Yes, I am."

There was more.

"Your son came up to me today and told me I was drunk," Mr. Davidson said.

"What?" I was horrified.

"That's right, walked right up to me, pointed in my face and said, 'You're drunk!'"

"Why did he say *that*?" I asked.

"I don't know," Mr. Davidson said, and laughed heartily, "because, you know, I hardly ever drink in front of the kids anymore."

"Oh, ah, ha, ha . . ."

And Blaze kept pushing on.

"He told me he wanted to punch me in the nose," Mr. Davidson said.

"That's really unacceptable," I said. "I don't know why he would say such a thing. He's never done that before."

"He's staking out his territory," Mr. Davidson said. "He's trying to figure out what it means to be a young man. This is how he's trying to determine his role. This isn't a bad thing."

"You're not worried about this?" I asked.

"Oh no. He's coming out of himself, giving himself a context. He'll figure it out. He's a bright kid."

Before this, Blaze had found no brick wall to butt up against. He had alarmed, cajoled, or simply worn down his teachers. In Mr. Davidson, Blaze had finally met his match, a person more obdurate than himself. Someone who would never give up.

Because it wasn't in Blaze's nature to concede willingly, he continued to grumble about the tyranny and injustice in Mr. Davidson's class. He took advantage of every opportunity he got to avoid working and never ceased trying to use his considerable powers of manipulation to get what he wanted. Under all of this, though, he was happier and more content than I'd ever seen him at school. I understood the full measure of this when I read his dream journal. I'd encouraged

Blaze to start writing his dreams down because he'd been talking about them to everyone who'd listen. While they were vivid and fanciful, I told Blaze, it would be better to keep them on paper. Some time in the spring of fifth grade, while he was still carping regularly about what a difficult teacher Mr. Davidson was, Blaze wrote:

> *I dreamed that one time when I went to school, I saw a tower and it was scary. And then Mr. Davidson came out of his room and carried me past the tower. And then the sun came out.*

The tower came up again in Blaze's dreams a couple of times after that. Each time, Mr. Davidson was there teaching him how not to be afraid.

Spring turned into summer and, once again, I worked the summer session with the preschoolers. Blaze was next door in his own special-ed class and Mr. Davidson's class was one door beyond that. In my experience, the summer-school session for special-ed students served mostly to give the special-ed parents five additional weeks of a break from their kids. That is to say, not much actual learning went on. Mostly, there were games involving water and lots of "crafts," such as constructing picture frames with cardboard and lima beans. The regular-ed kids got much more actual remediation in their classes. Since Blaze wasn't getting much academic time in his own class, I asked Mr. Davidson to start including Blaze in some of his lessons. In this way, I saw firsthand how effectively Mr. Davidson worked with all the children in his class. There was no doubt in my mind that I'd found the right placement for Blaze this time. I even began to allow for the possibility that Blaze might be able to go away to sixth-grade camp in the fall.

"What do you think about camp?" I asked Mr. Davidson one July afternoon.

"What about it?"

"Blaze. Do you think he'll be able to go?"

"I don't see why not."

"But the boat trip?"

"Ancient history," Mr. Davidson said. "It's a new day."

"But it's five days, isn't it? Away from home?"

"Yes it is." Mr. Davidson was smiling.

"And I can't go with him, can I?"

"No, ma'am, you cannot. No parents allowed. Kind of defeats the purpose."

"But, I don't know. . . . It's a long time. I don't . . . What if . . ."

"I'll be with him," Mr. Davidson said. "I'll be with him the whole time."

Blaze started sixth grade in the fall of 1999. I went back to work at school as well, but in a slightly different capacity. I had developed a real affection for the preschoolers and, in working with them, I had learned quite a bit about basic behavior modification and the efficacy of different teaching strategies. When the kids did well, started to talk, learned how to use the bathroom, blow bubbles, hold a pencil, or sing a song, I was as joyful as any parent. I *liked* being with the preschoolers. This was one thing Dr. Roberts had predicted quite accurately.

Despite all of this, though, the physical demands of the job were too much for me. As a veteran waitress, I'd spent years on my feet, hauling trays of food and drink and sprinting through busy dining rooms, yet none of that had adequately prepared me for the kind of lifting and carrying I had to do in the preschool. There was a big difference between a loaded tray of dishes, however heavy, and a rigid, sixty-pound child who didn't want to be lifted onto a changing table. I quickly developed a bad back. Worse than that was the almost constant assault of bacteria and viruses that we were all subject to every day. I was sure my body couldn't handle another year of flu, strep throat and bronchitis. I'd been sick more often in the preschool than I'd been in my whole life and I didn't want to risk doing permanent damage to my health.

I transferred to the resource specialist program, which had been helmed by Blaze's nemesis, Mary. It had expanded to include another credentialed special-ed teacher and dozens of children, spanning kindergarten through sixth grade. The range of abilities and disabilities in this group was staggering. On any given morning, I'd be working with second-graders reading on a kindergarten level, first-graders reading on a fourth-grade level, and third-graders who couldn't read at all. Unlike the preschoolers, these kids could talk and were quite skilled at using conversation to keep the adults around them off-task. Tony, an eight-year-old with an uncanny resemblance to Opie, was especially good at keeping the conversational ball rolling.

"Hey, Ms. Ginsberg, how old are you?"

"Tony, didn't your mom ever tell you not to ask a lady how old she is?"

"My mom's, like, *forty*. You're not that old, are you?"

"I'm pretty old."

"Are you, like, *thirty*? That's pretty old."

"Close enough."

"Are you married?"

"No, I'm not married."

"You got a boyfriend?"

"Tony, we don't talk about these kinds of things at school."

"Yeah, okay. But how old are you, really?"

Every one of these kids was fully included in a regular-education class, so each day I spent a portion of my time "shadowing" one or more of the students in their classes. In this way, I was exposed to the classrooms and students of every grade level.

A few weeks into the school year, I was forced to meet my fears about sending Blaze to camp head-on. It would have been easy to say no had Blaze been unwilling to go, but the opposite was true. Blaze couldn't wait to go away and talked about it almost every day.

"You'll be sleeping away from home for four nights," I told him.

"That's okay," he said.

"I won't be there. You can't call me or come home until it's over."

"That's okay, Mom."

"You have to eat what the other kids eat and do what the other kids do."

"Of course I will."

I was thrilled that Blaze was showing such independence and, more than anything, wanted his camp experience to be a good one, but I drove myself almost insane worrying about what might happen.

"You've got to let him go," my father said. "You've got to let him grow up. Don't be so overprotective."

"I *am* letting him go," I said. "But five days is a long time for a kid like Blaze."

"No, five days is a long time for *you*," my father said.

Blaze received a journal in which he would write down his camp experiences while he was away. In the front part of the journal, there were several questions that he had to answer before he left. The journal asked what he expected camp to be like. Blaze wrote: *I expect camp to be fun. I expect the classes not to have a lot of work. I expect the food to be cooked properly and the cabins to have a lot of beds.*

The journal asked if there were any special concerns he had about camp. Blaze wrote: *I am worried that some kids I don't know might laugh at me if I make a mistake at something.*

This particular bit of self-awareness convinced me more than anything that Blaze was ready to go.

In the week before camp, I conferred with Mr. Davidson almost every day, making a complete pest of myself. With the patience born of twenty years of experience with frantic mothers, Mr. Davidson explained every detail, discussed every possibility, and offered every reassurance.

"If anything bad happens," Mr. Davidson said, "and the kid really can't stay there, I will personally bring him home. But I really think it's going to be okay."

"I appreciate all that you're doing," I told Mr. Davidson. "It's above and beyond the call of duty."

"He's worth the investment," Mr. Davidson said.

"And you'll call me, right? Let me know how he's doing?"

"I will call you. It's a promise."

Blaze left for camp, along with all the other sixth-graders in his school, early on a Monday morning. I couldn't remember him ever being as excited as he was that day, tossing his bedroll and backpack onto the giant pile in front of the school bus and hopping aboard with glee. He didn't hover around me or linger for a second. After he offered me a perfunctory "bye, Mom," he didn't even give me so much as a backward glance.

Once Blaze was gone, it didn't take me very long to realize that I had completely forgotten what it was like to have ever been without him. All of a sudden, there were vast chunks of the day that were simply empty. I was completely unable to distract myself. Many of the mothers I worked with had assured me that I would relish my time alone and probably become addicted to it in short order. I was absolutely free to go anywhere, do anything and be home at no particular time. But I did nothing and went nowhere. I felt woolly and limbless. Without Blaze, all my internal structures were missing. I did manage to come down with a raging flu, which conveniently eliminated the necessity to think about anything, especially how totally vacuous my daily life seemed without Blaze in it.

On Tuesday evening, as I lay in an antihistamine haze, imagining fires, floods, and other possible camp disasters, I got a call from Mr. Davidson.

"You sound terrible," he said. "What happened to you?"

"Got a pretty bad cold," I said. "Probably psychosomatic."

"Well, I'm calling to tell you that your boy is doing fine. He missed you a little this morning, but he's having a great time. No problems."

"Really? Is he eating?"

"Oh, sure. Tater tots, pancakes . . . I was at dinner with him tonight. He had a cheese enchilada."

"My son ate a cheese enchilada?"

"Yes, ma'am, although not very gracefully, I'll admit."

"And he's okay, really?"

"He's fine. He's singing camp songs, going on hikes. He's one of the guys."

"Thank you," was all I could think of to say.

"You can stop worrying," Mr. Davidson said. "I'm not going to call you again because I'm not going to need to call you. We'll see you on Friday."

By Friday, my voice was almost gone from the flu and I was reduced to croaking out my words. Both my parents and Maya came with me to pick Blaze up from school and we stood there, with dozens of other parents, at the curb, like some kind of receiving line. Mr. Davidson pulled up first, before the buses, and got out smiling as he saw our party.

"Never had an entire family here to meet me before," he said.

The crowd at the curb burst out cheering as the yellow school buses pulled up and the kids tumbled off. And there was *my* kid, dusty, chapped-lipped, and tan from the sun, dragging his jacket along the ground, wearing Mr. Davidson's baseball cap on his head. He looked beat. He looked happy.

"Hi, Mom," he said. "I had a great time at camp."

I was so proud of him I could barely breathe.

We celebrated Blaze's success at camp for months. The fact that he could take care of himself for almost a week, away from me and away from home, was something I couldn't have envisioned only months before. Ironically, this very success was what got me thinking about the challenges Blaze would face in his next year of school. For some time I'd been ping-ponging from one school crisis to another with Blaze. Now, in a quieter time when he was making steady progress, I had the space to look ahead and try to avoid losing the ground it had been so hard to gain. Middle school was looming and I had no idea what to expect. Those middle grades were difficult under the best circumstances, I knew, and Blaze was most definitely not a kid who would just fit in. In addition, there would be no Mr. Davidson to smooth the path in seventh grade and beyond, and that worried me more than anything.

Mr. Davidson, it turned out, had similar thoughts.

"So what should I do?" I asked him. "What can I do to prepare?"

Mr. Davidson suggested that maybe I should try to have Blaze evaluated once more by someone I had faith in.

"Chances are, whoever I find will recommend medication," I said. "What do you think about that?"

Mr. Davidson paused before answering me, as if he were choosing his words carefully. "You know, when Blaze first came to my class, I was told *never* to mention medication to you," Mr. Davidson said.

"Dr. Roberts?" I asked.

"Yes."

"I guess she *was* listening, after all."

"Are you reconsidering now?"

"Well, I don't know," I said. "I've always been opposed to these drugs, but if there's something . . . If you *know* of something. . . ."

"Well," he said, "you shouldn't do anything you're not comfortable with but there really are a lot of very good medications out there now and maybe, well, you just never know. I've seen a lot of kids do really well. For some, it's like night and day."

So, once again, I tried to open my mind to the possibility of a magic bullet in both diagnosis and medication.

My long resistance to drugs wasn't born of ignorance. Over the years, Blaze's odd medical issues had thrown me into a world I knew almost nothing about and I wanted very much to become educated. So, in addition to researching growth hormone and prednisone, I started reading about a whole other class of drugs that was moving into the limelight just as he was starting school. I am referring now to the seratonin reuptake inhibitors, or SSRIs. The SSRIs are antidepressants that influence the amount of seratonin present in the brain. An older class of antidepressants, the tricyclics, influence all the brain's neurotransmitters. The first of these SSRIs to enter into the mainstream was Prozac but there were many more to come, including Zoloft, Paxil, Celexa, and Luvox. Intrigued, I read *Listening to Prozac* when it was published and then read the answer to that book, *Talking Back to Prozac*, which I found much more convincing. I saw what seemed to me to be a trend toward the "Prozac nation" that Elizabeth Wurtzel addressed in her book of the same name. Every doctor I'd had since the early 1990s (and these were general practitioners, mind you, not psychiatrists) had recommended one of the SSRIs for me—and not because I was depressed, but because I had a backache or stomach trouble or occasional difficulty falling asleep. At a certain point, I noticed it was almost impossible to avoid some kind of contact with these new antidepressants. Talk of them was everywhere (ads in *TV Guide*!), prescriptions for them were profuse, and periodically, some kind of article either denigrating them or extolling their virtues popped up in the papers and magazines.

I had a deep distrust of these medications. Part of this distrust stemmed, no doubt, from my upbringing and my parents' attitudes. But another component of my wariness came from the fact that, often enough, many drugs touted as cures later turned out to be more dangerous than the maladies they sought to address. Who hadn't heard of thalidomide? DES daughters? And who hadn't seen at least one article blaming various school shootings on the fact that many of the shooters were taking prescribed antidepressants? I had too many unanswered questions about the long-term effects of most drugs to feel comfortable with the claims of short-term benefits. But, of course, this was just my opinion. I was free to take or not take any drug prescribed to me and feel vindicated if my concerns were borne out or happily surprised if they weren't. The real problem, for me at least, was that whether or not *I* took the drugs was not the issue. It was whether or not I chose to give them to my son.

Although I'd been hearing about medication since Blaze started school, the pressure to give it to him had been fairly subtle at first. But he started school in 1992, when Prozac was making its first appearances in the mainstream and before diagnoses such as pervasive developmental disorder, not otherwise specified; Asperger's Syndrome; and bipolar disorder were being regularly applied to children. By the time Blaze was in sixth grade, Asperger's Syndrome—on the autism spectrum of disorders but with several markedly different characteristics—was cropping up all over the place. In addition, bipolar disorder, which I'd previously been told was never diagnosed in children, was becoming the new "hot" diagnosis for kids. There was also sensory integrative disorder, which usually got tacked onto a more established disorder as a sort of bolster. Obsessive-compulsive disorder (OCD) was mentioned more than ever before as well. Gone were the simple days of ADHD (attention deficit hyperactivity disorder) and eating disorders (although those often joined the party as "components"). Now there were newer, better, and bigger fish to fry. And it seemed that there was a drug to go with every one.

Had it not been for Mr. Davidson and the stunning success he'd had with Blaze, I would never have considered another visit to a psychiatrist, much less medication for Blaze. It wasn't that Mr. Davidson pressured me or even suggested that I medicate Blaze. But he believed in medication and I trusted him implicitly. Because of this, I opened my mind.

On a recommendation from a psychiatrist friend whose opinion I respected, I took Blaze to see Dr. B., another psychiatrist in another high-rent office. Dr. B. had a lousy bedside manner, if "manner" was even the correct word to use for his gruffness. I gave him the abbreviated version of Blaze's trials at school and flung out all I'd garnered from time in special ed about childhood psychiatric disorders. After a forty-five minute session, Dr. B. told me that Blaze had all the classic signs of ADHD and prescribed Ritalin.

"Gee," I told him, "I've heard just about everything but ADHD. That's a new one for the smorgasbord."

Although I was slightly suspicious of the rapidity with which Dr. B. arrived at his diagnosis, I was almost happy with it. In the face of all the strange, dark maladies on the table, ADHD seemed like a lucky break and Ritalin like a gift. What I found disturbing, though, were the reactions I got from those I told that I'd finally caved on my antidrug stance. "I'm proud of you," was the most common statement I heard from the teachers and school staff. My friends applauded the decision. My family was less enthusiastic but, like me, only wanted to make life easier for Blaze. Helen congratulated me on my decision and then added, "You know they're having really good results when they combine Ritalin with a little bit of Prozac. You might want to think about that option." Her enthusiasm was astonishing to me. It was like I had finally decided to become part of a club. A cool club.

At first, Blaze seemed to have little reaction to the Ritalin. Mr. Davidson reported no real improvement in his behavior. Blaze was still leaving class when he felt like it and still refusing to work when it didn't suit him. When I asked him how he felt after taking the pill, Blaze shrugged. I called Dr. B. and after speaking to his answering service a few times, he called back and suggested I raise the dosage. I added a pill at lunchtime. Blaze didn't mind traipsing off to the nurse's office before lunch and taking a pill. After all, there were plenty of his peers doing the same. After upping the dose, Mr. Davidson told me that Blaze seemed a little more focused. I held out hope.

Soon after, Blaze started showing some physical effects. His sleep patterns became erratic. Sometimes he'd have nightmares and sometimes he'd wake up in the middle of the night and not be able to fall back asleep. His eating habits changed too. He was either famished or refusing food altogether. And then he started to become irritable in the afternoons. When I was in college, we had a word to describe his condition: crashing.

"I'm just not sure about this drug," I told my father.

"Well, have you tried it yourself?" my father asked. I admitted that I hadn't. The thought hadn't even occurred to me. I felt my father had a valid point. I had spent Blaze's whole life trying to make his environment safe. I put plugs in sockets and tested jars of baby food. I wouldn't let him watch violent TV shows and trained him to look both ways before crossing the street. I wouldn't let him eat candy he'd dropped on the floor. But I'd been giving him a powerful stimulant without having even an inkling of its effects.

So I took a single dose, no more or less than Blaze got every day. After the subsequent sleepless night, I was deeply divided about continuing to give my son this drug.

As luck would have it, I had some help in making a final decision. The *Journal of the American Medical Association* came out with a report on psychotropic drug use in very young children just as Blaze was in the middle of his course of Ritalin. The report, which was profiled in *Newsweek, Time, U.S. News and World Report*, and newspapers around the country detailed an astronomical increase in prescriptions for

Ritalin in the years between 1991 and 1995 for children as young as three and four years old. Ritalin, however, wasn't the only drug the report mentioned. They were all there—Prozac, Zoloft, and Paxil plus some newbies: Clonidine, Risperdal, and Depakote. Clonidine is used to treat high blood pressure in adults. Risperdal is an anti-psychotic. Depakote is an anti-seizure medication. As for the antide-pressants, the *U.S. News and World Report* article said that the total prescriptions for SSRIs (adults and children) in 1999 were no less than 84 million.

Although I'd seen the *JAMA* report on my own, I started receiving all kinds of articles from friends who knew about my struggles getting Blaze through school. By the time it was all done, I had an inch of paper on my desk. There were articles about the role of HMOs in overprescribing psychotropic medications, articles about the decline in psychotherapy and behavior modification. There were articles profiling desperate parents for whom drugs had restored a sense of normalcy in their lives and the lives of their children and articles by doctors who swore by the efficacy of antidepressants versus doctors who vilified their evils. Most interestingly, I read an op-ed *New York Times* piece by Elizabeth Wurtzel describing her horrifying addiction to Ritalin as an adult.

I began to think I'd had some kind of lapse of sanity myself. Clearly, Ritalin hadn't worked any magic for Blaze. Rather, it was having a bad effect on him physically. What the hell was I doing giving him a drug that I didn't believe in for a condition he probably didn't even have? When I questioned Dr. B. about this, he shrugged and asked if I wanted to try something else.

I asked the doctor if he could please speak with Blaze's teacher. Mr. Davidson knew Blaze better than any teacher he'd ever had, I said. Perhaps after a conversation with this teacher he'd have a clearer insight into Blaze's behavior at school. Dr. B. said he'd try to fit it into his schedule, which I probably didn't know was quite packed because he was going on vacation; and he looked down at his watch.

I left his office and never went back. I also took Blaze off the Ritalin. Again, Mr. Davidson reported very little change. But this time, he went a little further. He suggested that perhaps Blaze needed a stronger drug, that he didn't think ADHD was the problem.

"Forget it," I said. "We're done with this. Nobody knows what's going on with these drugs or what kinds of long-term effects they might have. I'm not using my son as a guinea pig for psychiatrists and drug companies."

Mr. Davidson never mentioned drugs to me again.

I took quite a bit of heat for my little trial with Ritalin. Aside from my family, nobody thought I had done the right thing by ingesting the drug myself. How could I gauge the effects the drug had on Blaze by taking it myself, they wanted to know, when it was *proven* that children responded differently to it? This, of course, was exactly my point. Why would I give a drug that was too strong for *me* to my own child? Besides, I argued, Blaze was obviously reacting badly to it. The risk/benefit ratio seemed indisputably tilted toward risk.

I wish I could say that our brief encounter with Ritalin marked the end of our long day's journey into pharmaceuticals, but it wasn't. Nor could I ever settle the issue that easily. The problem was that I could see both sides of the dilemma quite clearly.

When Blaze was taking Ritalin, almost every child I worked with at school was on one or more of the drugs mentioned in the various articles on my desk. There was a line at the nurse's office at every lunch and recess. Parents were constantly "adjusting meds" and teachers were consistently reporting on subsequent behaviors. Some of these behaviors were fairly easy to report. Some of the kids just couldn't keep their eyes open and conked out on their desks. Some of them had stomachaches. Some drooled. A few showed no signs at all. There were some familiar refrains among the staff:

"Did Mom switch his meds?"

"Is she off her meds again?"

"Isn't he doing great on those new meds?"

There was an almost overwhelming relief among teachers when children were started on a course of drugs. And who could blame them? Their arguments were undeniably convincing. With a class of thirty kids, how was it possible to teach the prescribed curricula in the time allotted when a few of them were disruptive, inattentive, unfocused, and unmanageable? Teachers complained bitterly about having to cater to kids with special needs when, clearly, they shouldn't be mainstreamed in the first place. So many of these kids were so much easier to teach when they weren't jumping out of their skins—when they were on medication. And, really, wasn't that in the child's best interest? Many teachers and staff were taking antidepressants themselves. At one point the teacher of an ADHD student said frankly, "It's an absolute sin that this child is not on medication." The student's mother had tried Ritalin and, like me, had decided that it was having a negative effect on her son.

Although their attitude seemed harsh and uncaring on the surface, I understood the teachers' point of view. Most of the time they were grossly underpaid, understaffed, and overworked. Almost every teacher I knew regularly shelled out her own money for class materials. To top it all off, the teachers were expected to make sure all their students performed well on the standardized tests that were the worshipped conduits of public funding. Added to this were children whose ability or behavior was totally off the scale, and their overconcerned or underconcerned parents who fluctuated between extremes of denial, anger, grief, and self-righteousness. The teachers in regular education had no training at all with which to combat this kind of onslaught. As for the aides (of whom I was one), they got paid barely above minimum wage to teach, toilet, comfort, paint, soothe, discipline, and, of course, make copies. I had met and worked with teachers who were gifted, indifferent, devoted, talented, ignorant, stern, and loving but I had yet to meet one who wished harm on her children. Most were simply burned out and the issue of jumpy kids with learning problems or newly fashionable disorders was one more match to the embers. Yes, it was easier when they were medicated. For everyone.

I had no problem with the way teachers, school psychologists, and special-ed administrators felt about medication. What I did have difficulty reconciling was that teachers and school staff often found themselves in the position of tentatively diagnosing the kids in their classes and then suggesting possible medications to parents. If not quite as overt as this, many teachers certainly encouraged parents to "explore options," and school psychologists, although not medical doctors, definitely mentioned specific drugs by name and offered up diagnoses as if they were doughnuts.

I could understand why teachers and school staff became so involved in this cycle of diagnosis and medication. I was tempted to try my hand at it, too, while I worked with the kids in my program. After all, teachers spend a lot of time with the children. But I didn't think—had never thought—it should be the teacher's job to venture into the business and practice of psychiatry as so many of them seemed to do. I couldn't assign blame because I didn't see the cycle as being anybody's fault. But I wondered if there was a subtle drift toward putting teachers in the position of doctors. In the end, I thought, who would do the actual teaching?

The drug question was not a simple one for me and was made even more complicated by the fact that I had no idea what the future held for my son. I couldn't say if he'd be able to handle the pressures that would come with adolescence. All I knew was that, as his mother, I was painfully limited in orchestrating his destiny. If, at some point in the future, we were offered a drug that was tested, proven safe and addressed exactly what made navigating the social and academic milieu so difficult for Blaze, I wouldn't hesitate to give it to him. Hell,

I'd take it myself. Nor did I have any quarrel with parents who gave their children medication. That was just one of the choices we had to make as parents and we had to make them based on our faith and what our hearts dictated. All I really wanted was to be able to make this particular choice without pressure or derision. That was what my heart told me.

Blaze's graduation from sixth grade was a big deal at his school. Although they stopped short of donning caps and gowns, the students participated in a ceremony as full of pomp and circumstance as any graduation I'd ever attended. There were songs, a processional, and the awarding of signed diplomas (albeit half-sized). I tried to sit as far away from the rest of my family as possible to avoid crying in front of them and everybody else. I've always hated crying in public places. One might as well be naked. In fact, being physically naked might even have the edge over that kind of emotional nakedness. Unfortunately, complete removal from my family was impossible, so I settled for donning my sunglasses instead. That's always been one of the advantages of living in southern California: sunglasses are appropriate at every occasion.

Once the ceremony began, and I saw my son sitting quietly and proudly with his classmates (all of them together, no special-ed separations here), the tears began to roll down my cheeks, splashing wetly onto the program in my hands. And, of course, one of my sisters had to comment, "Look, Debra's *crying*. Aww," and further loosen the tenuous grip I had on my emotions. Family can always be counted on for these things.

I wasn't weeping out of a sense of sentimentality, although that would probably have been justification enough to shed a few tears. Rather, as I watched Blaze walk across the stage and shake hands very properly with the principal (who then abandoned decorum and gave him a big hug), I was thinking about what a struggle it had been to come to this place and about how many battles had been fought and won and lost.

When Blaze first came to his class, Mr. Davidson had explained his motto to me this way:

"You know the expression, 'Going for the gold'?" he said. "Well, in my class, we're going for the beige. Everybody blends. The biggest danger for these kids is the fact that they stand out. They are treated differently and then they become targets. I don't treat my kids as though they are different. It's amazing how kids can rise to your expectations, if only you have expectations to hold them to."

Although this seemed like such an obvious philosophy, it had taken so long for somebody to apply it to Blaze. He'd gotten so little time to show that he, too, could blend. In a sense, I felt he'd been a little cheated, that over the last seven years he should have been allowed more moments like this one to gird him for what was to come. I kept thinking about the scary tower from his dreams. I could still see it looming in the distance. And I wondered, hopeful and anxious, if, without Mr. Davidson to carry him to safety, he would be able to walk past it on his own.

Chapter 13

WATERLOO

October 2000

$\mathcal{W}$hen I was in the throes of labor, sweating, gnashing my teeth, and wondering how I would ever make it through the experience alive, the labor nurse looked at me comfortingly and told me, "Don't worry, you won't remember any of this later. The first time that baby looks up you, it will be all gone, not even a memory of this pain." That labor nurse wasn't entirely wrong; it was true that my body forgot the pain almost immediately. But she left out a few things. She didn't mention what else I would remember and ponder, years later, in ever-narrowing concentric circles of thought. She didn't predict what the rhythm of my life would be and how complicated the simplest acts would become. She couldn't have known, of course. She was sure I wouldn't remember that pain. But my mind, at least, has remembered and those complicated simple acts happen every day.

This is what it's like now.

I drop my son off at school and walk home in a state of total misery. I don't want to leave him there and he doesn't want to stay. At home, I waste hours folding clothes and writing letters. At ten o'clock, afraid that the phone is going to ring at any minute with bad news from my son's school, I decide I've got to get out of the house. I walk to the postal store to mail the useless letters I've spent all morning writing.

I round the corner where there's a Baskin Robbins and I see a man standing outside, peering in. I think, can he really be that in need of ice cream at 10:45 A.M.? Why is he waiting there for someone to open the door and set the bells on it jangling? Why is he waiting to be ushered in as if he's an expectant kid on a warm summer morning? So I take a closer look and see that he's wearing a pink shirt and navy pants and, in his hands, he clutches a baseball cap. And on the baseball cap is the 31 Flavors logo, the same logo that's on the shirt he's wearing. So, oh, I think, he works there and he's waiting for someone to let him in. But this poses a whole other set of problems.

Why is he working at Baskin Robbins for what must surely be minimum wage? He's a grown man. Actually, more than grown. By the looks of it, he's in his forties or maybe even early fifties. Is this the only job he can get? Has he been laid off by his company? No, impossible; no man of this age works scooping ice cream for minimum wage, unless . . . Well, unless this is the pinnacle for him. Unless this is what they meant when, at school, decades earlier, they said he would probably lead "a productive life." I slow down and steal another glance at him but I can't see his face as he leans into the door, staring into darkness.

And then I think what has been brimming over in my brain since the second I saw the hat with its logo. I think it in the liquid, wordless sense that I reserve for these kinds of thoughts. They never really formulate, but then, suddenly, there they are.

Is that my son a few years from now? This is what I think.

Suddenly, I start concocting all kinds of other scenarios and then shoot them down just as quickly. He's the manager or owner and that's why he works there. No, that doesn't make sense, because if he were the manager, why doesn't he have a key? Maybe he forgot his key today. No, if he forgot his key, he wouldn't be standing at the door, peering in. Maybe he's waiting for his partner. No, you don't need two partners working in one little ice cream store. It has to be that he can't have any other kind of job.

But is this such a bad job? Is it a terrible thing to work at an ice cream parlor at the dawning of a new millennium and wear a pink shirt with a logo? I think of phrases like *honorable profession* and *self-supporting.*

I wonder, could this be my son?

I have to wonder, because every day there are moments like this. Every day now, I straddle the line between faith and the impossible. Yesterday, my son told me not to worry, that most of the time he speaks metaphorically. Yes, *metaphorically* was the word he used and I know he understood its meaning. Yet, two days ago he ran screaming from his seventh-grade classroom because he heard the sound of distant sirens. I wonder because now we might as well be starting all over again, in that kindergarten classroom, with nothing "they" say matching what I feel. Only now it is so much worse, because now it's not new, *he's* not new. He's a big boy, on the verge of adolescence, not the cute little five-year-old who started kindergarten so long ago. This time it feels like an ending, not a beginning.

I wonder if this man's mother knows where he works and what he does when he's not here. I wonder what this man thinks when he's alone. I want to ask him but more than that, I want to see his face. I want to see if there is an expression of vacancy there. I want to see if he's smiling. I want to see if he looks . . . I can't help it . . . the word *normal* springs into my head.

My son looks normal, I think. My son is beautiful. Is this, could this be, my son?

I keep walking and wondering and I don't look back to see if the man gets into the store. I mail my letters and I think about my son. I wonder what kind of day he's having in school. I wonder if, when I pick him up later today, I'll hear that he "did a great job" or that "we are quite concerned about him." I think about how my son, with his undiagnosable differences, has allowed me to see the divine not just in himself, but in everything. I try to understand how *divine* consistently translates into *damaged.* I wonder what I've done wrong. I wonder what I've done right. I wonder if he'll be able to make it through seventh grade, through high school, get a girlfriend, have a family, play guitar, discover a cure for cancer, support himself working in a Baskin Robbins getting minimum wage. I wonder if he'll live with me forever. I wonder, finally, how long I will live myself. I can't die, I think to myself. I simply can't die. Not while he is alive.

I'm still contemplating my own mortality when I find myself rounding the Baskin Robbins again on my way home. The door opens suddenly and out comes the man, holding a scarecrow. He positions it in a flowerpot outside the store. Decoration, I think. It's fall now, almost Halloween. He turns when he hears me pass and smiles at me. He's got a pleasant face, not a trace of vacancy in it. I wonder again if he's the owner. I think maybe I should follow him inside, get myself a cone, and seep up some more information. But I second-guess myself again. I don't really want to know more than I do at this moment. And besides, I think, I've never really liked ice cream that much anyway. I only come to these places when I bring my son along with me.

I wasn't entirely unprepared for Blaze's entry in to middle school. I knew that not only were we changing schools, but districts. Blaze's new school district encompassed only middle schools and high schools and covered a much broader territory than his elementary school district. I knew too that a high school district has a different set of directives than an elementary school district. Conventional wisdom says that the kids here are not the chubby cherubs of grade school. They are big and gangly, flooded with hormones and confusion. Middle school and high school are the last stops before adulthood. In the best circumstances, these are not the halcyon days of childhood by anyone's definition. I knew all that and I also knew that, for us at least, special education in middle school and high school would be a much dicier proposition than in elementary school. The feeling I got was that, by seventh grade, whatever disabilities a special-ed kid had should be clearly defined so that he could be placed accordingly. If your kid was autistic, there was a special program for him with other "severely handicapped" children. If your kid was visually impaired, he got a note-taker and computer technology to help him with class work. If your kid was SED (severely emotionally disturbed), he was put in a dead-end program for fire starters and window breakers. Next stop, juvenile hall.

As always, Blaze fit none of the standard categories and I worried about how he would fare in a new system that seemed to have less tolerance for the gray areas between categories and diagnoses. I'd long since stopped trying to catch my flies with vinegar so, by the time Blaze was in sixth grade, I adopted a sweeter approach and called the administrative office of the new district and tried to voice my concerns about the next year as well as offer my help. I might as well have been trying to arrange a private meeting with the president. I was referred to three different administrators and left messages on several answering machines. Nobody called back.

In the spring of Blaze's sixth-grade year, I attended a "transition meeting" with Helen, Mr. Davidson, and the teachers and administrators from Blaze's new school. This gathering did very little to bolster my confidence. The school itself was brand new and, after less than a year in operation, was still in the process of determining the needs of its student population.

Mr. Davidson, Helen, and I (my parents, alas, were out of town and so this was one meeting my father did not attend) sat in a tight little knot on one end of a huge, polished conference table, while the representatives from the new school sprawled across the rest of the space. Even with Mr. Davidson there, I felt intimidated. I had never been in the company of so many large women at one time. By large, I don't mean overweight. This was a collection of amazons: giant women with big, blond, perfectly streaked hair, sharp lacquered nails, and serious business suits in muted shades of gray. They had Palm Pilots, cell phones, and leather-bound appointment books. Each one introduced herself to us, but it was pointless trying to separate them out. I felt like I'd wandered into a female superhero convention by mistake. By contrast, Mr. Davidson, Helen, and I looked a little like their hick relatives visiting the big city for the first time.

Mr. Davidson did most of the talking at first, describing the progress Blaze had made over the previous year and a half and delineating what he thought was most important for Blaze in the classroom (a feeling of security, a measure of success, a sense of belonging). He said he thought it would be a good idea for there to be a classroom aide. He said that Blaze was a good reader and worked best in small groups. It would be ideal, Mr. Davidson said, if Blaze could have all his classes in a small, highly structured classroom. Mr. Davidson was charming, but I didn't notice his charm registering in that room. These were clearly very busy amazons.

Helen spoke very little, but she did mention that I had been working in special education for the last couple of years and was doing an excellent job so that, as parents went, I was definitely in the top tier. One of the amazons gestured to me and leaned backward in her chair.

"Are you looking for a new job?" she asked me in a stage whisper. "We could really use someone with your talent in this district."

"I'd be interested," I whispered back. "But maybe we should talk about it when I'm not sitting right next to my boss."

After our corner had presented its case, one of the women got up and started drawing the interlocking, shaded circles otherwise known as Venn diagrams on an easel. "The kids will be spending this portion of their day in the mainstream classes," she said, shading one portion of the interlocking circles. "This portion here will be for special day class and then this," she leaned across the board with a nice show of athleticism, "will be for electives."

"Will you be Blaze's main teacher?" I asked.

"Oh no, I'm not teaching the special day class."

"Who is the teacher, then?"

"We don't have a teacher yet. But we're in the process of interviewing several candidates right now."

"Can you tell me about how the program will be set up?"

"Well, we think it's better not to focus on specifics yet. We're planning to design our program around the needs of the kids coming in."

It all sounded good and the diagrams were pretty, but we were talking about children here, not pork bellies, and my mind immediately translated the meaning of her words as: *We have no teacher, we don't know what we're doing, and there really isn't a program to speak of.*

"I'm not sure about this," I told Mr. Davidson when the meeting was over. "They don't seem to have much of an idea about the kids or the program."

"It'll be all right," Mr. Davidson said. "It's not necessarily a bad thing that they're forming a program around the kids. This way it'll be tailored to their specific needs."

Although his words were reassuring, I got the feeling that Mr. Davidson was even less confident than I was. Unlike me, though, his job was done after sixth grade. No matter how carefully he tried to prepare and nurture his kids, after sixth grade they were in somebody else's hands.

I made a valiant effort to get a job at Blaze's school before the start of the year. I had already decided that I would have to leave my current position in the elementary school because, by the looks of things, Blaze was going to need plenty of help in his new school and I needed to be available for him. I had been lucky enough to publish my first book by then (not the novel I'd been working on, but a memoir about my life as a waitress) and, for the first time in my life, was making a living as a writer. I figured that if I worked at his new school, I would be able to keep an eye on him *and* help some of the kids I'd been working with over the last year.

No such luck.

I went through a series of interviews at the district office and took a battery of tests reminiscent of the SATs ("Does everybody have a number two pencil? Please do not mark outside of the lines."). After all of this, I received a call from an administrative assistant informing me that there was a position available for me in a local high school. The job description involved copying, filing, and record keeping for a couple of different teachers. There wouldn't be much interaction with actual students. I mentioned that I'd asked for an aide position at Blaze's middle school.

"Oh, we're all full up there," the woman told me. "We don't need any aides at that school."

I told her that I appreciated the offer, but I'd have to decline. If anything opened up at Blaze's school, I said, I would appreciate it if she could consider me for that. She said she would and I knew she wouldn't. Once again, it seemed, I was on the outside looking in.

It was the end of August, a week before school started, by the time a teacher was hired for Blaze's class. My father and I had a hastily arranged meeting with the new teacher and Clark, the school psychologist (another one, I thought—if I lined up all the school psychologists Blaze had seen over the years, I'd have enough people for a bowling team), who pointed out that he was not just a plain old psychologist, but a *neuropsychologist*, thank you very much.

"You know," my father said, "I really think that, for the right person, Blaze could provide a whole new perspective. He's such a unique case, such a unique individual, that he could make a fascinating study. You could learn from him. I predict that he'll be very interesting for you."

Clark looked unimpressed. "I think I've seen just about everything," he said.

The new teacher seemed scattered and unprepared. His room was still in a state of chaos and he had only just received the files for the kids in his class, all of which were several inches thick.

"We're going to do our best," he said. "Things are a little disorganized at the moment, but we'll all get into a good rhythm pretty soon. How does Blaze feel about starting middle school?"

"He's anxious," I said.

"Well, that's natural," the teacher said.

"You know, I'm always available," I said. "You can call me anytime and I'm willing to come in, help out, whatever you need."

"That's great," the teacher said. "I'm sure we'll be fine."

"What do you think?" I asked my father as we left the meeting.

"The shrink seems reasonable," my father said. "I don't know about the teacher."

"Me neither," I said.

Months later, I looked back and tried to find a few grains of optimism in Blaze's first few weeks of seventh grade. I kept thinking that there must have been something positive in his initial experience there, there must have been some happiness in the beginning. But there wasn't. Day one was bad and from that inauspicious start, things only got worse.

Perhaps it was ridiculously naive of me to expect the slightly fuzzy warmth of elementary school in an institution containing 900 seventh- and eighth-graders. Still, I was amazed by what seemed to be a feeling of guarded hostility among the staff at the middle school. Adults patrolled the grounds in the morning with walkie-talkies, barking at children to keep clear of the curbs, get to class, stop loitering, stop running, and report to the office. There were very few smiles. The office staff were surly. The administrators seemed as if they were waiting for the students to do something wrong, as if they were all just juvenile delinquents in training.

It was true that the kids didn't much *look* like kids anymore. They

were a mass of long legs, big pants, lip gloss, and Nikes. They were all
taller than I was. They were brushing their hair outside the bathroom
and spitting into the parking lot. They had headsets, water bottles,
and cell phones. They chattered in groups and clustered around the
flagpole. They didn't say good-bye to their mothers as they quickly
hopped out of their cars.

Standing in the middle of this twelve- and thirteen-year-old
throng with my son, I could remember what it felt like to be in middle school and be one of a hundred little dramas unfolding every
morning between homeroom and first period. I could even remember thinking, then, that I had no perspective, that everything seemed
oversized, physically and emotionally. I looked forward to being able
to look back on the experience with the viewpoint of an adult. What
I saw now, from that adult viewpoint, was a group of children who
were not children and not adolescents. They were in that perilous
nether region that had made me so uncomfortable when I'd passed
through it myself. Yet, it seemed to me that the grown-ups around
them treated them all as if they had already metamorphosed into
young adults and should behave accordingly. How could you demand
that of them, I thought, when you could still see the shape of their
children's bodies just under their skins—when, only three months
ago, they were still considered kids?

Blaze stood outside of all this, moving in his own space and time.
Would there be anyone here, I wondered, who could reach him?

From the outset, the answer to that question seemed to be a
resounding no.

In the first week, Blaze's teacher reported that he was "concerned"
about Blaze's anxiety over fire drills and other loud noises. I explained
that Blaze had been hung up on fire drills since kindergarten and
that the fire drill issue was something that had been discussed at
length in every IEP meeting and was written all over Blaze's file.

Blaze tended to wander off, his teacher said, and he was "concerned" about safety issues. Me too, I told the teacher. Blaze had a pattern of testing his boundaries this way, I told the teacher. He would see how far he could go before he would be brought back. This was all in his file, I said, and I'd discussed it at the meeting, didn't he remember? Blaze's teacher was "concerned" that Blaze wasn't taking notes in his science class. He can't, I said. He can't look at a blackboard, listen to a lecture, and copy notes. He just can't do that. That's part of the reason he's in special ed to begin with. For four days out of every week, Blaze's school was on a "block schedule," which meant three two-hour class periods a day. Blaze couldn't handle the two-hour blocks, his teacher said. He got up, walked around. I'm not surprised, I said. Can *you* handle a two-hour block? I didn't even have classes that long when I was in college.

"There are other programs in this district that might be better for Blaze," the teacher said to me after one of these conversations.

"Really? Like what?"

"Well, there's a regional program in one of the other middle schools."

"You mean the SED class?" I asked him. "The one for the emotionally disturbed kids?"

"Well, uh, that is, um, the program."

"Forget it," I told him. "Never."

I didn't even bother trying to figure out why this man would recommend a program like this to me, nor did I attempt to explain why I would never place Blaze there. Although I didn't think he was a bad guy, I had no respect for him as a teacher. After a career as a businessman, he'd suddenly decided to start teaching and this was only his second year in the classroom. He dressed with a studied casualness that came off as rather goofy and he had an awkward "good old boy" attitude that didn't inspire much confidence. I didn't feel that he knew what he was doing and his instincts weren't that good, besides. I sensed that he was practicing on my kid. Maya was rather less intellectual in her assessment of him.

"He looks and acts like a giant Easter bunny," she said.

That was about the size of it.

I didn't have too much time to dwell on his incompetence, because a mere six weeks after the school year began, just as Blaze was starting to form an attachment to him, the Easter bunny quit, throwing his class into total chaos. The Easter bunny's replacement was Mrs. M., a middle-aged woman who had been teaching for too long and whose attitude had the unmistakable odor of resentment at having been drafted into a position she clearly didn't want. Her antipathy toward Blaze was immediate and irrevocable. To be sure, I wasn't an objective observer, but I had come to know many teachers throughout Blaze's school career. I hadn't liked all of them and I was sure that many of them hadn't liked me much, either. Among them, they had been warm, cool, officious, loving, competent, gifted, inexperienced, hostile, and gregarious. But Mrs. M. was the first teacher I had met who simply didn't like my child. Blaze, sensitive in the extreme, picked up on her feelings almost immediately and responded in kind. He regularly exited his classroom and refused to come back inside. He screamed, he carried on and generally acted like a mental patient. Usually, this got him exactly what he wanted: a get-out-of-jail-free pass from class into the office of the school psychologist.

After she'd been teaching Blaze's class for two weeks, Mrs. M. told me, "I've tried everything with him and nothing works. He won't stay in class and I can't follow him out. I don't really know what to do with him. He's uncooperative and resistant. I've tried everything."

I thought, *two weeks* and she's tried everything? I started getting calls from Clark, the school psychologist who had indeed taken an interest in Blaze, although not at all the kind I wanted.

"We're very concerned about Blaze's behavior," Clark said. "His anxiety level is very high and it's impeding his ability to function in the classroom. I think he has some serious difficulties. Have you thought about medication? I think this is clearly a case where medication would be beneficial."

Trying to be as polite as possible, I explained my entire philosophy on and history with the psychotropic drug issue. Clark wasn't having any of it. He was fairly convinced that Blaze was hearing voices, seeing flashing lights, experiencing major panic attacks and, although he never said it, I knew he was thinking psychosis. I began to panic myself. I knew very well that Blaze's many visits to therapists had only helped his ability to manipulate a situation. He was telling Clark what he thought Clark wanted to hear. If it got him out of class and out of working, all the better. What made it all so complicated, and what I tried to explain to Clark, was that Blaze really *was* different, really didn't fit in, really couldn't function in the half-assed excuse for a special-education class he was in. He wasn't faking *all* of it.

"He told me that he heard voices," Clark said. "He said that he could hear his kindergarten teacher telling him to get on line. He said he wasn't going to listen to her."

"What were you doing when he told you this?" I asked.

"Blaze was describing what he felt like when he came to class in the mornings."

"Exactly." I took a deep breath and tried to calm my racing heart. It was so very difficult to speak quietly and with some semblance of control, but I knew that if I screwed up this conversation, I wouldn't have any allies at all in Blaze's school environment. "Look, Clark," I said, "I know why Blaze says those things."

"Really?"

"Yes. Blaze's kindergarten year was a time of major transition for him and it was also kind of rough. He didn't have the easiest time with his kindergarten teacher. Blaze has a steel-trap memory—he's got every experience locked in there. When he tells you he hears his kindergarten teacher, he's making an *association* between that year and this one. This transition to seventh grade is just as difficult as the one to kindergarten and this is his way of equating the two. He's not really hearing voices in the way you're thinking. You know, Blaze's handicapping condition is 'speech and language impaired.' He doesn't communicate in a conventional way. I'm telling you what he means."

"I don't know," Clark said. "He seemed pretty sure that he could hear somebody speaking. And that's the language he used: *I hear her.* Usually kids won't say that unless they really can hear something."

"Yes, but Blaze isn't a usual kid," I said.

"He sees flashing lights," Clark said. "He said he can't be in the classroom because of the flashing lights."

"Well, that's just nonsense," I said. "It's an excuse to leave the room and it obviously works. There is a light that flashes when the fire alarm goes off and that's where the flashing light thing started, but there's no way he's just seeing lights."

"I don't know," Clark said.

"Well, he doesn't hear voices and see flashing lights at *home*," I said. "I can tell you that." My voice had the tinny ring of petulance. I was starting to lose it.

"Well, Blaze is clearly not as anxious at home," Clark said. "I really think you should consider medication. There are so many medications available now, especially for anxiety . . ."

I realized that I was fundamentally exhausted. I searched, but I couldn't find the reserves of energy I needed to try to convince Clark that Blaze was not emotionally disturbed, that I was not in denial about his problems, and that what he really needed was not medication but a decent teacher and program, similar to those he'd had last year. I had been struggling through this morass for eight years. Every encounter with a new psychologist, administrator, or teacher had required me to refocus my speech and attitude. It had been like learning fifty new dialects of the same language. I didn't know if I could attain fluency one more time. Clark didn't seem particularly interested in changing his point of view, either.

At home, my relationship with Blaze was starting to take on an odd new shape. I often found myself angry with him. I felt he wasn't trying, wasn't even making an attempt to fit in. He was also amassing a disturbing collection of physical tics. He fidgeted with the zipper on his pants ("Totally unacceptable," I told him), he chewed on his lower lip until it bled ("You'll scar yourself," I told him) and—the worst one of all—he constantly licked his hand and touched it to his forehead ("Do you know how insane that looks?" I asked him. "You have to stop that."). The crazier he acted, I told Blaze, the crazier they were going to think he was at school and they would start treating him like a nut. Did he want that? No? Well, neither did I.

"What's with the flashing lights?" I snapped at him. "You've got to stop telling people you're seeing flashing lights."

"But, Mom—"

"And you *cannot* just keep getting up and walking out of the room."

"But, Mom, I can't stay there. I just can't stay there."

"You have to try, Blaze. You have to."

Soon after Mrs. M. told me that she'd "tried everything" with Blaze, I began to think about retaining an educational advocate. None of the school skills I thought I had were working now and every time I tried to convince Clark or Mrs. M. that Blaze really was all right, my son did his best to make me into a complete liar. We were about to reach an impasse, I thought, and I was going to need a lawyer. I called around and got a referral from the mother of one of Maya's violin students (Maya had recently begun teaching private lessons full time). I liked the sound of Dr. Jean on the phone. She was very smart and had a wicked sense of humor. But she certainly wasn't cheap. Dr. Jean's services ran $125 per hour, right around the going rate for educational advocates. At that point, though, I had decided that I would spend whatever money it took to get Blaze into a better situation and if that ran out, I would have to borrow the rest.

I explained my situation to Dr. Jean and told her that I didn't think Blaze was in the right school but I didn't know which one would be better. Dr. Jean said she would request a copy of Blaze's file and have a look. Take notes, she said. Don't sign anything you're not comfortable with. Document everything. I'm going to give it one last shot on my own, I told her. We've got a meeting coming up and I'm going to request a full-time aide for Blaze. I told Dr. Jean that I didn't think she needed to be at the meeting, but that I would call her afterward and let her know how it went.

It was supposed to be a short meeting. I was supposed to go in, ask for an aide, and receive a yes or no answer. That was all I was prepared for. My father came with me, but said he could stay less than an hour.

"Hopefully, it won't take that long," I told him.

There was not one friendly face in the conference room. I could understand why Blaze found it so difficult to stay in class. My father and I sat at one end of an oval table and everybody else sat clustered at the other. What would you call a group like this, I wondered. A band, as in gypsies? Definitely not. A swarm, as in insects? Maybe. A murder, as in crows? Closer.

There was Mrs. M. facing me with a large and frankly false smile. Clark sat next to her, rustling a pile of papers. The vice principal sat next to Clark, her walkie-talkie at the ready. Blaze had been taking drama as his general-education elective (and, really, it was the only class he seemed to get any enjoyment out of at all), so the drama teacher was there as well. The district administrator for special education was a woman I met for the first time at that meeting. I recognized her name from one of the answering machines I had left messages on the previous spring. She was tall, thin, and sharp in every respect.

The meeting began calmly enough. I said I felt that Blaze needed an aide because he was clearly having difficulty in class. Mrs. M. followed this up by reciting the litany of Blaze's behavior problems and how she had no idea how to handle them. The vice principal confirmed that Blaze wandered around campus and often had to be reeled back in. The administrator said that it was very difficult to find aides and, besides, it was a directive of special education that a child learn "in the least restrictive environment" possible. An aide was restrictive, apparently. I told the administrator that I had applied for a position as an aide at this very school and had been told that it was all full. The administrator replied, lips pursed, that she knew nothing about that. Clark piped in that Blaze heard voices. My father tried to explain what I already had; that Blaze was associating and that he didn't hear voices in the way that Clark thought. Clark remained unconvinced. The drama teacher said that Blaze was disruptive in her class, that perhaps drama wasn't the right elective for him.

"But he loves drama," I told her.

"Well, I can't tell that from having him in my class," she said. "I don't think he knows the difference between fiction and reality. I have over thirty kids in my class, so I can't spend every class period dealing with Blaze. The aide who comes in with him doesn't seem to have much control over him."

"You know," I said, "I've worked with many different kinds of children and I've found that sometimes there's just a personality conflict between a teacher and a child. I understand it can happen and it's not anybody's fault. Drama is the one class that makes Blaze happy. But if *you* don't think he should be there, then it will never work."

"I'm happy to have him in my class," she said, indicating, by her tone, that she'd probably rather be boiled in hot oil, "if *you* think it's the right place for him. I just wonder if drama is the right placement for somebody like him."

She stared at me, stone-faced, barely civil, without so much as an attempt to mask her distaste of the whole situation. I responded with a look of naked hatred.

"I'm not taking him out of drama," I told her. *And fuck you* and *the high horse you rode in on*, I added silently.

"Fine," she said.

"I think what we're missing here is the sensory piece," the administrator said. "Blaze is a child who has sensory issues and needs a defined schedule."

"How do you know that?" I asked her. "You've never even met him."

"I have observed him and his behavior," she said.

"Yes, she has," Clark said.

The administrator went on some more about the sensory piece and said that she couldn't promise an aide until Blaze had further evaluation. Somewhere in the middle of that discussion, my father apologized and left. All my instincts told me to follow him, but I overrode them, thinking that this abortive meeting was almost over anyway and I'd just tell them that we could work it all out with my advocate and be done with it. That, it turned out, was a bad miscalculation, because the minute my father left the building, the group at the other end of the table descended on me like a pack of wolves (yes, a pack, that was what they were) and tore me to pieces with their words.

"You know there is a safety issue here that we are not addressing," Clark said.

"What do you mean? Blaze's safety?"

"Well, actually, the safety of others. Blaze can be violent."

"*What?*"

"He has attempted to push Mrs. M. when she stands in his way and he has grabbed the arm of the aide who goes with him to drama. She has told me that she's afraid of him." Mrs. M. nodded her head up and down in vigorous agreement.

"I don't know what you're talking about. I've never heard this before. I see that girl every morning and she's never said anything of the kind."

"Well, she wouldn't. She's not supposed to."

"But she did tell me," Mrs. M. said. "I have heard that."

"He jumped out of the electrical closet at me," the drama teacher said. "I was coming in from lunch and he was in there and startled me. I'm concerned about the safety of the other students."

"What are you talking about? Blaze has never, ever, been violent in his entire life. If anything, he's reacting out of fear."

"He may be changing now," the administrator said. "Middle school is a different world."

"There's something else," Clark said. "Blaze has been touching himself and exposing himself in class."

"What?"

The aide has reported that, in science, Blaze has been touching his pants and opening his pants. Have you noticed that at home? Has he started to take an interest in—that kind of stimulation?"

"Is this a serious question? No, of course not. He would never do a thing like that. Blaze is playing with his *zipper*. It's a nervous habit he's picked up and I've spoken to him about it. He is not exposing himself. Did the aide say she saw him actually expose himself to her?"

"She said he opened his pants."

"You know, boys this age are beginning to discover themselves," the administrator said, eyebrows raised.

"No, that is not what is going on. And if this aide is so terrified to work with Blaze, why is she still with him?"

"Try not to get defensive," Clark said. "We're trying to help."

"I really think we need to address the sensory piece, guys," said the administrator.

"I'll be honest with you. I really don't know who this child is that you're describing. This is not my child."

And then they all started talking at once. I heard bits and pieces, as if their words were shards of broken glass falling around my head.

"—could use professional help—"

"—can provide you with a referral to the county mental health offices. You just need to sign—"

"—medications that have been very effective in cases like this—"

"—affects the other students—"

"—can't promise a full-time aide at this point—"

"—referral to the regional center. They provide respite care and—"

"—to address the sensory piece—"

"—referral to L.A. diagnostic center. If you sign—"

"—medication for his anxiety—"

"—too much stimuli for him in drama—"

"—and, then, with medication—"

"—have you given any more thought to medication?"

I stood up. "I can't do this," I said and I could hear my voice was full of tears. "I can't have this meeting. I need my advocate."

They kept talking, but I could no longer make sense of anything that was being said.

"No," I interrupted, "you don't understand. This meeting has to end now. I can't do this anymore. I don't know the child you're talking about, so I don't have anything else to say. I want my advocate present."

"Can you sign the team meeting notes?" the administrator asked.

"No," I said. "I'm not signing anything until I talk to my advocate. And I want you to know, in eight years, this is the first IEP meeting I've left without signing. This is the worst meeting I've ever had." My eyes were brimming.

"We're sorry if this is upsetting to you," somebody said. "Can you stay for another minute and look these forms over?" I looked in the direction of the voice. It was the vice principal. She had been quiet for almost the entire meeting and she was now looking at me with something approaching compassion. It was that brief hint of understanding that undid me.

"I have to go," I whispered, and tripped, half walking, half running out the door. I had a ten-minute walk home and I cried all the way, sobbing, out loud and in pain, in the middle of the street. I felt eviscerated, as if I were leaving my guts in a trail behind me as I walked. It wasn't so much the attack (by then, I was sure that *attack* was the only word for it) that had me contorted with pain and anger. Nor was it the fact that I would clearly never have a decent relationship with anybody at the school or even that I was *surprised* that they had pulled out a long list of complaints. What had destroyed me so completely this time was the nature of those complaints and my own helpless, agonizing fear.

What if they are right? What if that kid really is my kid? What do I do?

And if it wasn't my child now, exactly, how long would it take before Blaze became the child they were describing? He was certainly in distress, that much was evident. But what about the violence they were describing—the absolutely crazy behavior? How long would it take for him to mold himself into the profile they were creating for him? And then what would I do and where would I take my son? An institution? A juvenile detention center? I saw Blaze disappearing into a dismal future and I was terrified. I lost my way on that walk home and I lost my faith—in myself and in Blaze. I hated myself for my faithlessness and I hated the group in the classroom who had brought me to it. It was late October then. I didn't stop crying until the end of January.

Hang tight, Dr. Jean told me, after I'd calmed down enough to tell her about the meeting. Do your best to write down everything they tell you and every phone call you get from them. If Mrs. M. calls you or if Clark calls you, write it down. You must have records of everything, she told me, and while you're doing that, we'll investigate some nonpublic schools and other programs in the district and see what we've got.

It was easy to keep records. After the meeting, I told Mrs. M. that

I'd rather not talk to her without Dr. Jean present unless we were talking about basics like homework, tests, or assignments. This suited Mrs. M. fine since she didn't particularly enjoy talking to me, either, and preferred to communicate via e-mail and handwritten notes. Together, the e-mails and notes made quite an impressive record of her feelings for Blaze.

> Blaze was extremely disruptive today. Yelling loud in class. <u>Refusing</u>. No work completed. It was *very, very* difficult for the rest of the class. They were <u>not</u> able to finish their work. I tried kindness, strictness, earning points—nothing worked, he continued the whole morning.

> There is a fire drill on Friday. Please advise how you would like to handle with Blaze.

> In science, he was <u>mostly</u> out of the room. Licked his forehead several times—told me there was too much dust falling. He didn't unpack his backpack. He kept looking at the clock and announced every ten minutes how much longer the class was. Couldn't wait to leave class and go home.

> Wednesday is a block day which means science is two hours. Are you planning on picking Blaze up early? I have a meeting and need to leave around 1 P.M. If you are not picking Blaze up, I need to make other arrangements.

Getting Blaze through school every day soon became very much like trying to keep a bad marriage together. All the players were unhappy and every morning was a struggle. In eight years, despite all his troubles, Blaze had never told me he didn't want to go to school, had never faced the day as if he'd been condemned to a life in prison.

But now he told me, "Mom, you have to help me. I don't know how to be good in school. I don't know how to do it." He hated school, he told me. He hated Mrs. M. I told him and that he had to keep trying, that I was looking for another school for him and that somehow we would work it out. And, every morning, to his credit, Blaze did try. He put on his backpack like Atlas shouldering the world and trudged off to school. But every afternoon, I got a fresh disaster report. He wouldn't stay in class, wouldn't listen, wouldn't participate.

At night, I couldn't fall asleep. I lay in bed for hours, creating escape fantasies in my imagination. We'd move to an island. We'd fly away, fall down a rabbit hole, take a balloon to Oz. When I did fall asleep, I had recurring nightmares. In the worst one, Blaze was lost and I couldn't find him no matter how hard I looked. In the dream, the landscape was divided into many different levels, which I had to climb up and down. One was dry, one was snowy, one was wet. On each level were people who'd had contact with Blaze in some fashion. There were old teachers and new teachers, neighbors, psychologists. Mr. Davidson was there on one level, surrounded by the parents of his students. My family was nowhere to be found. I kept trying to get these people to help me find Blaze, but everyone sort of gave up after looking only a short while. Some even tried to distract me so that I wouldn't think about him anymore. I felt betrayed by all of them, but especially by Mr. Davidson. "Wasn't he with you last?" I asked. "Didn't you see where he went?" Mr. Davidson turned around and walked away. My panic escalated as the dream wore on and I woke up, my heart pounding, my eyes dry and painful.

In his own room, Blaze wasn't faring much better. I'd wake up at two, three, four o'clock in the morning and hear music seeping through the wall. He was awake in there every night, listening to Miles Davis's *Sketches of Spain*, creating his own sleepless escape.

By January 2001, I had attended three very long IEP meetings with Dr. Jean. The staff was, unsurprisingly, much more conciliatory with

a lawyer present, but continued to present evidence that Blaze was a
seriously handicapped child whose needs clearly exceeded their capabilities. I knew what direction they were headed. The district didn't
want to pay for a private school and, if we proved that they did not
have an adequate program for Blaze, that is exactly what they would be
forced to do. For them, the best bet was to prove that Blaze belonged
in one of their SH (severely handicapped) programs and ship him out.
Pretty soon, I told Dr. Jean, their case would be fairly airtight because
Blaze was having a nervous breakdown.

"I'm losing him," I told Dr. Jean. "And I won't be able to get him
back this time."

Although we never mentioned it to them, the district needn't have
worried about funding a private school. There was precious little available in the way of specialized schools. My choices were limited to two:
a school that admitted exceptional children with learning disabilities
but no behavior problems and a school that catered to children with
severe behavior problems. Blaze didn't fit either category. It was a
Gordian knot, getting tighter and more tangled by the day.

Just before the third and final IEP meeting, I finally stopped wal-
lowing and made a decision. I had come to pick Blaze up from school
early one Friday (by then it had been determined that he couldn't last
a whole day) and waited outside the office for Mrs. M. to escort him
over to me. I saw them approaching before they saw me. Blaze looked
more miserable than I'd ever seen him. His eyes were downcast and his
shoulders were slumped. Mrs. M. steered him toward the office and
then caught sight of me, waiting. The two of them stopped before me.

"Not a very good day, I'm afraid," Mrs. M. said.

"Blaze?" I said.

Blaze looked at me and, suddenly, his eyes filled with tears. "Oh,
Mom," he said. "Mom, I'm sorry. Don't be mad at me."

"Oh, honey, I'm not mad at you," I said. "Come here, I'm not mad."
I put my arms around him and he buried his head in my shoulder,

sobbing, his whole body shaking. "It's okay, Blaze, it's okay, honey," I said, but it clearly wasn't okay. Nothing was even remotely okay. I stared daggers at Mrs. M., and she smiled and shrugged her shoulders. "Well, I have to go now," she said and her smile widened. She gave Blaze an awkward pat on the back. "Have a nice weekend!" she said and walked off.

When we got home, I sat with Blaze on the couch for an hour in silence while his eyes continued to leak out tears. I held him and stroked his head. He was completely exhausted. Finally, he said, "Mom, are you sure you're not mad at me? School is just too hard for me. I'm sorry."

"It's all right," I told him. "I'm really not mad at you. You don't have to go back to that school again."

"Do you mean on Monday? I don't have to go to school on Monday?"

"You don't have to go back to that school ever. You're going to stay home with me. We'll do school here. I'll teach you. You're finished with that school and with Mrs. M. What do you think of that plan?"

"That's good, Mom. That's very good."

1/26/01
    Ginsberg, Blaze
    Continuation of three-year review
    IEP Team Meeting Notes

Parent rights were offered and signed. Introductions were done. The purpose of this meeting is to finalize some points of the IEP.

The technology specialist gave his report. He stated that when he did his observation Blaze was distractible and difficult to keep on task. Blaze is tuned in even though he appears to be disengaged. The technology specialist feels a spell-check is very important.

The school psychologist reviewed his report again. A neuropsychological evaluation was completed on Blaze. Blaze experiences sensory overload in the classroom. He tends to shut down in the classroom.

Blaze needs information presented to him using a multisensory approach. He cannot process information that is not relevant or meaningful to him. He benefits most from one-on-one instruction that is meaningful and functional. He has difficulty with abstract thinking. The curriculum needs to be integrated. Blaze is overwhelmed with too much sensory input. Too much inclusion is difficult for Blaze.

Blaze's mom and advocate indicate that Blaze is very stressed right now. Consequently, they have kept him home for the last few days. Home schooling does not entitle Blaze to services.

[This school] is not working for Blaze right now. A transition plan for Blaze needs to be implemented. Mom states that Blaze is ready for a change. The school psychologist and the special-ed coordinator do not feel that a home [program] would be a good option for Blaze. It is their recommendation that he begin to transition now into a new program. He could transition slowly and start with a shortened day. Blaze's case carrier is concerned that allowing Blaze to stay home may reward negative behaviors. Blaze's mom feels he really needs the opportunity to de-stress so that he is emotionally ready to go to a new school. Blaze's grandfather feels Blaze has gotten into some bad behavior habits. He needs the time at home to relearn some good behaviors.

Blaze will be on "home hospital" for the month of February. He will begin school in a special day class placement on February 26. During the month of February, Blaze will visit [his new school].

The team discussed his handicapping condition. His original condition was speech and language impaired. This is not an accurate description of Blaze. The team decided his handicapping condition will now be multiple disabilities (MD).

Chapter 14

HOME

March 2001

*B*laze has been out of school for almost two months. When I made it, the decision to keep him at home seemed desperate and extreme. Never once, in his eight years of schooling, had I seriously considered removing Blaze from school. I felt sure that there would be some sort of reaction from the district office, although I had no idea what that might be. Please send him back to school? Maybe. We're sorry, we were wrong? Perhaps. Of course, there was nothing of the kind forthcoming from the school or the district.

After the last IEP meeting, wherein Mrs. M., Clark, and the special-ed administrator had vigorously tried to dissuade me from taking Blaze out of school (not *their* school, mind you, just school in general), I made arrangements with Mrs. M. to pick up Blaze's books and a month's worth of classroom assignments.

When I arrived at her classroom, she greeted me with the same ridiculous fake smile she always gave me during IEP meetings, as if we were really secret buddies and could never let a little thing like my child get in the way of our friendship.

"Oh, you know, the children were disappointed that they didn't get a chance to say good-bye to Blaze," she said. "Maybe you could bring him around to say good-bye."

I stared at her in disbelief. There were so many names I wanted to call her, so many epithets I wanted to hurl in her direction. I held all of this back, but for the first time I could remember, I was actively rude to a teacher.

"Can I get those books?" I said. "I'd like to leave now."

On my way out, I ran into Clark.

"Howdy," he said. "How's it going?"

"About as well as could be expected," I said.

"Well, good luck," he said. "We'll be in touch."

I haven't heard from anybody at the school since then. It's almost as if Blaze and I have dropped off the radar and disappeared. Had I known it was this easy to create our own island, I might have tried it earlier. It is peaceful here. Both Blaze and I have finally started sleeping through the night and, slowly, we are patching the stress fractures that have occurred over the last few months. But islands are known for isolation as well as peace. These days, I feel like I might as well be living on Mars for all the contact I have with the outside world. I have been working at home for some time, with most of my professional relationships taking place through the phone or e-mail. There is hardly any need for me to leave the house, other than to go shopping or run errands. And now that Blaze is no longer in school, I have lost all connection with what my father used to call "out there." Of course, I do see various members of my family on a daily basis, but then again, none of us have ever been representatives of the real world.

This isolation worries me a little. For now, removal from the fray is allowing me an opportunity to recharge and Blaze a chance to heal. But I suspect it won't take long for either one of us to forget how to negotiate the social contracts "out there." This has never been Blaze's strong suit, anyway. If *I* lose myself in our little world, we'll both be falling without a net. But these vague fears are pale compared to the impossible stress of the last few months, so I'm allowing myself the time to drift, to avoid making any long-range decisions. My primary concern now is making sure that Blaze learns something while he is home with me and doesn't lose any of the academic skills he has worked so hard to gain.

Six weeks ago, my entire family pitched in to help me. As they had so many times before, my own personal village joined forces in an attempt to raise one child. After dinner one evening, we gathered for a family meeting and my father made an announcement.

"As you all know, Blaze has been *released* from school for the time being," he said. "Before he starts at another school, it's very important that he develop some good work habits. He was so off track at this school that he wouldn't even stay in class. Nobody knows how much he knows or what he knows, but one thing's for sure: he hasn't learned anything this year except how to behave badly. It's our job now to help him get into some good habits and learn some basics. We're all going to have to devote some time to Blaze every week. Every one of you has a special skill you can teach him and he has a unique relationship with every one of you.

"Debra has the toughest job here because she's the one who is going to have to do most of the work and the one who is going to spend the most time with Blaze. But all of us have to help her. So how about it?"

There were no dissenters in the ranks.

Over the next few days, we hammered out a schedule. Maya took two mornings a week to teach Blaze music. After a few abortive attempts with the violin (too much fine motor coordination required there), Maya found an inexpensive cello, an instrument that Blaze was much more comfortable with. Because cello was not Maya's instrument, she signed up for lessons as well.

My realtor sister Lavander expressed doubts about her abilities to teach Blaze anything of value.

"I'm not an artist like all you people," she said. "I don't write or play music or act or anything. What am I supposed to teach him?"

"That's why you're perfect," I told her. "There are altogether too many arty types around here. You're the most organized person in this family. I need you to show him how to write clearly and legibly, how to fill out a form, write a letter, enter information in a check register."

"But that's so easy."

"Not for him, it's not."

When Lavander showed up for her first Friday-afternoon session, she brought paper, envelopes, stamps, an old check register, sharpened pencils, and a list of assignments for Blaze. All of this was neatly tucked into a folder with one of her business cards clipped to the outside. It was a beautiful thing.

My brother, Bo, the baseball coach, took charge of Blaze's physical education. Once a week, he showed up and took Blaze out to the batting cages to hit and catch. Bo also versed Blaze in the fine art of male chauvinism. As a result, Blaze came back from his sessions glowing and invigorated, the remnants of red licorice staining his lips, spouting his new mantra: "I can't tell you what we did, it's between us guys."

My actress sister Déja decided to work with Blaze on playwriting. The two of them disappeared into his room and generated several one act plays together, which they would then act out.

My mother, who had recently begun developing her nascent talent as an artist, offered to teach Blaze how to mix color and how to approach an empty canvas with excitement as opposed to the fear of failure that he'd held since his days in kindergarten.

Aside from me, my father spent the most time with Blaze. On Mondays and Thursdays, he worked with Blaze on practical math skills. ("He can't even make change for a dollar," my father said, shaking his head in disapproval. "We've got a long way to go here.") I listened to them work and shuddered, having intense flashbacks to my own fourth-grade math lessons with my father.

"No, that's wrong," my father said. "You forgot to carry the one again."

"No, I didn't," Blaze said.

"Yes, you did."

"No, I did— oh, yeah, I *did*."

"Do it again."

"Okay, Papa."

"Why did you skip that problem?" my father asked.

"I don't want to do it, it's got a remainder of two."

"What are you talking about?"

"I don't do remainder twos."

"Why not?"

"Remainder two is boring. I like remainder seven better."

"Don't be ridiculous, Blaze. I'm not one of your teachers, you can't get away with that crap with me. 'I don't do remainder two!' What, are you kidding? Do the problem. I don't want to hear that nonsense again."

"Okay, Papa," Blaze said, laughing.

The rest of Blaze's education was left to me. After a week of wading through his seventh-grade textbooks and worksheets, I realized I was unable to teach the chaotic combination of science, history, and language arts that was laid before me. I'd had no time to prepare, no lesson plans, no time to brush up on my own skills. I didn't even know where Blaze was on an academic level. He knew the difference between DNA and RNA, but he didn't understand the concept of natural selection. He knew, and understood, the entire Bill of Rights, but he had no idea what the Revolutionary War was. He knew all the parts of speech, but he started sentences without capital letters and refused to use any kind of punctuation. I figured it would take me months just to untangle the strands of his knowledge and lay them in the right direction. So I fell back on what I knew best—words.

For me, reading was the key to everything else. I reckoned that if I could just get Blaze reading and comprehending what he read, the rest would come.

We started by going through the seventh-grade syllabus, which contained all the usual suspects: *Tom Sawyer*, *The Outsiders*, *Old Yeller*, and *The Hobbit*, among others. I started every one of these books with Blaze and even finished *Old Yeller*, but he didn't connect with any of them. It was agonizing trying to read with him when he was clearly getting nothing out of the text. Finally, I asked him what book *he* wanted to read.

"*Romeo and Juliet*," he said.

"Shakespeare?" I said. "You want to read Shakespeare?"

"Who's Shakespeare?" he said.

"Shakespeare *wrote Romeo and Juliet*."

"Oh, okay. Then I want to read Shakespeare."

Fine, I thought, we'll read Shakespeare. What the hell. I bought three books. The first was a narrative version of *Romeo and Juliet* in a kid-friendly format. The second was a play, written in modern English. The third was Shakespeare's version. I started with the narrative version. Before we began, I gave Blaze a lesson about sixteenth-century England and who Shakespeare was. I explained iambic pentameter and why it was difficult to read Shakespeare in the original. After he'd absorbed all of this, we began to read, alternating pages.

From the first page, Blaze was totally involved in the story. Every so often, we'd stop and have spirited discussions about the action and the motivations of the characters. Blaze took more interest in the minor characters than the two principals and asked me what was the deal with Mercutio anyway, why was he so mad at everything? And Lord Capulet, why was he so disrespectful to Juliet? That Lord Capulet is an idiot, Mom, don't you think? He understood the love story and could even appreciate the tragic elements of the play, but, ultimately, Blaze was fascinated by the action on the periphery. This, I thought, was not a huge surprise.

When we finished the book, I made up a test for Blaze to take. It took me all of one morning to write a test with thirty-five multiple-choice questions. I labored over the questions, not wanting to make them too easy or too difficult. Who was Mercutio? I asked. When a character is speaking, alone on the stage, what is that called? What was Juliet's family name? What metaphor did Romeo use to describe Juliet on the balcony?

It took Blaze ten minutes to run through the test by himself. He missed four questions. I decided to consider this a major success.

We finished *Romeo and Juliet* about a week ago. We've had to switch gears and I'm now in the process of trying to find another book that Blaze will like as much. He hasn't come up with any suggestions so far and, in my drier moments, I'm inclined to lean toward Beckett or Camus.

The search for a new book is not the only dilemma I've been facing lately. I am starting to realize that Blaze will have to return to school before this year is over. Although my family has provided incredible support since Blaze left his school, their schedules are starting to conflict with the times they originally set aside to work with Blaze. My brother has just been offered a position as a long-term substitute teacher in another local middle school and is now busy all the time. Lavander is in the middle of closing on three different properties and is bouncing between cell phones and appointments. Maya has added several students to her roster and has started teaching a music program in an elementary school. Déja is auditioning for parts and working double shifts at her restaurant job. Even my father is flagging, plagued by a sprained back and general exhaustion. Blaze and I have been together, around the clock, without separation, for days. The hours I had set aside for my own work have now dwindled down to zero and I'm approaching panic mode over my ability to earn a living. In a very short while, this situation will move from being claustrophobic to destructive.

I have begun to understand too that I will never be able to educate

Blaze at home without giving him the opportunity to mix with other children his own age. I can teach him every subject in the curriculum, but if he doesn't get out there and get some sense of himself as an individual in society, he won't know how to live in the world. The longer he stays with me, protected but isolated on our little island, the less chance he has to develop the skills he needs to function outside of his immediate family. For all my best intentions, I can't teach him how to live in the world. I keep thinking that if I tried harder, had it more together myself, I'd be able to do this, but I don't know how.

I talk to Dr. Jean on an almost daily basis now and I confide my fears to her.

"We will find a place for him," she tells me. "There has to be a program in this district for him. And, really, we have to do this now because we've got to start thinking about high school."

"High school?" I almost shriek. "I can't think about high school now."

"It's less than two years away," she says.

"I don't think this kid can survive high school," I tell her. "Not from what I've seen this year."

"Try not to worry," Dr. Jean says. "We *will* find something."

I don't share Dr. Jean's optimism, but I cling to it nevertheless. I start preparing for another round of meetings at the two schools in the district that look like they might have a suitable program for Blaze.

For his part, Blaze is, amazingly, eager to return to school. He assures me that it was "*that* school" that was the problem and he is sure the next one will be better. Déja attended one of the two schools I am looking at and Blaze tells me that he wants to go there, that "you'll see, Mom, it will be good at that school."

Although I don't want to pressure him, I feel I have to tell him that the next school he attends will probably be the last one if it doesn't work out. If he can't manage to get some basic classroom behaviors nailed, he will have to stay home with me *forever*.

"I've seen you work for me and Papa and everyone else," I tell him. "You can do this if you put your mind to it, Blaze. And I will help you as much as I can."

"I know, Mom," he says. "I know you will."

"We can't go through what we went through at the beginning of this year again," I tell him. "I can't take it and neither can you. Do you understand me?"

"Yes," he says. "Mom, can I tell you something?"

"What?"

"You're the best mom I've ever had."

Today we're going to visit the Scripps Aquarium in La Jolla. Blaze has been looking forward to this outing for weeks. We're going with Michelle, the mother of one of Maya's violin students, and her two kids—Sabrina, six years old, and Terence, eight. Every Monday afternoon while Sabrina has her lesson in Maya's room, Blaze and Terence play board games and toss things around Blaze's room. They seem to have a good time. Blaze adores Terence. I'm not sure what Terence thinks of Blaze. He seems like a pretty serious kid but he enjoys making Blaze laugh.

Michelle, a woman of exceptional kindness and grace, has taken Blaze out before; once to see a movie over the Christmas vacation and once with Maya and her own kids to see a play. She's the kind of mother I could never be. She works at her kids' school, takes them to an astonishing variety of lessons (violin, piano, and baseball, to name just a few), plans elaborate educational outings, designs art projects, sends them to enrichment summer programs and on and on. I get tired just thinking about it. I'm a little envious of her and vaguely guilty that I'm not nearly selfless enough to expend the amount of energy she seems to have in abundance. Blaze is absolutely mad about Michelle and her entire family. I am convinced that he would find Michelle a perfectly acceptable mother were I not around, which I find highly amusing because, among her many virtues, Michelle is overwhelmingly *normal.*

Terence appears at the front door at the appointed time and we find out that Sabrina won't be joining us for this adventure because she was badly behaved and is being punished for throwing a fit earlier in the day. Blaze is fascinated and wants to know all the details. What did she do? How long is she going to be punished? Who is with her? Is she alone at home? Michelle explains that her dad is there with her and he's the one who decided she should be punished in the first place. Sabrina's dad doesn't tolerate bad behavior, Michelle tells Blaze. To me, she says, "Not like me. I always cave in the end."

"Mothers," I comment. "That's our job, isn't it? To cave?"

After a twenty-minute drive we approach the aquarium and Blaze says, "I can't wait to see all the fish. And I'm not going to be scared. No, sir."

"Why would you be scared?" I ask him. "They're only fish."

"Yes, but remember that time we came before and I was scared because it was dark?"

"Yes, but you were only about three or four then," I say.

"Yeah, I'm a big boy now," Blaze says. "A *big* boy."

"Yeah, you're like eleven or something, aren't you?" Terence asks. He's been busily sketching rocket ships in the backseat throughout the drive.

"I'm thirteen," Blaze tells him.

"You're thirteen?" Terence asks, disbelieving. "*Thirteen?* Are you sure?"

Michelle looks over at me, smiling, and I smile back. I'm wondering how this outing is going to turn out and I'm experiencing the first hint of trepidation.

In the entrance, there is a giant tank filled with sardines swirling around in a slippery mass of silver flashes. Blaze doesn't want to look at the sardines, he's already darted off into the main tunnel leading through the aquarium.

Terence reads every plaque and seems to have an encyclopedic knowledge of the marine creatures we pass in their lighted boxes. Michelle asks him to find certain fish in the tanks and identify them and he complies with ease. Blaze, on the other hand, skips from tank to tank seldom stopping long enough to take a good look at anything. I have to tell him to stay with us one, two, three times. Michelle tries to be helpful.

"Blaze, take a look at the halibut," she says. "Look at the face on him."

"Look at the California king crab," I add. "Reminds me of you."

Blaze wanders into the kelp forest and we follow. He's starting to lick his hand and touch it to his forehead. All the other hideous tics he picked up over the course of this wretched year have disappeared since Blaze has been home, but this one remains for some reason. I can't get him to stop. I watch him touch the railings where a million people have left a million viruses and then put that hand in his mouth. I can't stand it.

Through gritted teeth I tell him to stop or he can forget ever going on another outing like this again.

"I can't help it," he says, "my hands are dry."

"Then why didn't you put lotion on them before we left the house?" I ask.

"I don't know."

I'm desperate for a minute. I can't let him continue to lick his hand but I don't have anything that passes for lotion in my purse. It occurs to me that Michelle probably does. She produces the perfect size bottle of hand lotion from her purse at my request and I slather up Blaze's hands in front of the nurse shark tank. We've avoided a major freakout, at least for the time being.

Although Terence shows no signs of tiring and methodically studies every tank, Blaze looks as if he is barely controlling an urge to flee and starts weaving dangerously through the clots of people lining the tunnel.

"Maybe we should go outside," Michelle says.

There's an outdoor piazza between the fish tanks and the museum section of the aquarium and we walk outside into the chilly March air and take in the view. The Pacific stretches out in cobalt glory below us, tiny diamonds dancing in the pale sunlight. Blaze skips around the cobblestones but Terence sticks close by, asking questions about how far away the city is and how can you tell, as he looks through the telescope at the pier.

"How's your writing coming along?" Michelle asks me.

"It's tough finding time for it right now," I tell her, "with Blaze being home and everything. But he's going to be starting at a new school after the spring break, so I guess, if it works out, I'll have more time then."

She looks over at Blaze as he makes his circles around the piazza. "Yes, that's got to be difficult," she says. She doesn't elaborate on what she means but I hear what's unspoken in her words. I have a moment of abject self-pity. Yes, it's all difficult. It's difficult raising this kid who will never be normal and who, at thirteen, is so much less mature than Terence, five years his junior. I'm thinking that, just for one day, I'd like to see what it's like to have a life like Michelle's, where things are what they ought to be—husband, two kids, family car, school—and days follow a predictable pattern. These are the things I will never have. Blaze was right, he *is* a big boy. Too big to run around like this without attracting notice. I'm disappointed in him and in myself and I'm very tired. I feel the edge of a major depression approaching and I want this outing to be over so that I can go home and stick my head in the sand where it belongs.

We visit a few more sights in the aquarium and then it's time to go.

Michelle wants to take us to lunch. "Where would be the best place?" she asks.

"Any place with french fries," I tell her. "That's probably all Blaze will eat."

We settle on Friday's, nearby, guaranteed to have french fries. The hostess asks us how many children's menus we need and Michelle says, "Only one, right? Blaze doesn't need a children's menu, does he?"

I smile at her, feeling a surge of gratefulness for her consideration. She's assuming that Blaze, at thirteen, would feel insulted being offered a children's menu and crayons at his ripe old age and she's trying to respect his feelings.

"No, it's fine," I tell the hostess, "we'll take two children's menus."

At the table, Blaze is not content to sit quietly while Michelle and I talk. Terence seems deep in thought again so Blaze starts asking Michelle a series of questions.

"So, Michelle, do you listen to Fleetwood Mac?" he asks.

"I used to," she says. "A long time ago."

"They're a good band," Blaze says. "You know that song 'Dreams'? It's about how sad a person gets when there's nobody around to help."

"I never thought about it that way," Michelle says. "I guess I never really listened to it very carefully."

"Stevie Nicks sings that song," Blaze goes on. "She's singing to somebody she knows who won't help her."

"Hmm," Michelle says and looks over at me, eyebrows raised. Blaze goes on some more about various other songs he's heard and what they mean. He gets to Billie Holiday and starts telling Michelle about what a tragic life she had and that's why all her songs sound so sad. Terence looks at Blaze as if he's speaking Greek, but he's listening and so is Michelle and we're all involved and we're all thinking about our own associations with what he is saying.

I let Blaze continue on his riff and I remember that this is what I love the most about him. Whenever I start feeling like it's all hopeless, that we'll never be normal, that our lives will be spent navigating social situations and trying to figure out what's appropriate, Blaze will pull something like this out of his hat. He taps into my feelings and worries with a sort of sixth sense and responds by demonstrating his sensitivity, his ability to find a common level with whoever he's with and hold his own. His conversations may seem tangential, but they make sense and they are thought-provoking and always, somewhere inside them, there is a deeper meaning. His conversation with Michelle is about more than pop-song lyrics. He is picking up on her mood, on my mood, and on the dynamic between all of us at this table.

Blaze leaves the topic of music and moves on to Michelle's husband. Does he often hand out punishments to the kids? What does he do for a living? Michelle tells him that her husband is a lawyer. Blaze wants to know if her husband ever finds himself in any dangerous situations.

"Gee, I hope not," Michelle says.

"What kind of law does he practice?" I ask Michelle.

"Personal injury," she says.

Michelle drops us off at home after lunch and I try to regroup and figure out what we're going to do for the rest of the day.

"That was great," Blaze says. "I love the aquarium."

"You didn't seem to be loving it so much," I say. "You were running all over the place for most of the time."

"I'm sorry," he says. "You know I don't like to stand still in one place."

"I sure do know that," I tell him.

He waits a few beats before he asks me, "Mom, do you wish you had a husband?"

I stare at him for a few moments, lost, not knowing what to tell him or even how I can respond honestly when I don't know the answer to his question.

"Well?" he asks. "Do you?"

"Hold on a second, I'm thinking," I tell him. "That's a difficult question, you know." I ponder it for a minute while he waits and then I tell him, "I guess sometimes I do wish I had a husband. It would be nice, sometimes, to have a partner in life. But I don't really think about it that often."

"Maybe it wouldn't be a good thing?" he asks.

"I don't know."

"Maybe you'd fight with him, if you had a husband. That wouldn't be good."

"No, it wouldn't, but if one goes as far as to marry someone, one would hope that one wouldn't be fighting all the time."

"Maybe you could have one sometime," he says.

"Maybe," I tell him. "Maybe someday."

Blaze gets up and goes off to another part of the house and that's the end of this conversation for now. It's been just enough to make me start thinking about most of the decisions I've made in my life. I sit, limp, for several minutes, pondering my future. What's in it for me, I wonder, and what's in it for him? How do we end up? Alone and weird forever? The depression I felt moving in earlier seems to have come closer now. I can sense it, heavy and dank, just a few thoughts away.

Just then, Blaze bursts in through the front door and stands before me. He's been in the garage, working out on the elliptical exercise machine I bought to keep myself from turning into jelly. He's shirtless and shoeless, wearing only a pair of gray sweatpants.

Flushed and triumphant, he says, "Hey, Mom! Remember Lord Capulet?"

"What?"

"Lord Capulet, you know. Remember him?"

"*Yeeees . . . ?*"

"Okay, just checking! I'm going back to work out some more now."

Then my tall, skinny, olive-skinned, beautiful, smiling boy darts back out the door and I just start laughing. It's a deep, helpless, tear-rolling laughter that goes on and on. I laugh until my heart and mind are clean and then I laugh some more. I am happily breathless by the time I finally stop.

Only Blaze can do this for me. Only Blaze can make me stop on a dime, turn away from self-pity and find the strength to keep pushing on. He has read me again, this child of mine. He has sensed my darkness and shown me the brightness within him. He has reminded me that I wouldn't change anything, wouldn't trade him, wouldn't trade any of this for a "normal" life. I chose this life, he is telling me, and he chose me. We have come to this place together. Today, like so many times before, Blaze has turned me around and shown me the view from over here.

And this is a beautiful view.

EPILOGUE

$\mathscr{S}$hortly after Blaze suggested that we restage his birth, I put the idea to my family. Every one of them seemed quite taken by it and we discussed various ways to implement it. My father was especially eager to replay the entire scenario. In a concerted effort at authenticity, we tried to round up the original players for the big event. This was difficult because, while everyone was present in varying degrees the night Blaze was born, my three sisters and my brother now had obligations, jobs, and responsibilities that made it impossible for them to be in my living room at the appointed time. I didn't want to wait until we could all gather together because I wanted to act on Blaze's idea as soon as possible and I didn't want it to escalate into a huge psychological event.

With all of this in mind, my father and mother arrived on a lazy fall afternoon and prepared to venture into unknown territory. I was nervous. This time around, I really wanted it to go the way Blaze wanted it to go.

I ordered a pizza.

Blaze was excited. When I looked over at him I could see that he was already halfway there, heading back to that place between floating sleep and conscious awareness.

I began by placing a pillow under my shirt and sitting on the couch. Blaze sat off to the side, unborn, watching. My father narrated.

"Now, Blaze," he began, "when you were born, you came out gasping. Let me show you how." My father sat down next to me on the couch, leaned over, and put his head in my lap. When I looked down, it was my father's face I saw staring up at me.

"Uh, Dad," I interrupted, uncomfortable, "this is getting a bit too Freudian for me."

"Yes, it is," my father said warningly, "but you're going to have to transcend your own neuroses for a minute and focus on what we're doing here."

I conceded reluctantly and my father demonstrated how Blaze panted at birth. I waited, anxious to get that part over with. Blaze watched, entranced and soundless.

"Now this time," my father continued, "you're going to come out when you're ready and you're going to take a deep breath and cry really loud. Okay?"

Blaze nodded in assent.

"Okay," my father said, "here's Mommy getting ready to have you. There you are inside her tummy." I made some noises indicating that I was in pain. It was no joke—I was having visceral memories of labor. "It's time to come out," my father said, "but wait until you're ready."

I made more noises. I started to sweat. I turned to my mother. "Why didn't you tell me it was going to hurt like this?" I asked her again. I never was satisfied with her answer the first time around. My mother looked at me somewhat disdainfully and said, "Don't start with me now."

"Mommy's in pain," my father went on, "and she wants to see you. Are you ready?" Blaze shook his head. I was finally starting to get it. He would never be ready. He didn't want to come out then and he didn't want to now. Minutes passed as I continued approximating labor.

The doorbell rang.

For the first time ever, a pizza deliveryman had arrived early. My father huffed, annoyed by the interruption, but Blaze didn't stir and didn't lose one iota of his concentration while the man was paid and sent on his way and the pizza was deposited on the kitchen table.

"Mommy's still waiting," my father picked up. "Are you ready?"

It seemed to me that Blaze might stay in his nether state indefinitely so I started "pushing" and pulled the pillow out from under my shirt. He's just going to have to come out and face it, I thought. Again.

"Look!" I shouted. "Here he is!"

Blaze moved over to me and placed his head on my stomach. When he looked up at me, I was startled by what I saw in his eyes. That look was exactly the same as it was the moment he was born. Once again, I could feel the tears starting.

"Cry," I told him.

"Cry!" my father shouted.

Blaze made a scratchy, strangled sound.

"Louder," we urged him. "Take a deep breath. Louder!"

It took Blaze three tries to let out a wail. I could see the struggle within him and was awed by the strength it must have taken for him to get to that level. We held our breaths, waiting to hear evidence of his. Finally, he burst out with a long, solid cry.

"Good, Blaze," my father said. "Good."

Instinctively, Blaze snuggled close to me and I cradled him as if he were a newborn once again. "How did that feel?" I asked him.

"Good," he said. "It felt good." He was grinning widely. I'd rarely seen him look so happy and contented.

We were all very pleased with Blaze's reaction and the fact that he seemed so reenergized. We were also completely wiped out. I couldn't help but think that our exercise was the sort of thing that had *don't try this at home* written all over it.

We ate pizza together, all of us unusually quiet and subdued. The big smile on Blaze's face never wavered, but he was mostly silent, drifting through that long-ago place from where he'd come. It was similar to when he'd been born, but different in a very important way. Back then, Blaze was physically present, but barely with us in spirit. He was an active participant in his life now and willing, in a very real way, to give it a go. I could only hope that whatever healing had come from his rebirthing would be enough to sustain him into the future.

My parents went home shortly after we finished eating, citing emotional exhaustion. Soon after that, Blaze started wheezing and became asthmatic. Once again, he was struggling for the breath he'd been denied at birth. It was only then that I realized how very important the event had been for him and how important it had been for me.

But he was breathing and, finally, he'd had his chance to cry out loud.

I had been given an extraordinary luck with this boy, I thought then. Twice, he had shown me the life and intelligence in his eyes. Twice he had given me a glance right into his soul.

When I was about seven or eight years old, I read and loved a series of Finnish fantasy novels in which the main characters are funny-looking creatures called Moomins. In my favorite story, the creatures find a magic hat that transforms everything put into it. Moomintroll, one of the main characters, hides under the hat and emerges as an unrecognizable version of himself. None of his friends know him in this form and everybody starts to treat him like an imposter and an intruder. In despair, Moomintroll beseeches his mother to tell his friends that he is the real Moomintroll. His mother looks deeply into his eyes and it takes her a minute because he really does look entirely different. Finally, though, she sees her child in his eyes. As soon as she acknowledges this, Moomintroll is transformed back into his usual form and his mother assures him that, whatever happens, she will always know him.

The story made a huge impression on me when I was a child and I never forgot this scene although it would be years before I really understood its practical implications in my own life. This is the way it is for me and my son. I will always know him. And I believe that he chose to come to me for that very reason.

I know that Blaze's birth was traumatic. Anyone who was there could have testified to that. Although I wished it could have been easier for him, I assumed, at the time, that all births must be traumatic. It's the nature of the process, after all. Who, in his right mind, would trade an existence of swimming in protected warmth for the cold, bright gravity of the world?

What I didn't understand then was what it could mean, on a deeper level, to have been born strangled. Perhaps if I had known that such extreme birth trauma could pose lifelong problems, I could have done something sooner to counter the effects. Perhaps I would have done nothing. I will never know.

I do know that I've searched for meaning in other places: with psychiatrists, teachers, counselors, advocates, and doctors over the years. Along the way, I've filled out countless medical history forms for Blaze, all of which ask about his birth. The questions are always the same:

Was the pregnancy normal?

How long was labor?

Complications?

Cord around neck? How many times?

Did baby need oxygen at birth?

Apgar scores?

There are answers to these questions, but none of them reveal any true meaning. In the end, meaning is found in faith. Blaze has taught me about faith and about so much else. In that first moment in the delivery room, and now, and in countless moments in between, Blaze himself has provided the answers—answers to questions that never get asked, but should be—answers I've been increasingly unwilling to share in the uncompromising glare of science and medicine:

Did your baby look at you at birth?

Did he show himself to you?

Did you see his soul?

Could you hear it singing?

AFTERWORD

In many ways, *Raising Blaze* was a difficult book for me to write. For one, most of it was written during a particularly challenging time for Blaze in terms of school and social adjustment. It was not easy to keep perspective on the events of Blaze's early years while actively dealing with the consequences of those events. On an emotional level too, this was a tough book. Writing authentically about Blaze's birth and the years that followed necessitated reliving some of the darker moments in our lives, as well as the times of triumph and joy. However, while challenging, these were surmountable obstacles. What wasn't quite as easy to put aside was the nagging feeling that, despite my proprietary rights as his mother, I was objectifying Blaze for public consumption and thus invading *his* rights and his privacy in a fundamental way. The obvious question, then, was why write this book at all if, at some point down the road, Blaze (or anyone else, for that matter) might see it as exploitative?

Aside from the fact that I saw our story as compelling enough to commit to paper, the answer to that question was that I had never found a book like this myself, although I'd been searching for one for many years. I spent most of Blaze's school years feeling entirely alone and adrift, although I suspected there were many others who were, if not in exactly the same boat, experiencing a similar situation. Unfortunately, the very nature of being "different" is that it sets us apart from each other and prevents us from sharing our experiences, lest we stand out too much, attract too much of the wrong attention, or appear too strange. I found plenty of journals, books, and articles that discussed specific mental, emotional, and physical conditions, but none that addressed the general uneasiness of being undiagnosably different in a world where everyone seems to be trying desperately to fit in. It is true that every human story is unique, yet it is also true that there are qualities we all share as humans. Among those qualities are our differences and thus our sameness. My hope for *Raising Blaze* was that others would find themselves in this perspective and in our story.

I explained all of this to Blaze before I started writing and I was convinced that he understood what the book was about and why I was writing it. My first book, *Waiting*, was also a memoir in which Blaze had been featured and he had become familiar, even comfortable, with readers (heretofore, strangers) knowing the details of our lives. Yet this book concerned him much more personally, and I continued to wrestle with doubts about volunteering aspects of his life on paper.

While I was writing the last few chapters, Blaze began hovering behind me as I wrote, reading over my shoulder in a most unnerving way.

"You can't stand over my shoulder and read," I told him. "I can't write if you do that."

"But I want to read it," he told me.

"Why?" I asked him in a stunning display of stupidity. "You can read it when it's finished. You don't have to stand there and read it while I'm writing."

"But I want to read it now," he said. "It's about me and I want to read it."

And, of course, he had every right to read it. I started feeding him pieces of the manuscript, from the beginning. I tried to give him passages that were heavy with description and dialogue, thinking that those would be the most appealing to him, but he soon caught wind of that and demanded that I give him everything and so I did.

The first surprise was that Blaze became entirely involved in what he read. He sat with hunks of the text for one, two, even three hours at a stretch. Sometimes he laughed out loud and sometimes he asked me to define words that he didn't understand, but he didn't stop until he was finished with every page in his hand. The second surprise was how I felt about my son reading the book I was writing about him. I was scared. I realized, in that moment, that if Blaze gave me any indication that the book disturbed, bothered, or hurt him in any way, I would not be able to finish it and it would likely never find a place between two covers.

"What do you think?" I asked him, finally.

"It's really good, Mom," he said. "I like it. I want to read more."

This was the beginning of a dialogue between us that went on until I wrote the last page. Blaze took the opportunity to discuss various past events, sometimes arguing about my interpretation of them. He loved certain scenes, but there were some that he asked me not to include. In all of these instances, I respected his wishes.

As it turned out, I needn't have worried about Blaze being reticent about sharing his life. Soon after he read the first few pages, Blaze was regaling all and sundry with, "My mom's writing a book about me. Do you want to know what's in it? Let me tell you this one part . . ."

I have no way of knowing how Blaze will feel about this book in the future. Then again, I don't know how I will feel about it then, either. I do know that, right now, this is a book that comes to you from both of us. For the rest, we will have to see. Ultimately, both raising Blaze and *Raising Blaze* are acts of faith.

{ ACKNOWLEDGMENTS }

I was fortunate enough to have had the guidance of three lucky stars with this book and I owe them all a huge debt of thanks—much more than I can adequately express here:

My agent, Amy Rennert, who never gave up on this book and never allowed me to give up, either.

Judith Moore, for getting me started again.

My editor, Marjorie Braman—just the absolute best. Bar none.

I would also like to offer my deepest thanks to: Susie Smith, Lisa Shepherd, Michele Chavez, Bill Porter, Lisa Ebner, and, especially, Don Birkett.

And to my mother, my father, my brother, and my three sisters, I can only say this: I am so lucky to be here with you. You are, and will always be, everything to me.